THE OFFICIAL HISTORY OF THE
RYDER CUP
1927-1989

THE OFFICIAL HISTORY OF THE
RYDER CUP
1927-1989

Michael Williams

Approved by the PGA

Stanley Paul
London Sydney Auckland Johannesburg

Stanley Paul & Co. Ltd

An imprint of Century Hutchinson Ltd
62–65 Chandos Place, London WC2N 4NW

Century Hutchinson Australia (Pty) Ltd
89–91 Albion Street, Surry Hills, NSW 2010

Century Hutchinson New Zealand Limited
PO Box 40–086, Glenfield, Auckland 10

Century Hutchinson South Africa (Pty) Ltd
PO Box 337, Bergvlei 2012, South Africa

First published 1989

Set in 11 on 12 pt Times Roman

Designed by Julian Holland

Printed and bound in Great Britain by Butler & Tanner Ltd, Frome and London

British Library Cataloguing in Publication Data
Williams, Michael, *1933 Oct. 19* –
    The official history of the Ryder Cup.
    1. Great Britain. Golf. Competitions: Ryder Cup,
history
    I. Title
    796.352'74'0941

ISBN 0 09 1739101

Acknowledgement
The author would like to thank the staff of *Golf Illustrated* for their research, the cooperation of the British Newspaper
Library, and Keith Rushworth for the excellent statistics he has supplied.
    He dedicates this book in memory of his mother, Norah Marguerite Williams.

The publishers would like to thank the following for the use of their copyright photographs in this book: Associated Press,
Sport & General Press Agency, Popperfoto, Hulton Deutsch Collection, AllSport, Bob Thomas, Peter Dazeley and Phil
Sheldon.

Contents

Foreword

The Ryder Cup — a seed merchant's dream that has become an amazing reality and a major sporting occasion eagerly anticipated by everyone with an interest in the game of golf.

Over the years the venues, the format, even the teams may have changed but one factor has remained throughout. The goodwill, good manners and sportsmanship that are so essential to the continuing fortune of these matches are a common thread running through all the 28 contests already played. Who will ever forget the conceded putt at Royal Birkdale in 1969 to see the first, and only, tied match.

The matches so lovingly created by Samuel Ryder started in 1927 as 'a crusade for the sake of the prestige of British Golf . . .' with the great triumvirate of Vardon, Taylor, and Braid chosen by the PGA, to whom they had contributed so much as the Great Britain and Ireland selection panel to take on the mighty Americans. Playing that day in Worcester, Massachusetts, was Aubrey Boomer, now in his nineties, and sadly unable to travel to The Belfry in 1989 to see the amazing transformation in the matches.

Over the years all the great names in golf have competed in the Ryder Cup. Giants like Ted Ray, Gene Sarazen, Henry Cotton, Christy O'Connor, Max Faulkner, Arnold Palmer, Jack Nicklaus, Sam Snead, and many others right up to the present time, with the introduction of European golfers from 1979 and the likes of Severiano Ballesteros.

It is true that in the late 70s the continued American successes almost made the matches a non-event. When played in America the crowds were sparse and only a small percentage of the population knew what the Ryder Cup matches were about. In England, I think it true to say that more people came to watch the great American golfers than they did with expectation of victory. However, with the advent of a European team and the enormous improvement in golf in Europe, the Ryder Cup matches are once again a great international event, and a jewel in the crown of the sportsman's year.

Read and enjoy this book which I commend to you with appreciation for the fine research and writing of Michael Williams, who has truly captured the spirit of this unique golfing contest as a memory to a man of vision.

RT. HON. THE EARL OF DERBY MC
President
The Professional Golfers' Association

Seeds of The Ryder Cup

There were two unofficial matches between the professionals of Great Britain and the United States before the birth of the Ryder Cup in 1927. Both were won by the British, by 10½ to 4½ at Gleneagles in 1921 and then by 13½ to 1½ at Wentworth in 1926. It was the second of these occasions that was undoubtedly the more significant, for among those in the gallery was a small man with a rather bushy moustache. His name was Samuel Ryder.

This amateur golf 'nut', as he might now be called, was born in 1858, the son of a Manchester corn merchant. He was educated at Manchester University and went into the family business. Like most young men he had ideas of his own, and one of them was that there was a fortune to be made in selling penny packets of seeds to the garden lovers of England. When the senior Ryder doubted the wisdom of such an enterprise, the younger Ryder decided to set up business on his own.

Towards the end of the nineteenth century he moved south to St Albans in Hertfordshire and formed the Heath and Heather Seed Company. His business quickly prospered, as did his standing within the local community. In 1906 he became mayor of St Albans, and as the years went by and his packets of seeds sprouted all over the land, so Samuel Ryder began to think of ways in which to spend the more relaxing hours of his life.

He was past his fiftieth birthday when he took to golf, joining the Verulam Golf Club, St Albans, in 1910 at an annual subscription of four guineas, which is about what one now pays for a modest round of drinks. Within twelve months he was elected captain, an office he was to hold on two further occasions, in 1926 and 1927. While it was too late in life for Ryder to become really good at the game, he was nevertheless enchanted by it and he marvelled at the skill of the professionals.

In 1923 he sponsored a Heath and Heather tournament at Verulam. It was restricted entirely to professionals and it is claimed to have been the first of its kind in Britain. Among those who took part was Abe Mitchell, a one-time gardener himself, and it may have been this common background that encouraged the close affinity between the two men. Mitchell has often been described as the best British golfer never to have won the Open championship, and Ryder, still a man of golfing dreams, appointed him his own personal tutor at the then princely sum of £1000 a year.

Perhaps, therefore, Ryder was among the first laymen to recognise the potential earnings of the professional golfer, whose status in life until then had been little better than that of the caddie. If it was inevitable that Ryder should be in the gallery for that unofficial match against the Americans at Wentworth in the summer of 1926, it was nevertheless only by chance that the fixture was held at all.

Such was the size of the entry, including as it did many Americans, for that year's Open championship at Royal Lytham and St Anne's that the Royal and Ancient decided there should be regional qualifying rounds – one at Sunningdale, which is just down the road from Wentworth, another at St Anne's Old and a third, much smaller one, at Western Gailes. The Sunningdale qualifier proved a notable one for it was there that Bobby Jones had what is still held to be one of the most flawless rounds of golf there has ever been – a 66, all fours and threes, 33 out, 33 back, 33 putts and 33 shots, many of them with the long irons and brassies that were then needed to reach greens now within the compass of one irons (let alone drivers!) and pitching clubs.

Jones went on to win the championship at Lytham, but in the meantime there was a certain amount of time for the professionals to 'fill in' after Sunningdale and it was because of this that a second unofficial international was held at Wentworth, the British winning it comprehensively. Samuel Ryder was as enthralled as he was delighted to see Mitchell team up with George Duncan in the foursomes and defeat Jim Barnes, who had won the Open at Prestwick twelve months earlier and was now back to defend his title, and the great Walter Hagen by nine and eight, and then repeat the 'dusting' by crushing Barnes again in the singles, this time by eight and seven. Charmed as well by the chivalrous atmosphere that existed between the two sides, Ryder remarked in the bar afterwards: 'We must do this again.'

With that already inherent professional instinct of striking while the iron is hot, Samuel Ryder was promptly prevailed upon to donate a small but striking gold cup that today epitomizes all that is best in international competition. It cost the then substantial (although now fairly paltry) sum of £250 and the small golfing figure atop the lid is, as the donor predictably insisted, a lasting memorial to Abe Mitchell.

The first official Ryder Cup was arranged for 3 and 4 June 1927 at the Worcester Country Club, Massachusetts, less (now) than an hour's drive from The Country Club, Brookline, where in 1988 Curtis Strange defeated Nick Faldo in a play-off for the United States Open. In 1925 it had been here at Worcester that Willie McFarlane, a native of Aberdeen but since domiciled in America, had defeated Bobby Jones in a play-off for the US Open.

Getting a British team to the States by sea nevertheless involved considerable expense and a £3000 appeal fund was launched by *Golf Illustrated*, whose editor, George Philpot, was to accompany the team as manager. This was warmly received by the PGA, whose secretary, Percy Perrins, commented in an official statement:

I am glad to hear that the £3000 fund is going ahead very satisfactorily. Subscription lists are being sent very shortly to the secretary of every club, asking for donations both from the clubs and from individual members. It is in this connection that I ask every pro to do his bit by judiciously talking about the appeal and thus getting it known amongst the golfing public. A little enthusiasm will make all the difference between failure and success.

The similarly optimistic editor wrote in the same issue:

I want the appeal to be successful because it will give British pros a chance to avenge the defeats which have been administered by American pros while visiting our shores in search of Open championship honours. I know that, given a fair chance, our fellows can and will bring back the Cup from America. But they must have a fair chance, which means that adequate money must be found to finance the trip. Can the money be found? The answer rests with the British golfing public.

Within these wishful words there was nevertheless an undertone of caution, and rightly so. The long reign of golf's triumvirate — Harry Vardon, James Braid and J.H. Taylor — at the turn of the century was over and in the immediate post-war years Hagen had already twice come over to win the Open, as had Jock Hutchison and Barnes. The warning signs were up, despite the intermediate successes of Duncan in 1920 and Arthur Havers in 1923.

For all the urgings, the appeal was not altogether successful. Though £400 was raised within a week of the launch being made public, which was reported as 'gratifying', donations became increasingly sluggish and the target was never reached, there ultimately being a shortfall of some £500. This produced some strong words of condemnation in a subsequent *Golf Illustrated* editorial. While acknowledging gifts from as far afield as Ceylon, the Transvaal,

Australia, Canada, Nigeria and the United States itself, the editor declared:

> It is disappointing that the indifference or selfishness of the multitude of golfers should have been so marked that what they could have done with ease has been imposed as a burden upon a small number.
>
> Of 1750 clubs in the British Isles whose cooperation was invited, only 216 have accorded help. It is a deplorable reflection on the attitude of the average golfer towards the game. At a very conservative estimate there are at least 500,000 golfers in this country. If only one in every five had given a shilling [5p] − surely not a lot to expect − a sum of £5000 would have been raised.

And in another edition:

> We are reluctant to think that this represents the attitude of a great section of the golfing community towards a matter in which the nation's credit is at stake. If it were so, the reason for the present-day American supremacy on the links would stand exposed in bold − but not very happy − relief.
>
> When our professionals are undertaking a crusade for the sake of the prestige of British golf, an expedition in the spirit of amateurs, the people of this country might reasonably be expected to help as a duty. After all, they ought not to pursue the principle of taking everything out of the game and giving as little as possible to it.
>
> No doubt it is mainly slackness, the traditional British way of beginning slackly and muddling through, which has caused so many clubs to allow their imaginations to slumber when it is their active assistance that is needed.

The biggest single contribution of £210 had come from the Stock Exchange Golf Society while sums of £100 had also been received from Samuel Ryder, the Lucifer Club, the Dunlop Rubber Company, the manufacturers of the Harlequin and Silver King golf balls and Spalding Bros. There was a donation of 2s 7d (about 12p) from a 'boy golfer'.

Samuel Ryder may not have made his mark as a golfer but it is a game with which his name will always be associated

However, the public apathy was nothing new. In 1922, when the Royal and Ancient had asked clubs throughout the country to subscribe towards the expenses of sending the first British team of amateurs to the United States for the Walker Cup at the National Golf Links of America, Long Island, there had been another poor response with the result that the members of the committee had had to make up the large deficit out of their own pockets. *Golf Illustrated* concluded:

> Clearly golfers need to wake up in their active support of national causes. But whatever the remissness of the people in this practical matter, it is certain that their sentiments and their whole-hearted wishes for success are with the nine players who will set sail.

In those days there was no order of merit or money list from which the British team could be chosen, and instead the Professional Golfers' Association appointed golf's famous triumvirate of Vardon, Braid and Taylor to act as its selection committee. This was warmly received, as was the team itself: Abe Mitchell (captain), Aubrey Boomer, Archie Compston, George Duncan, George Gadd, Arthur Havers, Ted Ray, Fred Robson and Charles Whitcombe.

'This team is a well-considered blending of experienced skill and rising skill,' wrote Harold Hilton, one of the most respected golf writers of that time and himself a fine player. Besides twice being Open champion many years earlier, he is still the only British golfer to have won the US Amateur championship, in 1911. He went on:

Every man in it has, at some time or other, exhibited the capacity to achieve the big thing in golf. They look every bit as capable of winning the 'Ryder' Cup — a keen affair in which each country will be represented by eight players — as the British party which so signally triumphed in the experimental event of that character at Wentworth last season.

The team was chosen well in advance to give the players time in which to get leave of absence from their clubs, and their mission also included the US Open at Oakmont, a week after the Ryder Cup. No British player had won that since Ted Ray in 1920. The team embarked at Southampton on the *Aquitania* on Saturday 21 May 1927. If they sailed then in high hope as well as expectation, it was not long before reality struck home.

United States 9½ – Great Britain 2½

Played at Worcester, Massachusetts, 3, 4 June 1927

The great adventure, as it might be called, had a disastrous start, even before the British team set sail on the *Aquitania*. Abe Mitchell, who had been appointed captain, had been suffering from stomach pains and appendicitis was diagnosed. Regrettably, therefore, he had to withdraw from the team, though he was well enough to be at Waterloo Station, together with Samuel Ryder, to see the pioneers off and wish them *bon voyage*.

On the rail journey to Southampton the team gathered for an informal meeting and, at the prior suggestion of Mitchell, Ted Ray, who had won the US Open at Inverness, Toledo, seven years earlier, was appointed to take over as captain. Nevertheless it made the team dangerously short in manpower and it was left to the secretary of the PGA, Percy Perrins, to come up with a replacement. Herbert Jolly, one of a number of fine golfers to emerge from the Channel Islands (notably Harry Vardon), was called upon and sailed later on the *Majestic*, arriving in New York four days after the rest of the team.

The voyage lasted six days – as opposed

A sinister looking bunch but that was the style of dress when the first British Ryder Cup team went to Worcester, Massachusetts, in 1927. Left to right: George Duncan, with hands in pockets, Archie Compston, Fred Robson, Ted Ray, Sam Ryder with his dog, F.G. Gadd (secretary of the PGA), Charles Whitcombe, Arthur Havers, Abe Mitchell and George Philpot, the team manager

to the six hours it would take by Concorde today — and almost the only man seemingly unaffected by the occasionally rough passage was Ray, whose considerable appetite was entirely intact. The Americans were out in force when the team docked, officials of the United States Golf Association, the American PGA and the Metropolitan PGA all being assembled on the dockside together with Walter Hagen, the American captain.

It took a day or two for most of the British team to find their land legs again. After a number of welcoming dinners, one or two played practice rounds on courses not too far out of New York before moving on to Worcester for the serious practice. There they found the course to be quite hilly, the fairways beautiful, the greens slower than they had been led to expect and the whole place littered with bunkers of every conceivable shape, depth and size. George Philpot, the manager, was at once reminded of St George's Hill in Surrey.

Aubrey Boomer was quickest to find his game, while a curious American public also soon took to Charles Whitcombe, who was making the first of his six Ryder Cup appearances before the outbreak of the Second World War. One of three golfing brothers, the others being Ernest and Reg, he twice won the Match-play championship, which was not then far short of the Open in the matter of prestige. One man who found his form particularly elusive was George Gadd. He had proved the poorest sailor of the lot. However, he was the first to admit to his sub-standard performance and it was on his own recommendation that he was omitted from the team, in both the foursomes and the singles.

The understanding had been that this inaugural Ryder Cup match be played precisely along the lines of the Walker Cup, which had begun five years earlier. However, on the eve of the match an American deputation arrived with four counter suggestions. They were that fourball matches be staged instead of foursomes — the Americans tend

to call them 'Scotch foursomes', for this is a form of the game seldom played in the States; that any match finishing all square after 36 holes be continued to a definite result; that two points instead of one be awarded for a foursomes victory; and that both teams should be allowed to substitute a player in the singles on the second day. The British conceded only on the last point, for it was thought that Al Watrous, who had a damaged thumb, might not be able to play in the foursomes for America. (In fact he played in both singles and foursomes, winning both.) Furthermore, there had been a Walker Cup precedent for this.

The Americans soon had their tails up for they took the foursomes 3—1, the British being as overwhelmed on the course as they had been off it. There could be no complaints about the weather, however. It was sunny, but by no means as hot as it can be in these parts.

'Everywhere we went,' recalled Arthur Havers later, 'we were submerged by hospitality and kindness. Suddenly we were in a world of luxury and plenty — so different from home. It was something we had never expected. Even the clubhouses were luxurious with deep-pile carpets, not like the run-down and shabby clubhouses at home.'

However, Ted Ray was far from disheartened at the loss of the foursomes. 'It has not killed our team spirit,' he told the *Worcester Telegram* at the end of the first day. More explicitly, he added that: 'One of the chief reasons for our failure was the superior putting of the American team. They holed out much better than we did.' How often in the ensuing years did one hear exactly the same sentiments expressed. What also impressed Ray was how much better the Americans were with the long irons. 'If the same number of holes had required brassie shots to reach the green,' he said, 'I would certainly look more favourably on our chances.'

Ray and Fred Robson had had a fairly close game against Hagen and Johnny

Abe Mitchell (right), who had to withdraw as captain because of illness, wishes Ted Ray the best of luck on the SS Aquitania prior to the team's departure from Southampton

Golden, the match turning when the Americans took the twelfth, thirteenth, fourteenth and fifteenth holes in the morning to go from three down to one up. By then Hagen, who had been in indifferent form at first, had come on to his game and it was largely because of his play in the afternoon that the Americans got home by two and one. It might have been closer had Ray been able to get the ball up to the hole on the greens, but he could not. The only salvation had come from Boomer and Whitcombe, whose impressive golf in practice was maintained as they defeated Leo Diegel and Bill Mehlhorn by seven and six. Boomer made the game look almost ridiculously easy and they were a most impressive level fours for the 31 holes they took to win. However, for the most part the British team simply did not give of their best. Gene Sarazen and

Watrous, for instance, were nine over fours and yet beat Havers and Jolly by three and two.

Ray's lingering hopes of a big recovery in the singles were disappointed. Match after match was lost and the only win came from Duncan, who showed typical spirit in fighting back to beat Turnesa on the home green. One down at lunch and two down with nine to play, Duncan slowly got back the holes until he was level coming to the last, a short par four with the green on a crest just beyond a cross bunker. There he made a birdie three, and the British cupboard was not entirely bare.

Still, Whitcombe was unbeaten for he halved his match with Sarazen, who to this day recalls what a lovely swinger of the club Whitcombe was. Even so it was, from a British point of view, a disappointing result, for at one point Sarazen had been five down but typically clawed his way back. He had already twice won the PGA championship, then played by match-play, and was later to win it a third time.

The post mortem produced no excuses, though it was felt that the result could have been closer had Abe Mitchell not been taken ill before the team left England. However, George Philpot did add that 'several Mitchells would have been needed to alter the result'. There was some feeling that the British team did not have enough time in which to acclimatize before going into the match, though the truth of the matter was that this was a serious international contest as opposed to the 'exhibition' the British had won so comprehensively at Wentworth the year before.

Furthermore, the Americans had originally been prepared to play the match a week later. It was at British request that the date was brought forward to suit their travel arrangements before going on to the US Open – which was won by Tommy Armour at Oakmont, Compston being the leading British player, joint seventh. Indeed, the Americans bent over backwards to be accommodating, accepting quite readily the rebuff to their proposition that fourballs and not foursomes should be played on the first day. They recognized, according to *Golf Illustrated*, 'the British tradition that the foursome represents as true a form of golf as the single, and that counting the better ball is merely a mongrel way of pursuing the game, amusing though it may be in some circumstances'.

The size of the Ryder Cup defeat was, of course, disheartening but some encouragement was drawn from the fact that of the nine games the British lost, five of them went to the thirty-fourth, thirty-fifth or thirty-sixth greens. It was inescapable that the Americans had proved to be the better finishers, the only exception to that having been Duncan. Ray summed up the situation in a cable to the *Daily Express* in London:

Our opponents beat us fairly and squarely, and almost entirely through their astonishing work on the putting greens, up to which point the British players were equally good. We were very poor by comparison, although quite equal to the recognized two putts per green standard. I consider that we can never hope to beat the Americans unless we learn to putt. This lesson should be taken to heart by British golfers.

A postscript came from the manager.

If our young players profit by their experience, we can reasonably hope for a happier fate in the next match for the Ryder Cup. It is a soundly established truism that experience is a good teacher and the British professionals have every incentive to make the most of it.

UNITED STATES		GREAT BRITAIN
	Foursomes	
J. Farrell & J. Turnesa 8 & 6	beat	G. Duncan & A. Compston
L. Diegel & W. Mehlhorn	lost to	A. Boomer & C.A. Whitcombe 7 & 6
W. Hagen & J. Golden 2 & 1	beat	E. Ray & F. Robson
G. Sarazen & A. Watrous 3 & 2	beat	A.G. Havers & H.C. Jolly
	Singles	
Mehlhorn 1 hole	beat	Compston
Farrell 5 & 4	beat	Boomer
Golden 8 & 7	beat	Jolly
Diegel 7 & 5	beat	Ray
Sarazen	halved with	Whitcombe
Hagen 2 & 1	beat	Havers
Watrous 3 & 2	beat	Robson
Turnesa	lost to	Duncan 1 hole

United States 9½ — Great Britain 2½

Great Britain 7 — United States 5

Played at Moortown, Leeds, 26, 27 May 1929

Much has been made in recent years of the partisan behaviour of British crowds, notably at the The Belfry in 1985 when there was some condemnation of the occasional cheer which went up whenever an American missed a crucial putt. In fact, it was nothing new. It happened as long ago as 1929 at Moortown, the first official Ryder Cup match in this country, Britain gaining their revenge for defeat at Worcester, Massachusetts two years earlier, winning by 7—5 and therefore squaring the series at one all.

Although once again there had been lacklustre support to the public appeal fund to finance the match, more than 10,000 spectators were nevertheless present (including some who had crawled through various hedges) on both days and their fervour was

The 1929 British team at Moortown. Left to right (back row): Stewart Burns, Abe Mitchell, Charles Whitcombe, Fred Robson; (front row) Ernest Whitcombe, Percy Alliss, George Duncan, Henry Cotton; (seated) Archie Compston, Aubrey Boomer

15

rapidly evident – comparing, indeed, to the noise invariably associated with a football match. Whereas in tournaments in those days the silence was normally broken only by the curse of a player when he missed a short putt, now at once it was totally different, a very definite cheer going up when on the first green in the top foursome Johnny Farrell, partnered by Joe Turnesa, missed from not much more than a foot. There is no indication that the Americans took this other than in good part – a different attitude, it seems, to that which exists today.

Walter Hagen had again been appointed captain of the American team but George Duncan took over the leadership of the British side from Ted Ray, who in 1927 had stood in for Abe Mitchell. The match also marked the appearance of two brothers, Charles and Ernest Whitcombe, as well as the first by Henry Cotton, who was in due course to win three Open championships. Cotton, then twenty-two, received his invitation while on tour in America, not only competing in events but, with his thirst for golfing knowledge, also studying American methods in his firm belief that they knew something the British did not. 'It was a big thrill when I got the invitation,' Cotton later recalled, 'and I hastily cabled back my acceptance.'

The British team's headquarters were at the Majestic Hotel, Harrogate, just north of Moortown, and one of Cotton's more abiding memories was of long evenings spent in their private sitting room listening to the team's 'funny man', Fred Robson, as the floor waiter provided a steady flow of whisky. Cotton was in fact a teetotaller and with every round, the bill for which was to be divided equally among the players at the end of the week, he would order instead a Comice pear, to which he had a particular addiction. His leg was pulled unmercifully as glasses were raised to him with each round, but the last laugh was his since, when the final tab was delivered, much the most expensive item on it was the pears,

which were out of season.

There was still widespread concern at the public's financial support for the match. Though it was nothing like as costly as the trip to America, when £3000 had been the target, donations from outside the trade amounted to only £284 16s. However, the PGA, who had set out to raise £500, still had something in hand, if not a great deal, since the trade had donated £521 4s, making a grand total of £806. There were also difficulties for the Americans. They had set their public appeal fund target at £15,000 and obtained little more than £10,000, almost half of which came from 'exhibition' matches.

Golf Illustrated, still closely involved in the match, was critical of the organization of the appeal and summarized by stating that as an international match, the Ryder Cup ought to be run by the Royal and Ancient. 'If this is not done, the match will either die or develop into a private match with little or no interest,' it declared. Its recommendation was that the only way to get the message across to the average golfer was through his club committee, 'and if you wish to do that, you must pass through the proper channel of St Andrews and the various unions'.

Much of all this tended to be forgotten in the heady atmosphere of the British victory, as too were Ted Ray's strictures after the inaugural match that the main difference between the two teams lay in the putting. Now the attention switched to long and medium iron play to the green from between 150 and 180 yards. This was the key to what was described as 'class golf'. The Americans tended to be 'inside' their opponents in the foursomes, which they won 2–1, and the British 'inside' in the singles when they turned the tables by beating the Americans 5–2.

Duncan was the braver captain in that he decided right away to play only eight of the ten men at his disposal, since he regarded these 'as the men in form. Consequently

Walter Hagen (left), captain of the 1929 American team, returns the Ryder Cup on arrival in England to J.H. Batley, of the welcoming committee. It stayed in Britain for another two years

Percy Alliss and Stewart Burns were left on the sidelines, though both got honourable mention in dispatches for their wholehearted support of the team. Hagen, like many a succeeding American captain, opted to give all his men a game on at least one of the two days and this may have had a direct bearing on the overall result since it led to his leaving out the great Horton Smith from the foursomes. How damaging this was is hard to gauge but Smith, the first Masters champion in 1934, did rather highlight his absence by winning one of America's only two singles very impressively, even though he had had to switch for the first time to hickory-shafted clubs. Though steel had been legalized in America in 1926, it was not until 1930 that the Royal and Ancient followed suit and, since the match was in Britain, local rules applied.

It was cold and rather raw for the time of year on the first day, and the British had their first disappointment when Charles Whitcombe and Archie Compston failed to bring home a point in the top match, despite being one up on the thirty-sixth tee. The initial culprit was Whitcombe, who cut his drive into a bush from which his partner could only drop out under penalty. However, it was still a tough hole for the Americans to win since Turnesa, after a perfect drive by Farrell, hit a wicked hook that came back off an out-of-bounds fence, his ball finishing behind a marquee. There was apparently no 'line of sight' relief in those days but Farrell, with just enough room to swing, played the shot of the day over the marquee close to the flag.

So that was a halved match, and there was no joy at all behind as Leo Diegel and Al Espinosa, who a month later was to lose a play-off to Bobby Jones for the US Open at Winged Foot, went round in the morning in 68 to lunch seven up on Duncan and Aubrey Boomer. It was a lead they preserved to the end, poor Boomer having one of those days when he found every part of the clubface except the middle.

Mitchell and Robson, whose combined ages amounted to eighty-six, brought home the first British point, the 'grand old men' as they were called still being too wily for Gene Sarazen who, for all his experience, was unable to carry the visibly nervous Ed Dudley. They won by two and one. However, it was the Americans who led at the end of the day as Hagen and Johnny Golden got the better of Ernest Whitcombe and Cotton by two holes in the bottom match. One of Cotton's memories of this particular game was that his partner, normally the steadiest of drivers, skied his tee shot both morning and afternoon at the eighteenth, which meant that Cotton, even with one of his piercing fairway woods, could not possibly get home in two.

There was nevertheless fulsome praise for Cotton, Britain's new white hope. The benefits of his learning experience in America had done him the world of good and the woodenness that marked his earlier style had been replaced by a much more flexible swing that had added another 30 yards to his driving without any loss of accuracy. Cotton also looked an improved putter, but Whitcombe was not at his best and he was the weak link. Nor was Hagen exactly on his game at first, but Golden, a thoroughly dependable golfer and particularly strong with his irons, putted marvel-lously, this eventually rubbing off on Hagen as well.

With only a point between the two sides overnight, the whole match was nicely balanced on the Saturday, by which time the temperature had gone up, to the relief of the Americans, who had brought in Al Watrous and Horton Smith in place of Dudley and Golden. However, the impetus was all on the British side, the example coming straight away from Charles Whit-combe. Having halved the first in birdie fours, he made a glorious three at the second, won the third as well and Farrell never saw him again. Whitcombe strode home at his mechanical and imposing best by eight and six.

Here was the inspiration the British needed, and right behind came even more of it as the determined Duncan made mincemeat of the formidable Hagen, beating him by ten and eight. 'This guy has never beaten me in a serious match,' Duncan had declared, 'and he never will.' Hagen never stood a chance, Duncan being round in 68 and five up in the morning and then out in 31 in the afternoon.

In a way this huge defeat was not untypical of Hagen. He seldom did anything by halves, either in victory or, as in this case, defeat. Nor did it have the slightest effect on him. Just as the year before he had been beaten eighteen and seventeen in a 72-hole challenge match with Compston before winning the Open championship the following week, now he went straight to Muirfield and won it again, almost by a street in heavy rain, sun (when he set a championship record of 67) and then a furious storm when his two 75s on the last day were a thing of wonder.

There was also what was described as a 'black hatred' in the heart of Archie Compston as he brought about the downfall of Sarazen, though there had been little between them through the first eighteen holes. Then Compston, never one to shirk a rough and tumble, cut loose and was home by six and four.

Admittedly it was not all plain sailing and Mitchell, no doubt to the disappointment of the watching Samuel Ryder, could certainly not handle Diegel, who beat him by nine and eight in the third match. The American was highly impressive and very long with his deep-faced driver, despite a somewhat stilted method. His putting, with both elbows at 90 degrees, was also seemingly infallible and though Mitchell got round in the morning in 70, he was still five down. Nor did his 35 to the turn do any good, for by then Diegel had won another two holes and was out of reach.

But there was the bonus of a slightly unexpected win from the unpredictable Boomer against the more talented Turnesa, and this was a most valuable point for behind them Robson was always struggling against the wonderful golf of Horton Smith. The American was both longer off the tee and closer to the flag with his second shots, somehow 'holding the ball on the clubface' and seldom wavering in flight. Robson said afterwards that he had never met anyone who left him feeling so tired — a rare compliment.

By then the British were close to victory and it came, not from Ernest Whitcombe, though it should have done since he was dormie two on Espinosa only to throw away both the final holes. Instead it came from Cotton, the youngest member of the team, against Watrous. This was a fine performance, for Cotton had begun by losing three of the first four holes. But he slowly got the them back, squared the match at the eighteenth by chipping in with his niblick to go into lunch all square, and in the afternoon grew in stature until he closed the door on the fifteenth green.

For all the praise that Moortown received, for both the condition of the course and the arrangements in general, notable help having come from the adjacent Sandmoor club, there was a strong body of opinion that this was not the best venue, good though the gate had been. The contention was that for an event such as the Ryder Cup only the very best would do, and the best was to be found only on a seaside links. While this has always been Open championship policy, the same has not been true for the Ryder Cup.

GREAT BRITAIN		UNITED STATES
	Foursomes	
C.A. Whitcombe & A. Compston	halved with	J. Farrell & J. Turnesa
A. Boomer & G. Duncan	lost to	L. Diegel & A. Espinosa 7 & 5
A. Mitchell & F. Robson	beat 2 & 1	G. Sarazen & E. Dudley
E.R. Whitcombe & T.H. Cotton	lost to	J. Golden & W. Hagen 2 holes
	Singles	
C.A. Whitcombe 8 & 6	beat	Farrell
Duncan 10 & 8	beat	Hagen
Mitchell	lost to	Diegel 9 & 8
Compston 6 & 4	beat	Sarazen
Boomer 4 & 3	beat	Turnesa
Robson	lost to	H. Smith 4 & 2
E.R. Whitcombe	halved with	Espinosa
Cotton 4 & 3	beat	A. Watrous

Great Britain 7 — United States 5

United States 9 Great Britain 3

Played at Scioto Country Club, Columbus, Ohio, 26, 27 June 1931

Though that rising young star, Henry Cotton, had sealed Britain's victory at Moortown in 1929, he was not in the team which suffered as much in the heat of Scioto as it did at the hands of the United States in the unsuccessful defence of the Ryder Cup. Nor, for that matter, were Percy Alliss and Aubrey Boomer, both in their golfing primes but now ruled out because of a Trust Deed that declared that all members of both teams must be natives of, and resident in, the country they represented. Alliss was ineli-

gible because he was then attached to the Wansee Club in Berlin (though he was to move back to England later that year with his wife and newlyborn son Peter), and Boomer because he was successively at St Cloud, Paris, and the Royal Golf Club, Belgium. Cotton's absence was for a different reason, and it is a sad fact that he did not appear in the match again until 1937, the year in which he won his second Open championship. Short, therefore, of three of their best players, the British were ill

The 1931 British team which lost at Scioto. Left to right: (standing) Ernest Whitcombe, Percy Alliss, Bert Hodson, Fred Pignon (manager), Abe Mitchell, William Davies, Syd Easterbrook; (seated) Archie Compston, George Duncan, Charles Whitcombe (captain), Arthur Havers, Fred Robson

equipped for this second visit to the States and sections of both press and public condemned the whole sorry affair as a fiasco.

There is no doubt that Cotton would have played at Scioto if, firstly, the PGA had been more sympathetic towards him; and secondly, if he himself had been a little less intransigent. Cotton was a highly ambitious man and even tended to be regarded with a certain amount of suspicion because, unlike his contemporaries, he had received a public-school education. He was, in other words, a 'cut above' the rest. He was therefore less prepared to be dictated to than the traditionally subservient professional golfer and when he received his invitation to be a member of the 1931 team, he objected to the clause that declared he must also return to Britain with the team. This was like a red rag to a bull as far as Cotton was concerned, for it had been his intention to stay on in America afterwards. His game had already benefited from earlier visits to the States and he was anxious to further his career by playing in more tournaments with the ultimate ambition of one day winning the Open championship.

Furthermore, he backed his argument by pointing out that when the Americans had visited Britain, they had remained as a team until the conclusion of the Ryder Cup match. 'After that they have become individuals, free to do as they please. I think we could with wisdom take a leaf from their book.' Cotton therefore refused the invitation and justified his action in a lengthy article in *Golf Illustrated* to which he had been contracted. He declared:

Two courses remained open to me. I could have signed the contract and when the time came to make the return trip have repudiated my signature. I dismissed this thought as being one quite dishonourable. Thus the only course left open to me was to point out to the Association that it was my intention to remain in America after the date the team was due to return to England, and to ask them if this was permissible. The Association answered in the negative, and I replied that in that event I did not feel disposed to accept the conditions laid down.

It was pointed out to me that if I enjoyed the benefit of a free passage, it was not fair for me to use that benefit for my personal gain by staying after the team had returned and playing as a freelance. It was this that caused me to intimate to the Professional Golfers' Association that I was quite prepared to pay my own passage out and back. Here again the Association found my suggestion unacceptable.

By then it was also known that Alliss and Boomer, both of whom had been in the 1929 team, were not in the side either because their overseas residence was now seen to be against the rules of the Trust Deed. (We will come to that later.) Consequently Cotton approached Alliss and Boomer and the three agreed to embark upon a private American tour, Cotton now intending to be at Scioto not as a player but as a journalist.

The next unofficial move was from the PGA, who made it known to Cotton that if he was prepared to write a letter of apology for the stance he had taken, they would be prepared to overlook his rebellion. 'I could not in fairness to myself accept that offering of an apology,' wrote Cotton. 'I could not see that I had anything for which to apologise.' Even so, further overtures were made to Cotton on the eve of the Open championship at Carnoustie, the PGA now agreeing that provided he went out with the team and remained under the management of the PGA during the Ryder Cup and subsequent American Open at Inverness and, indeed, until the team sailed for home, they would give permission for him to remain in the States, provided he applied for such permission out there.

It was then that Cotton dug in his heels. He, Alliss and Boomer had by that time become engaged to play in a number of events and he maintained that it was now impossible for him to cancel his passage ahead of the main party. However, he was prepared to place himself under the management of the PGA when they arrived in America. Evidently this was not satisfactory to the PGA, and though they made one final effort through a third party to make Cotton change his mind, it was to no avail and that was the end of the matter.

We must now turn to the Trust Deed which prevented the selection of Alliss, who had been selected for the 1929 match but had not been called upon to play, and Boomer, who had played in both the preceding matches. There was confusion over this as well. According to Percy Perrins, secretary of the PGA, the original Trust Deed did not provide for any residential qualifications, though it was Samuel Ryder's recollection that 'when the first team went out [in 1927] the United States golf authorities decided that their team should consist of players born in America and residing in America'. Perrins was at variance with this belief. He wrote in a letter to *Golf Illustrated*:

I am under the impression that it was not before the *first* Ryder Cup match in 1927 that the Americans decided to play only American-born players resident in the United States, but that this gesture came before the *second* match was played at Leeds in 1929.

The British team for that match was selected in January, and it was considerably after that date that we heard of the American decision, hence it was too late to alter the constitution of our team for that year's match. This explains why Alliss and Boomer were eligible to play in 1927 and 1929. It was, however, resolved that a new Trust Deed should be prepared, in which qualification should be the same for both countries.

Public opinion on the resolution appears to have been divided, attacked as 'insane' in some quarters and supported in others. One counter argument was that if it was proper to include both Alliss and Boomer in the British team, why not also Tommy Armour or Jim Barnes, who had emigrated to America from Scotland? And, indeed, any of the British-born professionals who were making their names in the States? 'I feel sure,' wrote F.H. Fostick, of Weybridge, in a letter to *Golf Illustrated*, 'that British golfers would not desire that the Ryder Cup should be won for Britain by a team of professionals, few of whom are resident in Great Britain—a position that could easily be brought about if it was not for this resolution.'

On the other hand, it was pointed out by F.H. Taylor, professional to the Oxford University Golf Club, that the Americans themselves 'were not acting within the spirit of the agreement' by their selection of Leo Diegel, for while he was a native of, and resident in, America, his place of business was in fact in Mexico.

But Samuel Ryder had made it clear that 'the Cup is the sole property of the PGA and that they can alter the terms in any way they think fit at any time'. *Golf Illustrated*'s answer to that was that if the Ryder Cup was a purely domestic affair, 'the public is entitled to say: "Very well, treat it as a domestic matter. But don't come to us when you are short of money."' Furthermore, they posed the question of what would happen in the case of a freelance golfer, one unattached to any golf club but constantly playing around the world in 'exhibition' matches. Such a golfer would then have no residential qualification. 'Has the existing Trust Deed provided for such an eventuality?', it asked.

It was against this background that the British team arrived in the torrid summer heat of Ohio, and while they may not have played in their familiar tweeds, it is not hard to imagine how ill equipped they must have been as compared with the present-day golfer in his ultra-light clothing. Bernard Darwin, in *The Times*, wrote:

So far as one can judge, our men, with one or two exceptions, played more or less as well as could be hoped against a very strong side under extraordinarily difficult conditions. The handicap of playing in the other man's country is not perhaps sufficiently appreciated by those who have not tried it. Cold is the one and only thing that is at all likely to beat the Americans, and when our team won so fine a victory at Moortown, they were greatly helped by the raw and bitter weather. Similarly, heat is our worst enemy.

While Walter Hagen continued as American captain, Charles Whitcombe had taken over the British leadership from George Duncan, who nevertheless kept his place in the side though there is not much doubt that he was by then past his best. Indeed, he was dropped after the foursomes when he and Arthur Havers were resoundingly defeated ten and nine by Hagen and Densmore Shute. America won the foursomes 3−1 and thereby quickly gained the necessary platform for victory by 9−3.

There was also a resounding defeat for Archie Compston and a newcomer, William Davies, by eight and seven against Gene Sarazen and Johnny Farrell, and the only British pair to win, as in fact they had at Moortown two years earlier, were the two veterans Abe Mitchell and Fred Robson. They knew one another's game almost as well as they knew their own, and from this grew a great trust in each other as they defeated Diegel and Al Espinosa by three and one.

But down at the bottom Ernest Whitcombe and another new man to the match, Syd Easterbrook, met more than their match in Billy Burke and Wilfred Cox, and Charles Whitcombe's wisdom in leaving himself out of the foursomes was revealed. There were many who felt that Duncan should have been a non-playing captain, thus leaving Whitcombe free of the off-course responsibilities that always lie heavy on the shoulders of the leader.

The long and short of it. Gene Sarazen (left), who at 5ft 5in is the smallest man to have won the British Open, and Fred Robson before their singles at Scioto in 1931. Note that it is Sarazen who wears a tie and he won by seven and six

There was never much sign of a British revival in the singles, for Burke swept Compston aside by seven and six in the top match while Sarazen shook hands with Robson just as far from home. Indeed, the only relief against an unstoppable tide was provided by Davies, who had, according to Darwin, 'once more given his proof of a power of rising to the big occasion', and Havers. Davies, equal seventh that year in the Open, defeated Farrell by four and three while Havers, who had also played well at Carnoustie, gained a fine victory over Craig Wood, who in 1941 was to win both the Masters and the US Open. Such was the ease of Havers' win that observers could only wonder how much better he might have done in the foursomes had he been partnered by Charles Whitcombe rather than Duncan.

Abe Mitchell, Sam Ryder's personal coach and, many said, the best golfer never to win the Open championship

The consensus of opinion was that the Americans had played as well as they had to. The three new men, Burke, Cox and Shute, all won twice and there was general pleasure in seeing Hagen come back to his best, following his foursomes victory with another in the singles against his opposing captain, Charles Whitcombe. It is doubtful whether the presence in the team of Cotton, Alliss and Boomer would have made the necessary difference towards prising an unlikely British victory, but there were still those who speculated how different it all might have been.

UNITED STATES		GREAT BRITAIN
Foursomes		
G. Sarazen & J. Farrell 8 & 7	beat	A. Compston & W.H. Davies
W. Hagen & D. Shute 10 & 9	beat	G. Duncan & A.G. Havers
L. Diegel & A. Espinosa	lost to	A. Mitchell & F. Robson 3 & 1
W. Burke & W. Cox 3 & 2	beat	S. Easterbrook & E.R. Whitcombe
Singles		
Burke 7 & 6	beat	Compston
Sarazen 7 & 6	beat	Robson
Farrell	lost to	Davies 4 & 3
Cox 3 & 1	beat	Mitchell
Hagen 4 & 3	beat	C.A. Whitcombe
Shute 8 & 6	beat	B. Hodson
Espinosa 2 & 1	beat	E.R. Whitcombe
C. Wood	lost to	Havers 4 & 3

United States 9 — Great Britain 3

Great Britain 6½ − United States 5½

Played at Southport and Ainsdale, 26, 27 June 1933

Though no one was to know it at the time, the 1933 Ryder Cup match at Southport and Ainsdale, which abuts Hillside and therefore forms with Royal Birkdale one of the great trinities of golf courses, was to prove a golfing watershed. By then America had not yet established their supremacy. They had admittedly won twice quite easily in the States, but now, amid huge crowds and scenes of great excitement, Britain were to square the series at two all. The joy would almost certainly have been tempered had there been warning that this was to be Britain's last victory for twenty-four years, six of which would be taken up with the Second World War.

While America persisted with Walter Hagen as their captain, the British made

No one knew it at the time but this was the last British team, in 1933 at Southport and Ainsdale, to win the Ryder Cup for another 24 years. Left to right: (back row) Alf Perry, Syd Easterbrook, who sank the winning putt, Arthur Havers, A.Stark (trainer), Alf Padgham, Arthur Lacey, Percy Alliss; (middle row) Charles Whitcombe, J.H.Taylor, Abe Mitchell; (front) Allan Dailey, William Davies

another change, appointing the great J.H. Taylor to lead them in a non-playing capacity. Taylor was then sixty-two, but as a member of the illustrious triumvirate which he had formed at the turn of the century with Harry Vardon and James Braid, he was still a revered figure and, indeed, had already acted as a selector.

Taylor was always regarded as a natural leader. He had played a major part in the formation of the PGA and was also a keen supporter of artisan golf, born no doubt of the fact that he had begun his career in the game as a caddie at Westward Ho! At the age of seventeen he graduated to becoming an assistant greenkeeper, but what made him was his defeat of the famous Andrew Kirkaldy in a challenge match. Kirkaldy generously spoke so highly of Taylor that when the Scot retired as professional at Winchester, it was Taylor who was appointed to succeed him. Later he moved to Wimbledon and finally to Royal Mid-Surrey, where he remained for forty years. Taylor, Open champion five times between 1894 and 1913, spent his retirement where he had begun, at Westward Ho! These were some of his happiest days for he had not only gone home but the view, he claimed, was the 'finest in Christendom'. In 1957 he was accorded the highest honour by Royal North Devon, the club electing him president.

Taylor had a year or two earlier remarked that the Ryder Cup was 'no picnic', and accordingly on arrival at Southport he employed the services of a physical training instructor who, each morning at 6.30, took the team down on to the broad stretches of the Southport beach (where, years later, that great steeplechaser Red Rum used to stetch his legs) for a pre-breakfast run. Quite what the more elderly members of the British team – the average age was thirty-three – thought about that, particularly Abe Mitchell, who was then forty-six, or Bill Davies, forty-one, is another matter, but a little discipline does help to weld the team into a unit, giving them a common cause.

Charles Whitcombe, who played in every Ryder Cup match between 1927 and 1939

Sir Guy Campbell, a noted writer as well as a golf-course architect, commented that the training 'marks a precedent that should prove of the greatest value in the future'.

Mitchell and Charles Whitcombe were the only survivors from the victorious team at Moortown in 1929, and there was again no place for Henry Cotton because he was now at Royal Waterloo in Belgium and, being resident outside the United Kingdom, that made him ineligible for selection. At least this time there was apparently no row about it, as there had been over his omission from the team at Scioto two years earlier.

There was, if anything, more interest in the content of the American team, five of them making their first appearance in Britain. They were Billy Burke, who had won the US Open two years earlier in 1931, Olin Dutra, Craig Wood, Paul Runyan and Densmore Shute, whose trip was to prove one of very mixed fortunes. Born of a family which hailed from Westward Ho! he was to take the three putts on the eighteenth by which America lost the Ryder Cup, but he then went on to win the Open championship at St Andrews in a play-off against fellow American Craig Wood.

There was no place in the American team in 1933 for their newly crowned Open champion of a week or so beforehand, for it had been won by Johnny Goodman, the last amateur to do so. Bernard Darwin described it in *The Times* as 'a very strong side, if anything stronger than that which our men so gloriously defeated on that freezing day at Moortown'. Nevertheless there was a tone of optimism in his writing as he pointed out that 'this match has provided us with the most cheerful, indeed almost the only cheerful, golfing news since Havers won the Open championship at Troon in 1923'. Curiously, however, Darwin made the mistake of regarding the series as already standing at two all, since he was counting the victory at Wentworth in 1926 as a Ryder Cup match, which it was not.

An unashamed partisan, Darwin declared that the 'raging patriot will pray for a raging east wind, not because he hopes for slices and hooks — the Americans can play in a wind as well as anybody — but because it gets at the heart and liver, killing those who are not used to it'.

In the event the weather was nothing like as inhospitable as it had been two years earlier at Moortown and the match proved to be an outstanding occasion, not only because of the result. In its wake Sir Guy Campbell wrote in *Golf Illustrated*:

Looking back over those two hectic, breathless, chaotic and intensely interesting days, one cannot fail to have gained impressions, forming a picture that will remain in the memory long after its more particular details have followed countless others into the limbo of things forgotten. There was the weather, ideal for players and spectators alike; there were the tents and booths, the flags, a megaphone and loudspeakers with J.H. Taylor acting as ringmaster, suggesting a fair on an August Bank Holiday rather than a golf match; there were the enormous crowds that, except for a sad lapse when the Prince of Wales arrived, behaved excellently; there were the stewards who on the whole discharged their duties conscientiously and with intelli-

gence, though never again should they be armed with dangerous lances; there was the links, which was in wonderful order, and in spite of a few dull and characterless holes, proved itself an adequate test of golf; and there was the golf itself, through which the figures of Hagen, Sarazen, Mitchell and the pale, perspiring Easterbrook will move clear cut when the others have become indeterminate though gallant shades.

Right from the start things went well for Britain, and for the first time they took the foursomes, a form of the game in which the Americans traditionally claim to be totally at sea — yet still play it rather well. The score at the end of the first day was 2½– 1½, though at lunch it had looked like being an even more favourable advantage since Britain were, in order, three up, four up, all square and four up.

The top match was a key one and had initially not looked like turning Britain's way on the inward half in the morning, for Whitcombe and Percy Alliss had been one down at the turn to Hagen and Sarazen. But they got a fortunate half at the tenth to avoid going two down and made the most of it with some inspired golf, winning four holes in a row from the thirteenth. Then, after brilliant halves in three at the seventeenth, Whitcombe hitting a bunker shot from 180 yards stone dead, Hagen putted short at the last and that was the British pair three up.

However, Hagen and Sarazen were a formidable and experienced pair and despite going four down with only nine to play, launched a fierce counter attack that had their opponents on the ropes. Hagen began it by holing the longer putt on the tenth green to get one hole back, and in no time at all the margin was one. Somehow Alliss and Whitcombe hung on with the help of some fine bunker play, but at the sixteenth, with the Americans in trouble, Alliss cut his second into a horrid place beyond the cross bunker and they lost the hole to a five. So that was all square, but British hearts began to beat more evenly when the Americans hooked at the seventeenth to go one down again; at least the British pair could not be beaten! However, at the last Alliss first pulled the second shot into a bunker and then, after Whitcombe had come out beautifully from the sand, Alliss missed the short putt and the match was halved after all.

If this was ultimately a disappointment, it was not the only one. An even more bitter pill had to be swallowed in the bottom match, for Padgham and Alf Perry, having been four up on Burke and Ed Dudley at lunch, lost in the end one down. It had been a match of two swings, the first Britain's way and the other, more tellingly, in favour of the Americans. At the eighth in the morning Dudley and Burke had looked about to go all square when Padgham, playing out of the rough, hit Dudley and, as this meant loss of hole, the Americans instead went two down. From that point the British pair had the better of the exchanges, Perry making up for errant driving with some fine chipping. Padgham was faultless and the Americans simply could not get the important putts in. The turning point probably came at the first hole in the afternoon, for the British pair had a putt for a two and five up but missed it. Making good their escape, Burke and Dudley proceeded to play beautifully while Perry continued to struggle from the tee. By the sixth (the twenty-fourth) the match was square and though Padgham continued to play his part nobly, he could not carry his side and the match was clinched, as it happened, for the United States when Burke holed a long putt to win the thirty-fifth, the last being halved. They had gone round in 70.

It was instead the middle-order pairs who stood firm for Britain. Mitchell and Havers dovetailed perfectly against Shute and the mighty sixteen-stone Dutra, first one and then the other pitching close for his partner to hole the putts. It seemed to get Dutra down, for though he hit the ball with dis-

arming ease, he also began to play a bad shot or two and the holes slowly slipped away. For once there was no American recovery and Mitchell and Havers held on to win by three and two.

The third match was always close, Davies and Easterbrook all square at lunch against Wood and Runyan but inching their way ahead in the afternoon until they stood dormie two and could not therefore be beaten. But there was still an alarm or two, for the British pair lost the seventeenth and then Davies erred again by driving into a bunker at the last. Though Wood was also in some mountainous country off the tee, Runyan managed to find the green and it looked as if the Americans might get away with it. However, Davies, following his partner's recovery from the sand, chipped to three feet and Easterbrook holed not his last telling putt of this particular Ryder Cup.

So that left Britain needing four of the eight singles for victory and, fifty and more years ago though it now is, the dramas of that second day have gone down in history as being of seething excitement, with various matches teetering on the brink of victory and defeat, crowds stampeding in every direction and among them all the famous 'Southport Lancers', stewards bearing lances with red and white flags.

There were two particular British heroes: Abe Mitchell, at forty-six the oldest man in the team, and Syd Easterbrook. It was Mitchell, Sam Ryder's great friend and hero, who must come first for he was playing in the second match and a bleak prospect it became as Olin Dutra, with eight fours and a three in his first nine holes, took a three-hole lead. Many were those who left him, but some time later there came news that Mitchell, far from being dead and buried, was instead five up. Indeed he was. He had won eight holes in a row, the seventeenth in bizarre manner when Dutra, having been laid a stymie, tried to loft his ball and instead knocked Mitchell's into the hole.

This sudden turn of events kept Britain

George Duncan, who took so little time over his putts that he was known as 'Miss 'em quick Duncan'

just ahead, for while at lunch Padgham, in the top match, stood three down to Sarazen, Arthur Lacey, who had taken Alf Perry's place, was one up on Hagen, Alliss one up on Runyan and both Davies and Havers all square against (respectively) Wood and Leo Diegel. The United States held the advantage in the last two singles, Shute one up on Easterbrook and Horton Smith five up on Whitcombe. Diegel and Smith had been brought in for the singles in place of Burke and Dudley.

First blood went to the Americans, for Sarazen, who had been reaping the fruits of his 1932 US Open victory with a number of 'exhibition' matches across the length and breadth of America and was somewhat short of real competition, was in merciless form against Padgham and drew steadily away to win by six and four. However, this was quickly balanced by Mitchell, now playing superbly and running further and further clear of Dutra until he won by the resounding margin of nine and eight. Immediately behind them the news was less good from a British point of view, for Lacey had been overhauled by Hagen and Davies was losing ground heavily to Wood. Both matches were lost, Lacey getting back to all square again but then going down after losing the fifteenth and making a real hash of the sixteenth, where he took four to get down from 50 yards.

This left four matches on the course and Britain needing three of them. With the Duke of Windsor now in attendance, all eyes were on Alliss, Havers, Easterbook and Whitcombe and it was Alliss who initiated the final surge after standing all square with three to play. He won the sixteenth, and then came a real bonus as Runyan, in coming out of a bunker at the seventeenth, caught the ball thin and went out of bounds. Hardly had the cheers died than Havers came striding home a four and three winner over Diegel and there were two of the necessary three points in the bag. But Whitcombe, though he had chased Horton Smith hard, at last succumbed on the seventeenth green and everything therefore depended on Easterbrook and Shute, all square and one to play.

There was not a vantage place to be found as the crowd crammed every conceivable dune, but rumour had it that both players were bunkered and on the green in three. Easterbook putted first and missed and then Shute, with a chance for the Ryder Cup, ran four feet past.

Years later, at an almost identical moment around a mile or so away at Royal Birkdale, Jack Nicklaus was to pick up Tony Jacklin's ball, conceding him the putt that tied the 1969 match. But Shute's second putt could not quite be given, and he missed it. Easterbrook tapped his in for a five, and the Ryder Cup was back in British custody. It would be almost a quarter of a century before it was again.

GREAT BRITAIN		UNITED STATES
	Foursomes	
P. Alliss & C.A. Whitcombe	halved with	G. Sarazen & W. Hagen
A. Mitchell & A.G. Havers 3 & 2	beat	O. Dutra & D. Shute
W.H. Davies & S. Easterbrook 1 hole	beat	C. Wood & P. Runyan
A.H. Padgham & A. Perry	lost to	E. Dudley & W. Burke 1 hole
	Singles	
Padgham	lost to	Sarazen 6 & 4
Mitchell 9 & 8	beat	Dutra
A. Lacey	lost to	Hagen 2 & 1
Davies	lost to	Wood 4 & 3
Alliss 2 & 1	beat	Runyan
Havers 4 & 3	beat	L. Diegel
Easterbrook 1 hole	beat	Shute
Whitcombe	lost to	H. Smith 2 & 1

Great Britain 6½ — United States 5½

United States 9 — Great Britain 3

Played at Ridgewood, New Jersey, 28, 29 September 1935

The 1935 match at Ridgewood, New Jersey, was unusual in one particular respect. For the only time three brothers, Charles, Ernest and Reg Whitcombe, were in the British team. Not that it made any difference to the result on what was coming to be recognized as the more difficult American soil. The United States won comprehensively by 8—2 with two halved, and many subsequently were the British recriminations, in stark contrast to the high hopes that had accompanied the team before they sailed to New York.

The Whitcombes were a remarkable golfing family. Charles played in all six Ryder Cup matches before the Second World War, three times as captain. He was the middle of the three brothers, Ernest being the eldest. Prominent as they all were, only Reg managed, in 1938, to win the Open championship; yet he was in many respects regarded as the least gifted of the three. Slow to mature, he had never managed even to finish in the first eight in the Open until 1937 when, aged thirty-nine, he came second to Henry Cotton at Carnoustie. Twelve months later, in some of the wildest weather ever known, he achieved the family

The 1935 British team at Ridgewood, New Jersey, notable because it included the three Whitcombe brothers. Left to right (standing): Bill Cox, Edward Jarman, Richard Burton, Commander Charles Roe (manager), Reg Whitcombe, Alf Padgham; (seated) Ernest Whitcombe, Percy Alliss, Charles Whitcombe, Alf Perry and Jack Bussell

dream at Royal St George's.

Ernest (father of Eddie, who continued the family line with many years' distinguished service at Chigwell and for the PGA) had his best chance of winning the Open in 1924 at Hoylake, leading at one stage by three strokes. But the 43 he took over the first nine holes in the final round let in Walter Hagen, who beat him by a stroke. Charles had his disappointment not long before sailing to Ridgewood in 1935, for he was only a stroke behind Alf Perry going into the final round at Muirfield but then took 76 and finished third.

Perhaps it was the very fact that the first three at Muirfield that year, Perry, Alf Padgham and Charles Whitcombe, were all members of the defending Ryder Cup team that imbued more optimism than was justified. Undue amount may have been read into the fact that Henry Picard, a newcomer to the American side, was beaten into sixth place. However, he was the only member of this United States team playing at Muirfield and was not even the leading American. That position was taken by the great Lawson Little, who had just won the Amateur championship for a second time, first at Prestwick and then at Royal Lytham.

At all events there was an air almost of euphoria when the Nineteenth Club staged a farewell dinner for the team at the Grosvenor Hotel in London. The general opinion was that no finer band of golfers had ever left these shores. Charles Whitcombe, who had taken over the reins so successfully held by J.H. Taylor two years earlier, spoke of his conviction of 'leading a winning team' and he was supported by Commander Charles Roe, the new secretary of the PGA and now team manager. 'Though my association with professional golfers in an official capacity is somewhat short,' he said, 'I feel that no team could go to America with a greater opportunity of success than Whitcombe and his boys.'

This tune was to change dramatically in the wake of the team's subsequent defeat

and also the manner in which it came. 'We are left with the knowledge,' thundered *Golf Illustrated* in its editorial, 'that the best team we have ever sent played about as badly as it knew how. Scores running into the high eighties tell their own tale, which must be one of summary defeat.' What rubbed even more salt into the stinging wound was that afterwards the British team went on to play Canada at Rosedale in Toronto and lost that as well, by 9½−5½.

Unlike Scioto in 1931, when the conditions had been so uncomfortably hot, the weather was much more temperate at Ridgewood and there could therefore be no excuses on that score. What did seem to bother the British players was the unusual amount of clover on the fairways, though it was hard to accept that it was this that contributed significantly towards the subsequent débâcle. Rather it was once again a case of the Americans making the better start and the most of the foursomes, which they won 3−1. The only successful British partnership was Charles and Ernest Whitcombe, who defeated Olin Dutra and Ky Laffoon, one of four newcomers to the American team, the others being Picard, Johnny Revolta and their new champion, Sam Parks. Understandably, if misguidedly, Charles Whitcombe then left himself out of the singles on the grounds perhaps that three Whitcombes were too much of a good thing. On the other hand Walter Hagen, who had partnered Gene Sarazen to a seven and six victory over Jack Busson and Perry, did the same.

With their usual mountain to climb, the British at one point in the singles still lived hopefully, for of the first four matches to complete eighteen holes, they were ahead in three: Jack Busson one up on Sarazen, Reg Whitcombe two up on Revolta (who some said looked more like a movie gangster than a golfer), and Padgham one up on Dutra. However, Paul Runyan, Craig Wood, Horton Smith and Picard were all between three and five up, and that looked

Charles Whitcombe watches the flight of the ball. Note the matting tee even in 1935, but this was not in the Ryder Cup but at an exhibition at Leatherhead

more than good enough for the United States—which it was.

Furthermore, the Americans still won the three games in which they were trailing at lunch. By the turn in the afternoon Sarazen, who earlier that year had won his celebrated Masters, had overtaken Busson and, putting beautifully, closed out his man on the thirty-fourth green. Sarazen was nevertheless wholehearted in his praise of Busson, declaring this to have been the hardest match he had ever played. Since in 1929 Sarazen had been beaten by Archie Compston at Moortown, his memory was apparently fairly short, a failing his critics were as quick to point out as they had been to condemn the extravagant claims he had made over his famous victory in the Masters. In *Golf Illustrated*, Brownlow Wilson wrote:

We have heard a lot lately about Gene's double eagle [albatross two at the fifteenth which forced a play-off he subsequently won] during the last round of the Masters. He did win through when his cause seemed utterly hopeless to snatch the title from Craig Wood after the blond bomber had already received the congratulations of the players and the crowd. So much has been written of this feat that I am sick of the very mention of it. It has been shown in advertisements to sell special spoons which, they would have you believe, ensure such phenomenal shots. Gene writes that it was not luck but a super shot played to within a fraction of an inch. Let us get down to the solid facts. First flight players will sink a full shot once in a while because they are putting them up so often close to the pin. However when Sarazen holed his, he was lucky enough to have this miracle happen when it really counted, so let us hear no more of it being the result of supernatural skill.

Meanwhile Runyan, though consistently outdriven by Dick Burton, had much the sharper short game and got home by five and three. By now there was no stemming the American tide, even Revolta, who had gone three down with nine to play against Reg Whitcombe, storming back and winning by two and one as his opponent seemed almost to throw in the towel. Padgham, too, collapsed over the last nine holes, losing four of them to go down by four and two against Dutra. So, in no time at all, America had their seven points and it was all over.

All that followed was immaterial, though this should not detract from the performance of Percy Alliss who, despite being three down at lunch, came back to beat Craig Wood by one hole. It was Britain's only point in the singles, though the best recovery came from Bill Cox who, having been five down at lunch to Horton Smith, took six of the next nine holes to lead. They finished all square but it was, even so, a fine effort by Cox. Furthermore there was a halved match, too, for Perry and the painfully slow Sam Parks in the bottom match between the Open champions of Britain and the United States respectively. Parks was not highly rated in the States despite his US Open victory that year on the difficult Oakmont course (299 was his winning total), but he did have pluck, holing from 40 feet at the last to draw level with Perry.

Charles Whitcombe made no excuses over the Ryder Cup. We lost because we played golf so very much below our usual standard. If we had played as well as we can, the result might have been different. The team, except Alliss, who had a stiff neck, were fit and had been playing well in practice.

They had plenty of time for preparations, so we cannot blame it on that. The Ridgewood course is difficult but not too difficult for our men. It demands a type of golf not usually played in Britain. There is clover on the fairways and we discovered that we needed clubs with much more loft to play shots to the green with success.

With the clubs we are accustomed to employ it is not possible to play this shot so well as the Americans. We could not therefore play the type of shots most effective. The crowd gave us a fine show. The spectators did not have any effect on us. They were as fair a crowd as anybody could wish to have following. They gave us every encouragement, but we needed more than that. We needed more clubs and a lot of luck to have won.

The lone victory of Alliss, stiff neck and all, in the singles did not escape the notice of Henry Longhurst. 'The unkind critic cannot help remarking,' he wrote, 'that if Alliss had a stiff neck, the best thing to do with the next lot would be to make them all sit in a draught before the match!'

Various explanations were given for the poor British performance, the two most popular being the clover on the fairways and the insufficient time the team was given in which to acclimatize and practise. They had had a week, but several observers, including the captain's wife (!), declared that this was not enough. She was supported by both *Country Life* and *The Tatler*, whose correspondent went so far as to say: 'Better not to go at all than to be beaten like this every year.'

Not that the *Glasgow Herald* agreed with that sentiment: 'If we cannot face up to the humbling of our pride in a sport which is spreading to every corner of the earth, we would be false to those who helped to make the British sportsman acknowledged as the most gallant loser on earth.'

C.B. MacFarlane, of the *Evening News*, made much of the clover on the fairways, describing it as 'a terror, as the ball may skid off the irons'. However, Sandy Herd, the first man to win the Open championship with the rubber-core Haskell golf ball in 1902, dismissed this excuse. 'The ball sits down quite nicely in clover and you can get under it quite well,' he declared. He was also supported by 'M.W.' in *The Observer*, who commented that 'a lamer excuse could not possibly be offered and from whatever source it sprang, the pity is that it was ever offered'. Instead he regarded 'stage fright' as a more plausible explanation. Robert Browning, author of the definitive *History of Golf*, was at odds with that opinion, stating that stage fright 'seems to me an unnecessarily harsh and unsympathetic term to apply to the mental handicap which besets inexperienced players under unfamiliar conditions'.

Tom Webster, writing in the *Daily Mail*, suggested that the British team 'could not hole out in a hole the size of the Atlantic', while one American analysis that 'the British were content to play for the green, but the Americans went always for the flag' was dismissed by Browning. 'No doubt the timid approach play of some of the younger members of the British team may appear to justify such a belief,' he wrote, 'but in my opinion that is sheer nonsense.'

Closer to the truth may have been the *New York Herald Tribune* which said quite bluntly: 'With the exception of the Whitcombes, the British players seemed to have left their form on the practice ground.' They could also have made an exception of Alliss. The *New York Times* felt that 'what probably bothered the British players more than anything was the amount of water on the greens. The Americans had the more trustful and more watertight short games.'

How many more times we were to hear that in the years to come.

UNITED STATES		GREAT BRITAIN
Foursomes		
G. Sarazen & W. Hagen 7 & 6	beat	A. Perry & J. Busson
H. Picard & J. Revolta 6 & 5	beat	A.H. Padgham & P. Alliss
P. Runyan & H. Smith 9 & 8	beat	W.J. Cox & E.W. Jarman
O. Dutra & K. Laffoon	lost to	C.A. Whitcombe & E.R. Whitcombe 1 hole
Singles		
Sarazen 3 & 2	beat	Busson
Runyan 5 & 3	beat	R. Burton
Revolta 2 & 1	beat	R.A. Whitcombe
Dutra 4 & 2	beat	Padgham
C. Wood	lost to	Alliss 1 hole
Smith	halved with	Cox
Picard 3 & 2	beat	E.R. Whitcombe
S. Parks	halved with	Perry

United States 9 — Great Britain 3

Great Britain 4 – United States 8

Played at Southport and Ainsdale, 29, 30 June 1937

Though it might be hard to believe more than fifty years on, the United States had until 1937 never travelled well as a team on their visits to Britain. In the two previous Ryder Cup matches this side of the Atlantic, at Moortown in 1929 and at Southport and Ainsdale in 1933, they had been beaten, as they had in the previous two unofficial matches at Gleneagles in 1921 and at Wentworth in 1926. It was a curious state of affairs, in stark contrast to their dominance of the Open championship between 1921 and 1933 when Walter Hagen won it four times, Bobby Jones (an amateur) three times and Jock Hutchison, Jim Barnes, Tommy Armour, Gene Sarazen and Densmore Shute once each. Only once in those thirteen years had a British golfer, Arthur Havers in 1923, prevailed.

That particular tide had begun to turn with Henry Cotton's celebrated triumph at Royal St George's in 1934 when he had opening rounds of 67 and 65 for a record of 132 that has still not been touched. Immediately, Alf Perry and Alf Padgham followed in his wake in 1935 and 1936, though it had to be admitted that the American entry had at the same time begun to decline, in both numbers and quality.

Now, however, the full force of American golf assembled once again, first for the Ryder Cup on the 'Flanders Fields' of Southport and Ainsdale and then for the Open itself at Carnoustie. Nor was there any doubt that this was going to be a serious mission, for this was at once a mighty team, America's strongest yet and selected in two parts. Hagen, now forty-five, had slipped into the role of non-playing captain and the first six places were filled early in the year by Densmore Shute, the PGA champion of 1936, Tony Manero, the US Open champion of the same year, Johnny Revolta, Henry Picard, Horton Smith and the ageless Gene

Sarazen. It was over the remaining four places that the Americans took notable care, with a shortlist of thirteen. They were Craig Wood, Dick Metz, Paul Runyan, Ed Dudley, Sam Snead, Vic Ghezzi, Jimmy Hines, Lloyd Mangrum, Harold McSpaden, Byron Nelson, Ralph Guldahl, Olin Dutra and Ky Laffoon.

The vacancies were to be filled by the four players with the best record over six rounds of medal play, the 36-hole qualifyer for the PGA (then still a match-play event) at Pittsburgh in May and the full four rounds of the US Open at Oakland Hills only four days before the team was due to sail from New York on the *Manhattan* on 16 June. The only possibility other than those thirteen would have been if an American-born member of the PGA were to win either of those two events. It did not happen. Shute retained the PGA, while Guldahl ensured his place by winning the US Open with a record total of 281. The other three vacancies were filled by Snead, second in the Open, Dudley, who was fifth, and Nelson. Just imagine four of the modern-day players accepting such short notice!

Thus did Snead make the first of seven appearances in the Ryder Cup. He was then twenty-five, having wandered down from the hills of West Virginia with a golf game that was to entrance not only America but the world itself. However, he was not the only player to make a lasting impact at Southport and Ainsdale, for into the British team for the first time came a little Welshman, Dai Rees, the reigning PGA Matchplay champion, who was all heart and guts and was the only player to emerge from this first home defeat with a bigger reputation than the one he had already made.

Sam King was the other newcomer in a team that also at last welcomed back Cotton, eligible once again on his return from Royal

Alf Padgham driving at Southport and Ainsdale in 1937. Dai Rees, who was making his first appearance in the match, is in the centre, hatless

Waterloo, and rightly so after his Open championship victory of 1934. There was, however, a divergence of opinion over the selection of Padgham, who had lost his game after winning the 1936 Open and, furthermore, was said to be overplayed since he had spent the previous winter competing in South Africa. His supporters pointed to his obvious 'class', but it was his critics who were proved right for in the end he was very much one of the weaker links.

Even before the start the signs were ominous, for in practice it was clear that only Cotton and Rees were in any sort of form, though some heart was taken from

the fact that the only American who appeared at home in inhospitable weather was Hagen, who was not playing. However, it was all very different when the 'gun went' in a stiff south westerly wind that was made more difficult by the brick-hard fairways. Even slightly errant shots would bounce uncontrollably into the thick rough, and the PGA, which kept for the first time an official record of the scores of each match, probably wished they had not, because they were not impressive.

Compared with 1933, the crowds were much smaller and this was put down, apart from the weather which was also wet on the second day, to the fact that the entrance fee for spectators had gone up to 5s (25p)! There was nevertheless some early encouragement, for at lunch in the 36-hole foursomes Britain were up in two and level in the other two. Thus the opportunity was there for the building of a solid platform. Alas, it was not taken. At the end of the day America led by 2½–1½.

The analysis beforehand was that while Hagen had packed his strength in the middle, Charles Whitcombe, the British captain, had placed his at the top and bottom and particularly on a firm leading foundation from Padgham and Cotton against Dudley and Nelson, America's 'sacrificial lambs'! The plan went sadly awry, for though the British pair began 3, 4, 3, to go two up, they then had a spell when for six holes they did not once find the green with their second shots and were soon caught.

Nevertheless, after a lot of scrambling on both sides, Britain edged two up again, only to finish the morning round rather weakly, first when Cotton pushed his second at the sixteenth and then, after Padgham had played a lovely spoon shot to within 12 feet at the seventeenth, they contrived to take three putts. It was not the best of aperitifs before lunch, and sure enough the digestive system suffered immediately afterwards when, after the Americans had driven into a bunker at the short first hole, Cotton followed them. Moreover, the British pair took another four to get down and in no time at all they were three down. Whenever they threatened a come-back they either made a mess of it or else Nelson or Dudley would hole a long putt. Cotton may not have been at his best, but Padgham was all over the place and even Bernard Darwin was moved to write in *The Times* that he had had an 'unquestionably bad match'.

The tables were also turned in the second match, Arthur Lacey and Bill Cox leading by a hole at lunch but subsequently going down by two and one to Guldahl and Manero. Within that game there had never-

theless been a spirited British recovery, for the Americans had taken two of the first three holes in the morning. Cox was the mainstay with his sure touch on the receptive greens, though it was his pitch to the eighteenth and Lacey's putt that fended off the prospect of the Americans drawing level when Manero played a lovely run-up to the same green for a matching birdie. After lunch the British pair extended their lead to two holes at the sixth (or twenty-fourth), but Manero's putting was always dangerously accurate and the match became level again when Lacey went out of bounds at the fourteenth. It proved a fatal mistake, for at once Cox and Lacey became erratic on the greens and Guldahl and Manero made the most of it to get home by two and one.

Charles Whitcombe, as the protective captain, had paired himself with Rees, his only instruction before the match being that his young partner should pay no attention to the Americans in practice for fear that it might put him off. Perhaps it was as well, for they drew the short straw in that they faced the most formidable pair of all in Sarazen and Shute. Later Rees was to write in his autobiography, *Thirty Years of Championship Golf*: 'They were certainly impressive and seemed, with their heavy build and air of conscious superiority, to be an entirely different race.' However, this only served to redouble Rees's determination, dented though it must have been when, as early as the fourth hole when trying to negotiate a stymie, he succeeded only in knocking his opponents' ball into the hole. Undeterred, Rees played magnificently. He produced the best golf of the four and largely carried Whitcombe, who gave his partner ample opportunity to explore the rough on the left.

The British couple took the last two holes in the morning to square the match and they remained pretty well deadlocked until the fifteenth in the afternoon when Rees for once erred, going through the green. This made Sarazen and Shute one up, but Rees

Lord Wardington presents the Ryder Cup to Walter Hagen at Southport and Ainsdale in 1937

got in a good putt to win the seventeenth, and it looked very much as if they might take the match as well when Sarazen was much too strong with his second to the last and landed on the practice putting green. It was an impossible place from which to get down in two and Rees was flabbergasted when the Americans called for a ruling and obtained a free drop at the front of the green, leaving them with a very straight-forward chip, which Shute laid dead. Whitcombe, having assured the agitated Rees that the ruling was correct, then putted rather feebly and the little Welshman was suddenly left with a putt of around six feet for a halved match. Down it went, and not

for the first time, nor the last, Rees was a hero.

Alliss and Dick Burton followed in even better style, beating Picard and Revolta. It was due in the first place to a great counter attack after they had been one down after nine holes in the morning but then lunched three up as Alliss holed a beauty at the home hole and Picard missed something of a tiddler. However, the margin was back to one by the turn in the afternoon and it took a lot of British character for them to hold on as half followed half before the match finished at the thirty-fifth.

The second day was full of more wind and now also torrents of rain that made the playing of golf as unpleasant as watching it. Misguidedly perhaps, Whitcombe dropped himself and also omitted Cox, who had played well enough in the foursomes to have deserved a second chance. Furthermore Whitcombe persisted with Padgham as his number one and that presented the Americans with the ideal start, for he was no match for Guldahl, a big man with not the most engaging of swings. Guldahl was, however, master of the conditions and, after even exchanges through the first five holes, he drew remorselessly away to be six up at lunch and ultimately the winner by eight and seven. The other games were much tighter, America up in four at lunch, down in three and the other all square.

King had a terrific tussle with Shute and was unlucky to be only all square at the break, for the American twice holed pitch shots as well as some unlikely long putts. But things changed swiftly afterwards as Shute shot into a four-hole lead with only eleven to play. It was then that King climbed back off the floor. Beginning with a two at the eighth he played those eleven holes in four under fours, finally drawing level at the last where, after Shute had shaved the hole, he sank a putt of five feet for a birdie and a halved match.

Next came the gallant Rees, who had been in deep trouble at three down to Nelson at one point in the morning. Once, Rees's club had slipped out of his hand altogether in the pouring rain, but he took four holes in a row to lead by the narrowest margin at lunch. Pressing on, this soon became three up and presently he was being carried back to the clubhouse by his exuberant Welsh followers.

Behind him came another point as Cotton, though by no means firing his second shots as accurately as he had done in practice, nevertheless always had something in hand against the painstaking Manero. Cotton was two up at lunch and drew further and further clear before shutting his man out by five and three.

Technically, of the matches finished, that was 4—4 but by then it was clear that the United States were going to win. At lunch they had held the advantage in three of the last four singles and just about the last hope went when Alliss, one up on Sarazen after eighteen holes and later three up, gradually had his lead eroded until they were all square with four to play. It was the fifteenth that was crucial. Alliss was always going to make three, but Sarazen had the great good fortune to see his tee shot bounce back off a spectator on to the green, and then he had the audacity to hole the putt for a two. It was a fortunate lead, but once he had got it Sarazen never looked like letting go.

Nothing much mattered after that, for Snead, clad between shots in a white mackintosh, led Burton by two holes at lunch and, with that easy grace of his, consistently outdrove a man himself considered to be a long hitter. It inevitably wore Burton down as Snead made a lasting impression in victory by five and four. If Perry, against Dudley, and Lacey, against Picard, could have plucked victory then Britain would still have forced a tie, but neither looked like it and both lost, albeit it gallantly, by two and one.

Britain had been beaten by much the superior team, and afterwards the analysts were soon at work. The conclusion was that the Americans were vastly superior near the hole, with the capacity to sink anything from 50 yards in, while the British had thoughts only of getting close. In brief: 'They attack the flag and we don't.'

There was nevertheless some consolation, for the two teams then moved on to Carnoustie and it was there, in some even more deplorable weather, that Cotton won what he always considered to be the best of his three Open championships. He scored successively lower — 74, 73, 72, 71 — the last two of which, on a course that was within a drop of being so waterlogged that it was unplayable, being matters of wonder; and the Americans were put to flight.

Immediately this gave hope that next time there might be a different Ryder Cup story to be told. But already across Europe dark clouds were forming above the armies Hitler was assembling. The match was scheduled, before war broke out on 3 September, for November 1939 at the Ponte Vedra Club, Jacksonville, and the British PGA got as far as announcing the first eight places. They were: Henry Cotton (captain), Jimmy Adams, Dick Burton, Sam King, Alf Padgham, Dai Rees, Charles Whitcombe and Reg Whitcombe. The remaining places were never filled.

The Americans also announced their full team of Walter Hagen (captain), Vic Ghezzi, Ralph Guldahl, Jimmy Hines, Harold McSpaden, Dick Metz, Byron Nelson, Henry Picard, Paul Runyan, Horton Smith and Sam Snead. 'Caps' were still awarded, even though the match was never played.

Furthermore, the Americans, presumably believing that it would not take long for Germany to be put in its place, even went so far as to announce a team for 1941. It read: Hagen (captain), Jimmy Demaret, Ghezzi, Ben Hogan, McSpaden, Lloyd Mangrum, Nelson, Gene Sarazen, Smith, Snead and Craig Wood. Unknown to them, however, the Japanese had already fixed their eyes on Pearl Harbor and it was not until 1947, ten years on from Southport and Ainsdale, that the Ryder Cup was resumed.

GREAT BRITAIN		UNITED STATES
Foursomes		
A.H. Padgham & T.H. Cotton	lost to	E. Dudley & B. Nelson 4 & 2
A.J. Lacey & W.J. Cox	lost to	R. Guldahl & T. Manero 2 & 1
C.A. Whitcombe & D.J. Rees	halved with	G. Sarazen & D. Shute
P. Alliss & R. Burton	beat	H. Picard & J. Revolta
2 & 1		
Singles		
Padgham	lost to	Guldahl 8 & 7
S. King	halved with	Shute
Rees 3 & 1	beat	Nelson
Cotton 5 & 3	beat	Manero
Alliss	lost to	Sarazen 1 hole
Burton	lost to	S. Snead 5 & 4
A. Perry	lost to	Dudley 2 & 1
Lacey	lost to	Picard 2 & 1

Great Britain 4 — United States 8

United States 11 — Great Britain 1
Played at Portland, Oregon, 1, 2 November 1947

After six years of war in Europe and the austerity that followed, Britain was undoubtedly ill equipped for the match at Portland, Oregon in 1947. The Open championship had not been played between 1940 and 1945 and when it was resumed in 1946 at St Andrews and won by Sam Snead, some of the British players could be seen in their service uniforms. There was also still food and petrol rationing as the country endeavoured to get itself back on its feet.

America had also been at war, though more briefly, and on looking up their tour records it can be seen that only in 1943 were no statistics kept on their money-winners. Ben Hogan was the leading earner for the three years beginning in 1940, and Byron Nelson his successor in 1944 and 1945. Only in 1943 was the PGA championship not played, though the US Open was cancelled between 1942 and 1945 and the Masters between 1943 and 1945.

A tour of sorts nevertheless did exist and Nelson, who was excused military service because he was a haemophiliac, played some golf the like of which had never been seen before. In 1944 he won 13 out of 23 tournaments, and, in 1945, 18 out of 31, including one astonishing sequence of 11 in a row. He was also runner-up seven times and never out of the top ten. At one point he played 19 consecutive rounds in under 70 with a stroke average for the season of 68.33.

To some extent it could be argued that Nelson did not have too much competition because many of the other leading players were away on active service. Furthermore, preferred lies were allowed on courses no longer groomed to their previous standards, while there were even concessions over the number of clubs players were allowed to carry. Even so, Nelson's record was as outstanding as his golf and it was a considerable loss to the game when, because of his less than robust health, he went into semi-retirement at the age of thirty-four, indeed not playing in a single tournament in the year of resumption of the Ryder Cup.

Consequently Nelson gained his place at Portland only by invitation. The American PGA had for the first time introduced a points scoring system, allocating 100 points each to the winner of the Open and PGA, 95 to the Masters champion, 70 to winners of tour events and proportional marks to those finishing in the top ten in the same events. They were also allocated over a two-year period, which still exists today. The system was greeted with a certain amount of scepticism in Britain, the argument being that it was too rigid and did not cater for the man who had run into some recent form. Amateur statisticians nevertheless went to work to see how the British team would have been made up on a similar league basis and discovered that it would have differed in only two respects, Reg Whitcombe and Richard Burton having a better record than Jimmy Adams and Eric Green, both of whom were in the team.

For all the businesslike approach of the Americans, interest in the match was not high. At such a time, the war only just over, the British PGA was unable to launch an appeal fund and there were doubts in many quarters as to whether it was advisable to resume the Ryder Cup so soon. Had the money not been raised, the match could have died there and then. It was saved, after some secret negotiations involving Fred Corcoran, an American promoter who was at the time executive director of the American PGA, by one man — Robert Hudson, an American industrialist who annually sponsored the Portland Open and was in addition a member of the American PGA advisory

Though the war was over, Britain travelled more in hope than expectation to the 1947 match at Portland, Oregon. Left to right: (back row) Commander Charles Roe (secretary of the PGA and team manager), Jimmy Adams, Max Faulkner, Eric Green, Charlie Ward, Reg Horne; (front row) Sam King, Fred Daly, Henry Cotton, Dai Rees, Arthur Lees

committee. It was Hudson, like Sam Ryder before him, who saw the value of these international matches and, single-handed, he came up with the money to keep the Ryder Cup afloat for some years. Hudson was also the benefactor behind the Hudson trophy, an inter-club match involving professionals and amateurs at the South Herts Club in north London, and he will be remembered too by some grateful professionals for the food parcels he sent each Christmas when supply in the shops at home was still short.

The British team sailed on the *Queen Mary*, where incidentally they consumed the biggest steaks they had seen in years, and Robert Hudson was at New York to meet

them and then accompany the party on the protracted three-and-a-half-day rail journey to the far north-west. The trip was relieved by some informed commentary by Max Faulkner, who had swotted up the route beforehand and was able to tell an at first disbelieving audience some of America's history. Faulkner also recalls the train arriving a few hours late and himself, tongue in cheek, explaining the delay to waiting reporters by saying that there had been some buffalo on the line that had stopped the train! It was just part of Faulkner's rich imagination, but it was swallowed hook, line and sinker and made headlines.

The ten years that had elapsed since the previous Ryder Cup match meant that there were many changes on both sides, and much the most significant was the inclusion for the first time of Ben Hogan as the American playing captain. Henry Cotton had taken over the reins of the British team, though there was a suggestion that as a player he might already be past his best. Since he was to win the Open championship again in 1948, this was obviously not the case! Among his new-comers were Fred Daly, the new Open champion, Arthur Lees, Charlie Ward and Faulkner, all of whom became household names in the years ahead.

On the American side there emerged 'Dutch' Harrison, Lew Worsham, Lloyd Mangrum, Jimmy Demaret, 'Porky' Oliver and Herman Keiser. Leonard Crawley, writing in the *Daily Telegraph*, described this American team as 'as good a side as any that has ever played against Great Britain, and probably better'. He said that if the British managed to win four games, he would be well satisfied. They did not even manage that, the 11−1 defeat being the heaviest yet.

In bringing the match to Portland, which was obviously part of the PGA's bargain with Robert Hudson, something of a risk was taken because winter starts earlier in Oregon than in other parts of the North American continent. Sure enough, rain greeted the arrival of the British team and it did not stop until after they had left. Conditions were appalling. Dai Rees described it as being like playing in India during the monsoon, while 'Toots' Cotton, the wife of the British captain, remarked that 'no club at home would consider even holding the monthly medal in such weather'.

With quite large crowds able to roam the fairways, conditions underfoot were worse than many experienced watchers had ever seen. There were pools of water everywhere, bunkers flooded and mud oozing up over the soft ridges of foot prints. Only the greens survived more or less unscathed, but for all the difficulties of playing golf in such conditions, the Americans were magnificent.

Hardly any of them were over par, and in the opinion of Leonard Crawley it was their short game and ability to improvise that separated the two teams. He wrote:

On the sodden greens their approaches pitched past the pin, sat down and then, as a rabbit temporarily stunned, scuttled back, often 15 feet before lying dead. The British approach shots seemed just as well struck but were usually on the short side and burrowed straight into the turf.

An American writer, Robert Caldwell, observed:

Since 1937, American professionals led by Byron Nelson, in my view the greatest golfer the world has ever seen, have set an entirely new standard in tournament golf. Golf clubs and golf equipment have improved and fierce competition in 40 weeks of season all over our continent has made it essential for the tournament player − if he hopes to survive − to mechanize his game and to learn to improvise for all manner of situations of play.

Compared with ten years earlier, he felt that the British had made some advance.

They drove just as straight as our players, if not quite as far. Their second shots were adequate but lacked the consistent accuracy of the Americans and consequently, over 36 holes, the British were all under far greater pressure on and around the greens. The modern American professional excels in the trap shot, the chip of any description and with his putter, which more than any other club earns him his living.

There were two unusual happenings before the match. On the last afternoon of practice Cotton asked for an inspection of the American clubs. Apparently there was no official reason for this, but the inference was that some of the clubs had grooves which put more spin on the ball and were therefore illegal. Hogan submitted to the inspection without complaint and the two captains were in attendance together with one of the

American officials. Nothing untoward was discovered, but the incident did have a sequel at Ganton two years later.

Then, the following morning, just before play was about to begin, Cotton called the British team to his suite for what the players thought was going to be tactical talk. Instead he held up a bible and said: 'Gentlemen, I think we should have a few moments for meditation.' Heads were bowed, but the call for outside help was unavailing.

Only briefly was the British team in with any sort of chance. At lunch in the foursomes they were narrowly up in two matches but heavily down in two, and in the end they lost the lot, which once again left them with a towering mountain to climb. In the top game Worsham and Oliver were quickly into their stride against Cotton and Lees, Cotton somehow always being faced with the important putts and missing the lot. They were six down at lunch and ultimately demolished by ten and nine.

Behind them Mangrum, who had been wounded and subsequently decorated in the D-Day landings, played beautifully in partnership with Snead. They were round in 71, one under par, and six up against Ward and Daly, who in the afternoon had a chance or two to cut the deficit. But by then they were so bruised and battered that they could not make the most of their opportunities, and they went down by six and five.

It was in the third foursome that Britain had their best chance, for Faulkner relished the prospect of playing the formidable Hogan and Demaret, announcing himself straight away with a thrilling two iron second shot to the first green, Adams holing the putt for a birdie. Indeed, after nine holes, which they covered in 33, the British were four up. Even so the impression was that Hogan, very painstaking on the greens, always had matters in hand, and by lunch the Americans had cut the margin to two.

Nor was there any holding Hogan and Demaret for a time after lunch. They got their own back by also playing the outward

Henry Cotton soon after he had been appointed captain of the 1947 British Ryder Cup team

half in 33, to go two up only to be caught again, first when Faulkner hit a fine mid iron close enough for a birdie at the eleventh and then when Adams returned the compliment with a pitch right by the hole at the long fifteenth. It was at the sixteenth that the match took its final turn. Demaret was bunkered from the tee but Hogan hit a glorious six iron as clean as a whistle off the top of the sand and Demaret made the maximum of it by then holing from 12 feet for a birdie. It was a telling blow, and the Americans made sure of a third point on the last green.

King was the steadying influence in the

last foursome, for though Rees was as full of dashing strokes, he also hit some destructive ones and a useful lead dwindled to a single hole at lunch. Barron was much the weakest of the four players and it looked as if he might become too much of a burden for Nelson when the Americans fell three behind again after only two more holes in the afternoon. However, Nelson then began to show his class and with telling putts on the eleventh, twelfth and thirteenth greens and a glorious tee shot right beside the flag at the seventeenth for a two, they closed the door.

The singles were consequently something of a formality, hastened immediately as Harrison, who had not played in the foursomes, caught Daly on one of his off days — 40 strokes to the turn. The American was well ahead at lunch, and with 34 on the outward half afterwards, soon won by five and four. Behind them Adams had a fine tussle with Worsham, finishing birdie, birdie in the morning to cut the American's lead to a single hole, and by the turn in the afternoon he was level. Yet there was no shaking Worsham, and with golf that grew in strength he won by three and two. A third American point quickly came from Mangrum who was round in 70 in the morning, six up on Faulkner and won with five holes to spare. Nor was Ward a match for the big-hitting Oliver, and when a counter attack of 34 for the first nine holes came in the afternoon, it gained him no ground at all as Oliver still breezed home by four and three.

The best scrap was that between Nelson, who was in great form, against the tenacious Lees. Nelson was round in 70 in the morning for a lead of two holes, and hard though Lees tried with some really splendid golf, he could make no further impression. So that was it, for Cotton, though he had begun promisingly, looked increasingly tired and drawn against the glorious golf of Snead and it showed in his putting. Three down at lunch, Cotton did close the gap again to one but the impression was very much of Snead

winning as he pleased.

Demaret was given something of a fright by Rees, one down at lunch and still one down with nine to play. But the American found an extra gear, playing the eleventh, twelfth, thirteenth and fourteenth holes in two under par, and Rees, for all his pluck, could not answer that. A whitewash was nevertheless avoided, for down at the bottom King, though held by Keiser for 18 holes, always looked the better player, particularly with his irons. Sticking religiously to par, King began to draw steadily away and finally finished his man off on the fifteenth green.

It had therefore been a sharp lesson for the British. Few had expected them to win, but a defeat of that size was a humbling experience, although one not uncommon in the barren years ahead.

UNITED STATES		GREAT BRITAIN
Foursomes		
E. Oliver & L. Worsham 10 & 9	beat	T.H. Cotton & A. Lees
S. Snead & L. Mangrum 6 & 5	beat	F. Daly & C.H. Ward
B. Hogan & J. Demaret 2 holes	beat	J. Adams & M. Faulkner
B. Nelson & H. Barron 2 & 1	beat	D.J. Rees & S.L. King
Singles		
E.J. Harrison 5 & 4	beat	Daly
Worsham 3 & 2	beat	Adams
Mangrum 6 & 5	beat	Faulkner
Oliver 4 & 3	beat	Ward
Nelson 2 & 1	beat	Lees
Snead 5 & 4	beat	Cotton
Demaret 3 & 2	beat	Rees
H. Keiser	lost to	King 4 & 3

United States 11 — Great Britain 1

Great Britain 5 − United States 7

Played at Ganton, 16, 17 September 1949

Ben Hogan again led the United States in the 1949 match at Ganton, a lovely heathland course in Yorkshire's Vale of Pickering, but not this time in a playing capacity. On a fog-shrouded February morning earlier that year Hogan, driving with his wife Valerie away from the Phoenix Open where he had just lost a play-off, had had a fearful head-on collision with an overtaking bus. He had instinctively flung himself across his wife to shield her from the impact, and it probably saved his own life as the steering wheel concertinaed into the back of the driver's seat. Even so, it took an hour to cut him from the wreckage.

Hogan suffered multiple injuries: a double fracture of the pelvis, broken collarbone, ankle and rib and extensive contusions to his left leg. However, it was the subsequent blood clot that very nearly ended his life. For some days it hung in the balance and when the crisis had passed, Hogan's recovery proved a very slow and painful process. He was in hospital for 58 days and when discharged was down to six and a half stone. He was out of golf as a competitor for the whole of that year and his return, just eighteen months after the accident when, still in discomfort, he won the US Open at Merion, was one of golf's fairytale come-backs.

The United States Ryder Cup team on arrival at Ganton for the 1949 match. Left to right: Johnny Palmer, 'Dutch' Harrison, Lloyd Mangrum, Sam Snead, Ben Hogan (non-playing captain), Clayton Heafner, Jimmy Demaret, Chick Harbert, Bob Hamilton

THE OFFICIAL HISTORY OF THE RYDER CUP

Nevertheless Hogan was fit enough, albeit still on sticks, to travel with the Americans to England and at some stage, as he rested his aching legs back at his home in Fort Worth, his mind must have turned to a small incident that had passed almost unnoticed during the 1947 match at Portland. It was then, on the eve of the foursomes, that Henry Cotton, his opposing captain, had called for an inspection of the American clubs. The amount of backspin the Americans were getting on the ball with their pitching clubs had been a matter of comment before, but the inspection, to which Hogan had made no protest, found nothing untoward and it was only after the match that it became generally known that it had even taken place.

Hogan had nevertheless not forgotten it, and on the eve of the match at Ganton he got his own back by demanding an examination of the British clubs. The request was made rather less discreetly. Even members of the public heard that the issue had been raised, and two golf club manufacturers who happened to be in the vicinity were asked their unofficial opinion. When the two could not agree, the PGA was left in a difficult position and hurriedly drove to Scarborough where Bernard Darwin, who was then chairman of the Royal and Ancient's Rules of Golf committee, was dining. Whether it caught him between the soup and the fish has been lost over time, but his verdict was swift and, in its way, classically to the point. 'Nothing that a little filing will not put right,' he said before resuming his place at table. Consequently the clubs were spirited back to Ganton where Jock Ballantine, the club professional, spent the evening in his workshop filing away.

Hogan was therefore proved to have been on solid ground in his request, and Ken Bousfield, who was making his first appearance for Britain, recalls Dick Burton's clubs coming in for particular attention. This in no way surprised Bousfield for he can recall quite vividly, even before departing for Ganton, Burton spending long hours in the professional's shop at Coombe Hill with a brace bit boring away at the holes rather than grooves which were then the feature of some iron clubs. Bousfield also remembers one of Sam King's clubs and another belonging to Arthur Lees being extensively scrutinized, while Dai Rees, in his autobiography, claims that 'for the rest of the day I made my fingers and thumbs sore with the chore of filing down the grooves. It seemed ridiculous, for filing simply sharpened the edges and made the clubs even rougher.'

Golf Illustrated concluded that the whole matter had been handled very clumsily and called for a compulsory examination of clubs before every event. 'The present arrangement is unbearable,' it proclaimed. 'No captain ought to be put in the invidious position of having to make the request.' However, it did not blame Hogan and nor did Leonard Crawley in the *Daily Telegraph*, who wrote:

> Too much emphasis has been laid on Hogan's insisting on an inspection of clubs before the match. The fact that Bernard Darwin saw fit to agree with Hogan's objections to certain British clubs is proof beyond doubt that Hogan was right. I would have done exactly the same myself in Hogan's position.

Nor was this the only note of discord. Aware of the food rationing still in force in Britain, the Americans brought with them a supply of their own: 600 steaks, twelve sides of rib for roasting, a dozen hams and twelve boxes of bacon. The only speculation beforehand was as to how so much could be consumed in so short a time! Well, the British gave them some help when they were invited to dinner one evening, but sadly there were some on this side of the Atlantic who felt that the Americans, by arriving to an extent self-sufficient, had insulted their hosts by indicating that the food they would have been offered would not have proved good enough. No doubt this had never even crossed the minds of the Americans, and

Sam Snead, in unfamiliar white cap, gets ready to practise at Ganton

it was unfortunate that their actions were misinterpreted.

In many ways the American team was an unknown quantity, for only three of its members – Sam Snead, Jimmy Demaret and Lloyd Mangrum – had played in Britain before. They would obviously miss Hogan. Byron Nelson had by then retired from serious competition and they could not even call upon their new US Open champion, Cary Middlecoff, because he was not at the time a member of the American PGA.

The British, even without Henry Cotton who had now entered semi-retirement following his third Open victory in 1948, still had the more experienced team. Seven of the players who had been at Portland in 1947 had not only kept their places but had apparently learnt from that chastening

experience, and they arrived at Ganton in some sparkling form. Charlie Ward and Sam King, in their final warm-up, holed the course in 62; the rest were not far behind them and the feeling was that if such golf could be maintained they were fully capable of facing any team anywhere and more than holding their own.

For once such high expectations did not fall on stony ground. Amid scenes of great excitement, with a big crowd on the first day scampering here and there after first one match and then another, Britain took the foursomes 3–1, maintaining every bit of the form they had shown on the practice days. It left them needing but 3½ points from the remaining eight singles for their first victory since 1933, and even the more pessimistic followers had to admit that this looked well within their capability. Instead the Americans, no doubt stung by some harsh words from their captain, rose from the ashes of potential defeat with an unsurpassed come-back to take six of those eight singles and snatch victory by 7— 5.

Right from the start it had looked good for Britain, for at lunch on the first day they had led by three up and two up in the first two foursomes, were square in the fourth and only one down in the third. Max Faulkner and Jimmy Adams set the best possible example at the top against 'Dutch' Harrison and Johnny Palmer, never looking back from the moment at the short fifth where Adams hit the stick with his tee shot. Faulkner holed the putt for a two and a lead they never subsequently looked like yielding.

Faulkner's glorious hitting of the ball won many accolades, and anything he lacked in the form of stability in the morning was more than made up by the cool generalship of Adams. They were round in 69 to the Americans' 73, and three holes to the good. Nor was there any let-up afterwards, for Adams remained as steady as rock while Faulkner's shots flew straighter and straighter. When they finished off the match on the seventeenth green, they were no less than five under fours.

Behind them Fred Daly and Ken Bousfield also took their grip straight away, out in 33, and with a three at the short tenth to their opponents' bogey, they were three up on Skip Alexander and Bob Hamilton. However, there was a nasty moment or two to come for the Americans took three of the next four holes, two of them with birdies, only to weaken at the end, losing the short seventeenth to a par and then, of all things, the eighteenth to a five. Even so, Daly and Bousfield were round in 69 and back in the driving seat at two up.

Bousfield had equipped himself splendidly in his first Ryder Cup match — almost his only bad shot of the morning was when he fluffed a little pitch off a bare lie at the fourteenth. Daly, as the senior partner, was

back to his best and the culminating blow to the Americans came at the fourteenth when, from almost exactly the same position he had fluffed in the morning, Bousfield this time pitched dead for a birdie. They were around four under fours, which was then the jargon, for the 34 holes they needed to win.

Nevertheless it was not all one-way traffic, for Jimmy Demaret and Clayton Heafner largely outplayed Ward and King, Demaret in particular appearing to be the master of every shot in the book. His pitching was quite deadly and Heafner made the most of it, putting like a demon. Even so, the British pair hung on to them like leeches and, at only one down at lunch, were still in with a chance. What finished them was the extra gear the Americans found in the afternoon. Beginning at the eighth, they went 3, 4, 3, 3, 3, 4, 3, 4, five of them birdies, and it was all over by four and three.

Though Burton had not been reunited with his filed-down golf clubs until shortly before driving off, he was quite unperturbed and may even have been put on his mettle. He was the strong man in partnership with Lees and they had a rare old tussle with Sam Snead and Lloyd Mangrum, whom Hogan was relying upon for a point. There was never more than a hole in it in the morning, the Americans looking the more likely to lead but being pegged back by a great chip from Burton which saved the seventeenth, and then a long putt from Lees which also saved the eighteenth.

All square therefore at lunch. The British pair at one stage went two up in the afternoon but the Americans caught them again at the twelfth and fourteenth, only to lose the fifteenth and sixteenth to pars. Even then British hearts missed a beat or two, for Mangrum's fine tee shot at the seventeenth brought the margin back to one and a great groan went up when Lees, not for the first time, found a bunker with his second shot to the last. However, Snead had pulled his drive and Mangrum, trying to find a gap between the pines, instead caught one of them. It made a crack like the firing of a pistol, but it was just what the crowd wanted to hear. The hole was halved and Britain had got their third point.

In some instances, both before and after the Ryder Cup match at Ganton, Britain could justly have been accused of beating themselves. Such could never be said on this occasion for, with hardly an exception, they played their hearts out in the singles. Yet it was not enough, for the Americans played even better, their golf being quite stunning as a whole barrage of birdies overwhelmed their opponents before crowds that could scarcely believe their eyes. Perhaps the best measure of the American performance, in which they won six of the singles and lost

only two, was that every man jack of them was under fours for the best part of their 36 holes. They had to be.

The lead came very properly from Harrison at the top, for he began 3, 3, 4, 3, 3, 3 against Faulkner to be four up in no time at all. A glorious striker of the ball with a lovely putting touch, Harrison was, on the day, in a different class to his opponent and in holing the course in 67 was a demoralizing seven up at lunch. That set the pattern, and at the half-way point the Americans were, in order behind him, one down, one up, four down, one down, five up, five up and one up.

Faulkner was clearly beaten already and so were King and Lees, both five down to Chick Harbert and Demaret, who were

After the 1949 Ryder Cup match, the Americans played in the News of the World *match-play championship at Walton Heath. Here Lloyd Mangrum is watched by Max Faulkner*

round in 68 and 67 respectively. However, there was still some hope for the British since Adams had clung to a narrow lead against Johnny Palmer, Ward had matched Snead's 68 to be only one down, and Rees had played brilliantly against Hamilton, round in 65 to stand four up. Surprisingly perhaps, Charles Whitcombe, the British captain, had left Rees out of the foursomes and it was not an easy choice for him to bring back the little Welshman and drop Bousfield, who had been largely responsible for a point on the first day.

The tail had had a tougher time, but Burton was just ahead of Heafner while Daly was involved in the best match of the morning, somehow holding Mangrum to a single hole despite the American having a 66 that made him look as indestructible as he had been when serving in the American Army in Normandy.

Faulkner was the first to fall, by eight and seven to Harrison, but Adams, though he was at one point overtaken by Palmer, then had a run of 3, 3, 2 from the tenth, played the closing holes steadily and got home on the seventeenth green. Ward, who had got the worst of any stymies that were going in the morning, was next, predictably eclipsed by Snead, who was seven under fours for the 31 holes.

So that was two points in the American bag, but Rees remained a man inspired, all fours and threes in the afternoon as he devoured Hamilton by six and four, twelve under fours for the day and only one five on his card in 32 holes. Everything therefore depended on Burton keeping his narrow lead on Heafner, and Daly perhaps making up his deficit against Mangrum; for elsewhere King had subsided to Harbert and Lees likewise to Demaret.

And how the two of them fought, Burton raising great hopes when he made the most of his opponent's lapses at the eleventh and twelfth to recover a lead earlier lost. The strain of it all was nevertheless showing, first with a tell-tale three putts and then with

his driver, though this should take nothing away from Heafner who, from the thirteenth, went 3, 4, 3, 3 to turn defeat into victory.

Similarly there were brief hopes for Daly, who had begun the afternoon with two birdies in his first three holes to overtake Mangrum, fallen behind again but then come back to square with a two at the tenth. It was a brief reprieve, for the American, as courteous an opponent as he was ruthless, promptly responded with a run of 3, 2, 4, 3, 4, winning four of them, and he was, twelve under fours on the day, as home and dry as were the United States.

It was, without question, a remarkable and stirring recovery by the Americans, for they had had their backs to the wall but with courage and skill had responded with the sort of golf to which there was very little answer.

GREAT BRITAIN		UNITED STATES
Foursomes		
M. Faulkner & J. Adams 2 & 1	beat	E.J. Harrison & J. Palmer
F. Daly & K. Bousfield 4 & 2	beat	R. Hamilton & S. Alexander
C.H. Ward & S.L. King	lost to	J. Demaret & C. Heafner 4 & 3
R. Burton & A. Lees 1 hole	beat	S. Snead & L. Mangrum
Singles		
Faulkner	lost to	Harrison 8 & 7
Adams 2 & 1	beat	Palmer
Ward	lost to	Snead 6 & 5
D.J. Rees 6 & 4	beat	Hamilton
Burton	lost to	Heafner 3 & 2
King	lost to	C. Harbert 4 & 3
Lees	lost to	Demaret 7 & 6
Daly	lost to	Mangrum 4 & 3

Great Britain 5 — United States 7

United States 9½ — Great Britain 2½

Played at Pinehurst, N. Carolina, 2, 4 November 1951

There had not been too much to cheer in British golf in the immediate post-war years. Not only had the Ryder Cup been lost twice, but so had the Walker Cup and the Curtis Cup, similar international competitions but in these instances contested by amateurs, both men and women. There had been a ray of sunshine with Fred Daly's Open victory, the first by an Irishman, at Hoylake in 1947, and cause for even more celebration when, in 1948, Henry Cotton captured his third title at Muirfield. However, Cotton, never blessed with the most robust of health, was by then beginning to limit his appearances, a victim in his early forties of the strain of competition. There also arrived on the scene a South African by the name of Bobby Locke.

Indeed, it was a scene Locke was to dominate, winning the first of his four Opens in a play-off against Harry Bradshaw at Royal St George's in 1949 and then another at Troon the following year. Hard on his heels came an Australian, Peter Thomson, who won four times in the 1950s and a fifth time in the 1960s. These were bleak years for Britain, relieved just once, by Max Faulkner in the 1951 Open at Royal Portrush in Northern Ireland, the only occasion on which the championship has been played outside Scotland and England.

What no one was to know was that another eighteen years would pass before next there was a British winner, and there may not have been quite the romanticism about Faulkner's victory then that perhaps there would be today. He was nevertheless a most colourful figure in his plus fours and the wide range of coloured socks, shirts and pullovers which suited his dashing style of play. He was also that week a man of supreme confidence, in contrast to his form in practice, which had been almost embar-

rassingly bad. Dai Rees recalled in his autobiography that 'to make a match of it we [Ken Bousfield was the third of the Musketeers] had to give him a three-hole start, and we still beat him out of sight. His chipping was nervous and weak and his driving off.' Yet Faulkner had a premonition that he was going to win and even beforehand went round signing autograph books 'Max Faulkner, Open champion 1951', explaining in his inimitable way: 'My dear chap, it's in the bag!'

And in the bag it was. Faulkner holed out like a demon, only 26 putts in one round, finished early, since the leaders were not out last at that time, and spent an anxious

Dai Rees — the heart, body and soul of ten British Ryder Cup teams

53

period in the clubhouse drinking endless cups of tea waiting to see if anyone could beat him – which they could not. Antonio Cerda, of Argentina, had the best chance but failed, and Faulkner's name, as Open champion, was consequently the first to be pencilled into the Ryder Cup team to play at Pinehurst, a wonderful golfing spa deep in the heart of North Carolina boasting three courses (whereas now there are seven). Set among a forest of pines over undulating sandy ground, it is reminiscent of Sunningdale, perhaps England's most treasured heathland course.

By then the British team was being selected by a committee, who drew up a short list of sixteen. The captain was Arthur Lacey, who had played in two Ryder Cup matches before the war. Rees described him as 'a large chap who had the bluff geniality and strength of a yeoman farmer'. Though Lacey had no more luck as captain in America than his British predecessors, it was nevertheless in one way a most happy trip for him, for it was there in Pinehurst that he met his future wife and where they later settled.

Just as Britain had two new players in their team in John Panton and Harry Weetman, so too did the Americans in Jack Burke and Henry Ransom, who was to play only in the foursomes. By then Ben Hogan had also made his comeback, winning his celebrated US Opens at Merion in 1950 and then, a few months before the Ryder Cup, at Oakland Hills where, on a course on which only two players broke 70 all week, Hogan was at his finest. After a last round of 68 he said merely that he was glad he had brought 'this monster to its knees'. It was possibly the fiercest examination the United States Golf Association has ever set.

Hogan had also won his first Masters that spring, but it was Sam Snead who was invited to become the new Ryder Cup captain and with Lloyd Mangrum and Jimmy Demaret they formed a mighty 'engine room'. No one really expected this to be the moment

for Britain to record their first victory in the United States. They sailed on the *Queen Mary*, and one of Bousfield's clearest recollections is of how unexpectedly cold it was. He remembers Hogan wearing pyjamas under his shirt and trousers, while Carlton Heafner took with him an overcoat to don between shots.

Pinehurst was likened by some British visitors to 'Carnoustie in early spring' and the course, at its full stretch just in excess of 7000 yards, was playing so long that some of the tees were moved well forward to give the players a better chance of 'getting up' in the accepted number of strokes. Even so, all the cards seemed to be in the American hands and so it proved, though there was broad agreement that the British did in fact play rather better than the overall margin of 9½–2½ indicated.

Leonard Crawley admitted that he had been wrong in his estimation that 'the British would be out-hit to such an extent that they would be unable to cope with their opponents on this fearfully long course', adding that 'they opened their shoulders and, though physically smaller, their second shots more often than not were inside those of the Americans. But it was the old story of American superiority near the hole'.

Hogan, a shrewd thinker on golfing matters, thought there must be some basic reason for this and came to the conclusion that the more heavily watered American greens bred better putters than those in Britain which, in the days before the 'pop-up' sprinklers, were sprayed by hand with the use of hosepipes. Similarly, Hogan suggested that the hard Texan fairways bred better swingers than the more lush and well-watered fairways in north America. Some substance to this theory was given by the fact that the whole United States team came from the South and had indeed dominated American golf for the previous ten years.

The most marked difference between the sides was nevertheless in their bunker play, and when the British team returned home

The 1951 British team which lost at Pinehurst. Left to right: (back row) Arthur Lees, Ken Bousfield, Harry Weetman, Jack Hargreaves, Jimmy Adams, John Panton; (front row) Charlie Ward, Dai Rees, Arthur Lacey, Max Faulkner, Fred Daly

loud calls were made for the installation of practice bunkers at golf clubs. No doubt the words were heeded, for these days there are many more practice bunkers and the once familiar sight of an enraged secretary descending on anyone bold enough to be found improving that part of his game beside some distant green is now very much a thing of the past.

No one learned this better than Dai Rees, who played Demaret in the singles and was duly beaten by two holes. He later recalled:

We had a tremendous match, with Jimmy performing wondrous things in bunkers. I regard him as the greatest sand player I have ever seen. He was in eleven greenside bunkers that day and on ten occasions he got down with a splash and a putt. At the thirth-fourth I scored a birdie to square and at the next I felt sure I would go ahead for the first time when

my opponent's ball was almost completely buried in a bunker near the green and I was on the green.

Instead Demaret, after a couple of hard looks at the flag, exploded straight into the hole. It was a two-hole swing if ever there was one, and with Rees driving into a bunker at the eighteenth, Demaret finished with more daylight between them than had looked remotely possible a few minutes earlier. Nevertheless there was a happy sequel, as Rees recalls in his autobiography.

After I had congratulated Jimmy on his bunker play he made a typically American generous gesture, handed me his sand iron and said: 'Keep it, Dai, as a gift. The one you've got has too sharp an edge and you'll never have any finesse with it.' It was a modern sand wedge, a broad-soled club, with the back edge lower than the front. Instead of cutting into the sand, as my sharp iron did, it lifted the ball out with real control. I took the club to Britain and had it copied for my own set so that, although I lost the match, I came away with a profit.

One man who came away from Pinehurst with a much enhanced reputation was Arthur Lees, a gritty Yorkshireman, for he was responsible for both the British victories, first partnering Charlie Ward to a two and one victory over 'Porky' Oliver and Ransom, and then beating Oliver again in the singles by the same margin. These were, however, small crumbs of comfort, only Daly escaping defeat in the singles as he halved with Heafner.

Even so it was Heafner, a sound if rather unattractive-looking player, who had given the Americans their impetus when he part-nered the youthful newcomer, Burke, to a comfortable win in the top foursome, five and three against Faulkner and Rees. Sur-prisingly on such a cold morning, a damp mist hanging low over the pines, they played wonderfully well, out in 34, round in 69 and yet only two up. Whenever one of the Americans made a mistake, his partner in-variably made up for it and their passage was made easier when after lunch Faulkner and Rees began badly and subsided to in-evitable defeat.

By contrast Lees and Ward played each of the first nine holes in par for a one-hole lead against Oliver and Ransom and then put on a real spurt, covering the last five holes in 3, 2, 5, 3, 3, three of them birdies, for a three-hole lead. Some of this momen-tum was lost after lunch as errors by Ward led to the loss of two holes and with seven to play they were back to only one up. How-ever, at the twelfth with the green wide open and the British already bunkered in two, Ransom had a 'head up' and the Americans lost their chance.

There was real splendour about the golf of Snead and Mangrum, the former hitting the cover off the ball and the latter quite

deadly with his putter. Adams did what he could but Panton, perhaps a little nervous on his debut, was not his normal trustworthy self. Not that there was much that could be done in the face of the American's outward half of 34, and with sixes at both the tenth and eleventh the Scottish pair slumped to five down, which they still were at lunch. Afterwards the Americans repeated their 34 to the turn and that was good enough, five and four being the eventual margin.

It was for Bousfield, partnered by Daly, a big thrill to face Hogan, who had Demaret at his side. 'He is the best I have ever seen,' recalls Bousfield. 'Such precision, he could put the ball just where he wanted it.' Demaret was slightly off his game and it did enable the British pair, perking up with 35 home against their 41 out, to cut the five holes by which they had trailed after nine holes to three. However, Hogan was not the sort of man to let that sort of thing go on for long and in the afternoon the Americans drew away once again, also winning by five and four.

Once again, therefore, the British, trailing 1−3, found themselves almost hopelessly in arrears going into the singles two days later (there was an unusual break in play when both teams were invited to a football game on 3 November) and their cause was far from helped when in the top match Burke ran right away from Adams, six up at lunch, the same margin by which Mangrum led the out-of-sorts Weetman. Furthermore Skip Alexander, who had made a miraculous recovery from severe injuries and burns in an air crash not much more than a year earlier, was five up on Panton and Snead four up on Faulkner. Indeed, at half-way America led in six of the eight singles, the only relief being provided by Rees, who was one up on Demaret, and Lees, four up on Oliver.

The end of Rees's brave effort has already been described, but Lees, out in 34 in the afternoon, more than held his own — which was just as well. Oliver came back at him towards the end, but too late for it to matter. There was an encouraging result, too, for the whistling Daly against the lumbering Heafner, two golfers in sharp contrast to one another. Three down at lunch, Daly was just as far behind with three to play, even though he had been much the superior player between tee and green, the weaker only on the greens. And then suddenly the Irishman got two holes back and was only one down with one to play. Rising to the occasion, he safely made the eighteenth green in two, Heafner was bunkered and the match was halved.

Elsewhere the American tide flowed with its customary strength, but mention must be made of the great fight Ward put up against the immaculate Hogan, who went round in 67 in the morning and was still only two up. Then Hogan began the afternoon round 3, 3 and still Ward, a little terrier of a Midlander, came back at him, out in 33 himself. Yet nothing would shake Hogan, and he also hit the shot of the day, a three wood covering the best part of 300 yards to the long fourth after he had had to chip out of the trees on the left. Inevitably he then holed the long putt for his four and a half, made another birdie at the next, one of the best and most demanding of par fours, and Ward hardly saw his man again.

Snead was no less magnificent against Faulkner, round in 67 in the morning and four up. Even so, the British Open champion somehow kept the flag flying for longer than many would have been capable of doing. Snead was in simply unbeatable form and he closed the door emphatically with a run of 3, 3, 3 through the thirteenth, fourteenth and fifteenth, and high though the praise was of his performance, so it was, too, of the fight Faulkner had put up.

UNITED STATES		GREAT BRITAIN
Foursomes		
C. Heafner & J. Burke 5 & 3	beat	M. Faulkner & D.J. Rees
E. Oliver & H. Ransom	lost to	C.H. Ward & A. Lees 2 & 1
S. Snead & L. Mangrum 5 & 4	beat	J. Adams & J. Panton
B. Hogan & J. Demaret 5 & 4	beat	F. Daly & K. Bousfield
Singles		
Burke 4 & 3	beat	Adams
Demaret 2 holes	beat	Rees
Heafner	halved with	Daly
Mangrum 6 & 5	beat	H. Weetman
Oliver	lost to	Lees 2 & 1
Hogan 3 & 2	beat	Ward
S. Alexander 8 & 7	beat	Panton
Snead 4 & 3	beat	Faulkner

United States 9½ — Great Britain 2½

Great Britain 5½ — United States 6½

Played at Wentworth, 2, 3 October 1953

Though golf is an individual game, the pressures of team golf are something special. A man is no longer playing for himself but also for others; in the case of the Ryder Cup, for his country as well. No one game is in essence any more important than any other. A win is a win in anyone's language and it does not matter whether the victory margin is ten and eight or a single hole. It still counts the same: a point for your side. Nor does it matter how many strokes are taken. A hole won in a five to a six carries no more value than another taken with a two against a three.

In some ways the lead players in competitions such as the Ryder Cup can be said to be under less of a responsibility than those down at the bottom of the order of play. A point lost early can always be made up by others following behind. But for the tail-enders there is no such cushion when the overall match gets tight. Everything then depends on them and a drive cut, a second shot mis-hit, a chip fluffed or a putt missed can, in the overall context, mean the difference not only between an individual game won or lost but in the whole destiny of the team, the rest of whom are probably grouped at the side of the green watching.

It was this culminating burden of responsibility that fell upon the young shoulders of Peter Alliss and Bernard Hunt in the 1957 Ryder Cup match at Wentworth where, thirty-one years earlier, Sam Ryder had had his dream of regular confrontation between the professionals of America and Britain. This time, however, the match was not played over the East course but on the now senior West which, in another ten years or so, was to become the home of the pioneering World Match-play championship, first sponsored by Piccadilly and later by the Japanese company Suntory. It is also at Wentworth, incidentally, that the PGA European Tour has based its headquarters.

As fate would have it, everything hinged on Alliss and Hunt. Furthermore, Alliss was only twenty-two and the first and still the only son of a Ryder Cup player, Percy, to follow in his father's footsteps, Hunt was twenty-three. Both young lions were on the foothills of golfing careers of many distinctions, but they will also be remembered, cruelly of course, as the two men who could have won the Ryder Cup and did not. Both, in tragic circumstances as the huge crowd held its breath, took six at the final hole, Alliss to lose and Hunt only to halve, and that made all the difference as America squeezed home by the narrowest margin, 6½−5½. Two fives, both of which had been there for the taking (how much easier it is to say that than do it!), and the result would have been reversed. It was a stinging blow, soon softened though it was by an historic British victory four years later at Lindrick.

Not since 1933 had Britain had such a great chance. Nor could there have been a better year in which to do it. Queen Elizabeth had come to the throne, Everest had been climbed by Sir Edmund Hillary and Tensing, England had won the Ashes at cricket, Gordon Richards had won the Derby, Stanley Matthews had won his only FA Cup Winner's medal with Blackpool, a popular Czech Jaraslov Drobny had at last won Wimbledon and Ben Hogan had won the Open championship. It was a year of fulfilment of promise, and in the Ryder Cup hopes were for once quite high, for the feeling beforehand was that this was not a vintage American team, principally because it did not include Hogan, at the time unquestionably the greatest player in the world and in the midst of his greatest year.

One of the two crucial putts missed in the 1953 match at Wentworth when Britain were so close to victory. Bernard Hunt's shoulders sag and Dale Douglas (left) walks across to commiserate.

Not only had he conquered his one remaining peak in the Open at Carnoustie, but in the spring he had won the Masters for a second time and in June he had won the US Open for a record-equalling fourth time. No man had ever come so close to golf's Grand Slam, but the last leg of the PGA was something he never even attempted. Hogan had neither the time to get back to compete because of the proximity of the dates, nor the inclination. Since his accident he had decided against playing 36-hole matches, which was then still the PGA's match-play format, and the same held for the Ryder Cup.

In Hogan's place, the PGA was won by Walter Burkemo, one of four newcomers to the American team. The others were Dale Douglas, the new Canadian Open champion, Ted Kroll, who had four times been wounded during the war, and Cary Middlecoff, a qualified doctor in dentistry, former US Open champion, but one who had had to serve a long apprenticeship before becoming a fully fledged member of the American PGA and able to play in the Ryder Cup.

Eric Brown, who was making his British debut and was to have a great record in the Ryder Cup, had a similar long wait, for the rules then were that anyone turning professional could not compete in a major domestic tournament for five years. Brown had left the amateur ranks in 1946 but, once let loose, he certainly made up for lost time. Into the team with him came Alliss, Hunt and Harry Bradshaw, the first golfer from Eire to be so honoured and runner-up to Bobby Locke in the 1949 Open championship.

Lloyd Mangrum had taken over as the United States captain in a playing capacity, and Henry Cotton was leader of the British team, in this case – and on doctor's orders – non-playing. Though Cotton was then forty-six, Hunt remembers being convinced, as indeed were others, that his captain ought to have been in the team as well. He partnered the great man twice in practice and can still see to this day the little 'cut up' wood he played from a hanging lie on the seventh fairway up to the green. 'I could never have done that in a month of Sundays; pure genius,' Hunt recalls.

The team stayed in the Dormie House at Sunningdale, where they had also undergone some trial matches, and Cotton, always a great believer in good food breeding good golf, made sure the team ate off the fat of the land in still not the most plentiful of times. He even took his players up to town to see *Guys and Dolls*, which was certainly the first time Hunt had been to the London theatre.

Cotton was quite convinced that the British had it in them to win, and was fearless in his selection. He left out the experienced Dai Rees and Max Faulkner from the foursomes and played instead all his newcomers, though not together. It was a plan that misfired, America taking a 3–1 lead that was just as important in the final context as the errors of Alliss and Hunt that later hit all the headlines.

'It was gloom and misery everywhere,' wrote Desmond Hacket in the *Daily Express*. The only crumb of comfort was that it might have been worse, for the three-up lead that the two Irishmen, Daly and Bradshaw, had enjoyed at lunch and still with nine holes to play against Burkemo and Middle-coff suddenly began to disintegrate until they

stood only one up and one to play. Furthermore, the three games ahead of them had already been lost. Hearts immediately missed another beat when, after Daly had hit the British second shot into a greenside bunker, Burkemo cut a brassie round the corner and on to the green. The odds then seemed to be on the Americans getting a half, but Bradshaw splashed out to four feet, Middlecoff missed by a fraction for a three from eight yards and it was all up to Daly.

Hunt recalls standing by the green with the rest of the team and counting Daly's routine of passing the putter head backwards and forwards over the top of the ball before eventually addressing it. 'We counted twelve before he got round to hitting the ball,' he said, 'but it went in' – with what Hacket described as 'the loveliest sound all day'.

Two of the foursomes were always lost causes. Brown and Panton lost the first four holes to Mangrum and Snead and were seven down after only nine. Indeed, the Americans were round in 67, eight up and cruised home by eight and seven. Yet even this terrific golf was eclipsed by Kroll and Burke, for they holed the course in 66 in the morning for a seven-up lead on Adams and Hunt and won far out in the country as well, this time by seven and five.

Weetman and Alliss had a closer encounter with Oliver and the tall and lanky Douglas, only one down at lunch and still in there fighting down the homeward stretch. It was Weetman who cracked, first with a bad pitch to the sixteenth and soon afterwards by missing a six-foot putt, and that made the Americans two up again. However, it was at the seventeenth, that long and twisting par five, that the depths of despair were touched. Oliver, with the honour, drove out of bounds into the gardens on the left, and this surely was a hole the British pair would get back. Not a bit of it. Weetman skied his drive 150 yards, Alliss cut the corner with a great second, Weetman thinned his pitch clean through

Not an easy lie for Sam Snead at Wentworth in 1953. Note how much the photographers' equipment has changed

the green and, after Alliss had chipped back, Weetman missed again from four feet for a win. So the Americans got a half in six for the match.

Legend has it that Cotton was so disappointed, even furious, that he let slip that he could 'kick the team's asses', and the quote, quickly picked up by the press, was all over the newspaper placards at the Wentworth the following morning with the result that 'Toots' Cotton spent some time running round tearing them all up!

True or not, Cotton got down to some serious talking back at the Dormie House at Sunningdale. In the belief that Rees could not wait to get stuck into the singles after missing out in the foursomes, he put the little Welshman out top, then Daly, who was in great form, and next Brown with the instruction: 'All I want from you is a point,' to which Brown is said to have replied: 'And you are bloody well going to get it!' Next came Weetman, then Max Faulkner (which was a gamble since his form had been poor in practice), Alliss, Hunt and finally the dependable Bradshaw. Panton, after another disappointing performance, was dropped along with Adams. Meanwhile Mangrum made only one change, bringing in Joe Turnesa for Oliver.

No doubt the Americans felt that their lead was a fairly comfortable one, but they were in for some unpleasant surprises once the morning fog had lifted, there being a

90-minute delay before Rees and Burke could see sufficiently far down the fairway to be able to drive. Even then it was almost a case of blind man's bluff and at both the first and second holes Rees mistook the line to the green; by the time the sun came out after five holes, he found himself two down.

By lunch Rees had nevertheless clawed his way back to all square and the state of the poll was then evenly balanced, both sides up in three matches and level in the other two. However, Rees soon fell behind again, very out of sorts with his putter. Even so, Burke was still only one up playing the seventeenth in the afternoon and sealed the match not by pitching from 80 yards short of the green but instead taking his putter and knocking his ball all along the ground to within less than a foot of the flag. The 'Texas wedge' has seldom been employed more usefully.

This was a heavy blow to the British, for they had been counting on Rees. However, Daly did his stuff magnificently in the second match, out in 32 in the morning, six up at lunch and walking all over Kroll, whom he duly beat by nine and seven. Brown, too, was as good as his word, taking the considerable scalp of Mangrum. Two up at lunch, it was nevertheless a close-run thing as Mangrum, who had earlier from the lower tier of the seventh green twice putted up and twice seen his ball roll all the way back to his feet again, came back at his man with birdies at the fifteenth and sixteenth to square. Brown's response was to hit a thrilling iron to the seventeenth to go one up again and, scenting blood, he hit two more great shots to the eighteenth and there was another point.

It was Weetman, though, who brought the whole match to life. Four down at lunch to Snead was a seemingly hopeless position against a golfer of that class. Still four down and six to play, however, Weetman's raw and muscular courage suddenly got its reward and, with the help of a steady stream of unexpected errors by the American, took

five holes in a row to lead one up. It was an extraordinary swing but, having been given his chance, Weetman clung on to halve the last and, despite the out-of-sorts Faulkner losing to Middlecoff, Britain were still in with a chance.

The news from behind was even better, for down at the bottom Bradshaw was accounting for Haas by three and two while Alliss, one down at lunch to Turnesa, had advanced to one up and three to play and Hunt was up as well. While accepting the attention always paid to the last hole, Alliss nevertheless contends that it was the sixteenth hole that was crucial. It was here that Turnesa sliced violently from the tee and his drive was destined for the trees when it struck a spectator. Even then the American was bunkered in two, but he still saved his par and won the hole as Alliss misjudged his pitch.

When Alliss then drove out of bounds at the seventeenth he became one down, but it was, amid the mounting tension, Turnesa's turn to hit a bad drive at the last, right into the trees on the right. Somehow he got it out but he was still well short of the green in three and destined for a six. Alliss had meanwhile driven perfectly and, with a two iron second just to the left of the green, looked safe for a five and a halved match.

In his autobiography, *Alliss Through the Looking Glass*, he describes the next few minutes.

As I walked round the ball, even as I stood by it, my mind was full of nothing but feet, rows and rows of feet − brogues, moccasins, sneakers, boots, shoes, spikes, rubbers, the shoes of the people perched on the front seats of the grandstand. The biggest pair of shoes belonged to Tony Duncan, the former Walker Cup captain. Why I should notice that I'll never know. The thought of Duncan, Duncan's feet and all those boots and shoes kept popping idiotically in and out of my mind. The ground between me and hole was not as simple as it must have looked. It was

Henry Cotton (right) has every reason to look wistful as Lloyd Mangrum hangs on to the Ryder Cup for another two years after America's close call at Wentworth in 1953

rather mossy and fluffy. The answer was to swing my wedge well back and slowly and carefully lob the ball well on to the green. Then of course I had the fear that if my backswing was a little too long, I might hit some of those damned shoes in the stand. I took a long steady swing at it, at the last moment forgot all about the ball and bumbled it a yard short of the green. I had to play again. This time I played a neat little run-up, just over a yard short of the stick. Turnesa was on and just missed his putt for a five. Then, from that short range, I missed. Half in six, and for Alliss, a ridiculous, incredible, childish, delinquent six.

He had lost.

But there was still Hunt to save the day, a lonely figure despite all the spectators charging around him as he trudged that last fairway. All square at lunch against Douglas, the game ebbed and flowed until Hunt at last inched his way ahead, one up and one to play. If he could just hold it, the Ryder Cup would be tied. Hunt's recollections are now almost totally lost in time, but he does remember pushing his second shot towards the big tree just short and right of the green and thinking: 'All I have got to do now is run the ball up to the flag and I've got him.' Tragically, he overdid it and, from the back of the green, he took three putts to lose the hole, halve his match, and thereby, see the Ryder Cup remain, shaky though the grip was, still in American hands.

GREAT BRITAIN		UNITED STATES
	Foursomes	
H. Weetman & P. Alliss	lost to	D. Douglas & E. Oliver 2 & 1
E.C. Brown & J. Panton	lost to	L. Mangrum & S. Snead 8 & 7
J. Adams & B.J. Hunt	lost to	T. Kroll & J. Burke 7 & 5
F. Daly & H. Bradshaw 1 hole	beat	W. Burkemo & C. Middlecoff
	Singles	
D.J. Rees	lost to	Burke 2 & 1
Daly 9 & 7	beat	Kroll
Brown 2 holes	beat	Mangrum
Weetman 1 hole	beat	Snead
M. Faulkner	lost to	Middlecoff 3 & 1
Alliss	lost to	J. Turnesa 1 hole
Hunt	halved with	Douglas
Bradshaw 3 & 2	beat	Haas

Great Britain 5½ — United States 6½

United States 8 — Great Britain 4

Played at the Thunderbird Ranch and Country Club, California, 5, 6 November 1955

After their narrow escape at Wentworth two years earlier, the United States were a little more circumspect about their prospects for the 1955 match at Thunderbird, one of those spectacular courses that, due to the marvels of artificial watering, were springing up in the golfing spa of Palm Springs. Lloyd Mangrum, who had said after the Wentworth match that he would 'never, never captain an American team again because of the 9000 deaths I suffered in the last hour', had handed over to Chick Harbert, who had missed the previous two matches but came back because he had won the 1954 PGA championship, a means of automatic selection.

Harbert had with him five newcomers to the match, beginning with Jerry Barber, who at five feet five inches was easily the smallest man on either side but, with justification, was building for himself a reputation of being an absolute wizard on and around

Eyes right and smile please. The 1955 British Ryder Cup team prior to departure to Thunderbird, Palm Springs. Left to right: Harry Bradshaw, Eric Brown, Christy O'Connor, Harry Weetman, John Fallon, Dai Rees, Syd Scott, Arthur Lees, Ken Bousfield, John Jacobs

the greens. Also playing for the first time was Tommy Bolt, who was building a reputation of another sort since he will always be remembered as having just about the 'shortest fuse' of anyone on the American tour, throwing so many clubs that he earned the nickname 'Thunderbolt'. Doug Ford, the 1955 PGA champion, Marty Furgol and Chandler Harper also came into the side to join the four Wentworth survivors in Jack Burke, Ted Kroll, Cary Middlecoff and Sam Snead.

Meanwhile Britain had at last abandoned their selection process by committee and introduced an order of merit from which the leading seven players gained their places automatically and then themselves sat down to pick the other three. It did not therefore imitate the American two-year process, and in the coming years there were many different permutations. But at least it was a step in the right direction.

For the first time Dai Rees took over the captaincy and there were new 'caps' for John Fallon, John Jacobs, who subsequently became such a fine teacher of the game that he is popularly known as 'Dr Golf', Syd Scott, not the longest hitter but seldom off the fairway, and Christy O'Connor, one of the greatest golfers ever to emerge from Ireland. In the team again, though he did not play, was Ken Bousfield, who as Matchplay champion was also an automatic selection. Jaded after a hard season, he did not feel well from the moment he arrived at Thunderbird, the fierce desert heat hardly helping. Arthur Lees had also won back his place to join the Wentworth survivors in Eric Brown, Harry Weetman, Harry Bradshaw and, of course, Rees.

Americans have always been complimentary and generous in their regard for the British players, and Snead was quoted beforehand as saying that this British team was the best he had seen and that the United States could have their 'work cut out to win'. He suggested that the fact that the course was on the short side (6314 yards)

might be of some help, though he did concede that the Bermuda grass around the greens took some getting to know, requiring a technique entirely different to that in Britain, and was therefore to America's advantage.

Nevertheless the lengthening sequence of American victories was beginning to cause a little concern, and Snead did suggest that the time was approaching when fourball play could profitably be introduced, claiming that it was 'better for the players and better for the spectators'. This was the first time any change to the traditional format of 36-hole foursomes and singles had been publicly aired, and while it did not have any immediate sequel, times of change were in sight, though fortunately without the abandonment of foursomes, which was at the time in Snead's mind.

In their five previous visits to America, Britain had never won more than three points. It was a dismal record, but there was some encouragement this time as they gained their biggest haul, going down by 8–4 and even giving the Americans something of a fright. This was particularly the case in the foursomes which, though they were taken 3–1 by the Americans, could very easily have been split 2–2. Indeed, it was the most thrilling day's golf anyone could remember in the States.

A shimmering early morning haze hung over the blue mountains which surround Palm Springs, and the two matches which stood out were that in which Fallon and Jacobs, having been two down at lunch, beat Barber and Harper on the last green and, in due course, that in which Burke and Bolt, of America, having been down at lunch, just got the better of Lees and Weetman. Only Henry Longhurst was wise enough to point out later that while it could therefore conceivably have been 2–2, 'it might just have easily been 4–0 to America!'

It was Fallon who was called upon to open the proceedings once the kilted band of the American Sixth Army had completed

The opening shot of the 1955 match at Palm Springs. Johnny Fallon drives off the first tee en route to a one-hole victory with John Jacobs against Chic Harbert and Jerry Barber

their marching drill on the first fairway. The initial few shots told a familiar tale. Fallon, having cut his drive into the palm trees, redeemed himself with a fine pitch for Jacobs to hole the putt for a four. But it was to no avail, since Harper hit a great second for America, Barber obliging with the birdie putt.

For once, though, this was no indication of what was to follow, for the British pair proceeded to play quite beautifully and, in reaching the turn in 35, were back to all square. The next six holes were halved, and then came one of those blows of which the British always seem to be on the receiving end. At the short sixteenth, whereas Jacobs

found the green with a lovely spoon shot Harper sliced badly into the bushes. Yet it was still the Americans who made a two, Barber finding a gap and chipping in. It was a cruel moment and, still suffering from the shock of it, Jacobs and Fallon also took five at the eighteenth, normally a par five but reduced this week to a par four, to lunch two down.

But the British pair kept nibbling away, and with nine holes to play were back to one up. There followed two apparently crucial holes, first when Fallon putted woefully short at the eleventh to lose the chance of going two up, and then at the thirteenth where Barber again chipped in to make the match square. Yet another marvellous chip by Barber looked like saving the sixteenth, but Harper unaccountably missed the putt and that presented the British with a glimmer of daylight. This seemed to disappear when Harper hit his second shot at the seventeenth only a foot from the hole, but Jacobs followed with a six iron just as good – even better, considering the pressure he was under. Nor was even that the end of the excitement, for at the last, after Harper had fluffed from the back of the green, Barber chipped in yet again. So instead of two for it from four feet, Falloon unexpectedly had to hole for the match, and he made it.

This was not the only cliff-hanger, for Lees and Weetman played superlatively, particularly over the morning's inward half, on which they had five threes and four fours to be round in 68 and yet were still only one up on Burke and Bolt. Then in the afternoon the British went out in 34 and had still not improved their position. Bolt seemed to revel in the challenge of it all and when the British did make a slight mistake or two, they were punished. One up playing the last, Bolt seemed to put the seal on things with a great second shot, but Lees followed him with one almost as good and Weetman sank the putt for a birdie. It was to no avail, for Burke promptly matched him and there was a third point for America.

Ford and Kroll had provided another, eased on their way by a 5, 5, 7 start from Brown and Scott, and were never other than in full control. Much the same was true of Snead and Middlecoff, for though Rees and Bradshaw came back from three down to be all square at lunch, the British pair were never at home on the greens and three-putted much too often.

The American writing was not quite as clearly on the wall in the singles as sometimes it had been in the past. Though Bolt was three up on O'Connor in the top match at lunch, Harbert six up on Scott and Snead five up on Rees, the remaining five games were more evenly balanced, Jacobs, Lees and Bradshaw all even against (respectively) Middlecoff, Furgol and Burke, Brown three up on Barber and Weetman only one down to Ford.

Indeed, at one point in the afternoon Britain were running neck and neck. The recovery, such as it was, was begun very properly by Rees, the captain, who had faced a veritable barrage of birdies from Snead in the morning – four in the first seven holes – and stood five down at lunch. But Rees was nothing if not a fighter, and after six holes in the afternoon he was back to only one down. Then Snead, in a black straw hat, hit his drive at the long seventh hard by a palm tree, and with Rees reaching the edge of the green in two, the chances were that the match would be level. Instead the genius of Snead prevailed, for he somehow found the room in which to swing a wood, not only reached the green but then rubbed salt into the wound by holing for an eagle three. This was a bitter blow and marked the end of Rees's fight back.

Nor could O'Connor, right in at the deep end in his first Ryder Cup since he was out top, make anything of Bolt, and though Scott made up ground against Harbert, time was never on his side. Jacobs, however, in his only Ryder Cup match, played wonderfully well. Not that it was immediately rewarded, for though he completed the morning round in 69, he was still two down to Middlecoff. But in the afternoon Jacobs rose to even greater heights with a deadly touch around the greens. His recall of the match is as clear now as it was at the time.

He remembers going out in 32 to square the match, making birdie threes at the twelfth and thirteenth to go two up, Middlecoff giving him a most generous putt at the sixteenth ('to clear his mind', Jacobs felt, before holing his own for the half), and then the American sinking a monster for a birdie at the seventeenth. So it all came down to Jacobs having to hole from five feet at the last to win. Across the slope there was a horrible right-to-left borrow of at least 12 inches, and yet Jacobs somehow always knew he was going to hole, and he did. He was round in 65.

The golf of Lees and Furgol was hardly of that class, but the little Yorkshireman, who had won both his matches at Pinehurst four years earler, pulled away to win with something to spare, as did the hard man of the team, Eric Brown. He led Barber quite a dance, round in 69 in the morning and three up. Even then he had to be on his mettle for, despite an outward half of 34 in the afternoon, his lead was cut to two. But he ran in a long putt for a two at the fourteenth and two holes later it was all over.

Had Bradshaw, all square after 18 holes having had a run of six successive threes, managed to get the better of Burke, and had Weetman, one down, overtaken Ford, then the match would have been tied. Alas, Bradshaw subsided towards the end and Weetman could not for the life of him close the gap on Ford.

All in all, however, it had for once been a good effort by Britain, and at the closing ceremony Lord Brabazon of Tara, then president of the PGA, in true Churchillian manner, spread wide his arms and said: 'We have learnt a lot, although we have lost, and we are going back to practise in the streets and on the beaches.' They were to prove prophetic words, for ahead lay Lindrick.

UNITED STATES		GREAT BRITAIN
	Foursomes	
C. Harper & J. Barber	lost to	J. Fallon & J.R.M. Jacobs 1 hole
D. Ford & T. Kroll 5 & 4	beat	E.C. Brown & S.S. Scott
J. Burke & T. Bolt 1 hole	beat	A. Lees & H. Weetman
S. Snead & C. Middlecoff 3 & 2	beat	H. Bradshaw & D.J. Rees
	Singles	
Bolt 4 & 2	beat	C. O'Connor
C. Harbert 3 & 2	beat	Scott
Middlecoff	lost to	Jacobs 1 hole
Snead 3 & 1	beat	Rees
M. Furgol	lost to	Lees 3 & 2
Barber	lost to	Brown 3 & 2
Burke 3 & 2	beat	Bradshaw
Ford 3 & 2	beat	Weetman

United States 8 — Great Britain 4

Great Britain 7½ — United States 4½
Played at Lindrick, 4, 5 October 1957

After twenty-four years of American domination, Britain at last reached the promised fairway with a glorious and emphatic victory at Lindrick. And by chance this first success since Southport and Ainsdale in 1933 all stemmed from a cancelled luncheon engagement that left Sir Stuart Goodwin, a Yorkshire industrialist, at a loose end. It was on the same day that Dai Rees was playing an 'exhibition' match at Lindrick with Fred Daly, Jack Jacobs, the local professional, and Jack Shanks, of Hillsborough. With nothing better to do, and though he had no particular interest in golf, Sir Stuart went along to watch, enjoying it all immensely despite heavy rain.

Afterwards he invited the four professionals, together with Commander Charles Roe, the PGA secretary, to dinner, and in the course of conversation said that he wished there was more top-class golf in the area. Rees, quick to seize an opportunity, immediately pointed out that a city the size of Sheffield was quite big enough to stage a tournament. Sir Stuart then asked how much it would cost, and when Commander Roe replied £5000, he promptly made out a cheque for £15,000 with instructions to organize one for the next three years. Thus came into being the Sir Stuart Goodwin Foursomes, a professional event held in the Sheffield area.

Some months later the PGA were still desperately seeking a sponsor for the Ryder Cup, and though the match was drawing ever closer they did not even have a venue. Sir Stuart came up trumps again, advancing a guarantee of £10,000 with the assurance that the PGA could take all the gate money. Just, therefore, as Robert Hudson had saved the match after the war, now it was saved again, and in return for Sir Stuart's generosity he was invited to nominate the venue.

He chose Lindrick and whenever the name of this delightful heathland course on the borders of Nottinghamshire and Yorkshire crops up in conversation, it is always the memories of the 1957 match that first spring to mind.

Never had there been such scenes of excitement as when the American invaders, after all their years of monopoly, were at last repelled. What is more, the hero of the hour was very much the captain, Dai Rees himself, as, by example, he inspired the team to its famous and conclusive victory after another near-disastrous opening day when once again they lost the foursomes 3—1. Rees, together, with Ken Bousfield, had been responsible for providing a slender lifeline as they beat Art Wall and Fred Hawkins while all around them were being submerged. Yet Britain came back to win the singles 6½—1½, not the least remarkable thing about it being the manner in which the team responded when their morale was seriously under threat — and not only because of their defeat in the foursomes.

Immediately after play had finished on the first day, Rees called a team meeting to decide who should play in the singles. Having been on the battlefield himself, he had had no opportunity to watch the others and had to rely on the scorecards for information. 'It required only half a look at the figures to decide who had played well and who had played badly,' he wrote later in *Thirty Years of Championship Golf*. 'There could be no argument that Max Faulkner and Harry Weetman had appeared to be sadly out of form in losing to Ted Kroll and Jack Burke by four and three.'

Nevertheless Rees was unwilling to make a decision single-handed, as a non-playing captain might have done, and while admitting that he had a good idea of the eight

The moment for which so many had been waiting. Dai Rees holds the Ryder Cup aloft after that memorable British victory at Lindrick in 1957

men he wanted in the singles, he asked for a free discussion. Faulkner immediately spoke up, saying that his play had been 'rubbish' and he should not be included. Weetman promptly said that he should stand down as well, and that apparently was the end of the matter, all amicably settled.

Having next decided his order of play, with Eric Brown out top in the hope that he would catch Tommy Bolt (which he did), Rees, after exchanging lists with Jack Burke, the American captain, was making his way back through the club lounge when he was approached by a journalist with the request: 'We would like a statement. Harry Weetman has announced that he will never play again

in a team captained by you.'

After their previous conversation, and as a long-standing friend and travelling companion of Weetman, Rees could hardly believe his ears; he was always convinced that it was a put-up job since Weetman's wife, Freda, was not only in the vicinity but was widely quoted in the following day's newspapers criticizing the fact that the players' wives were not allowed to stay in the same Worksop hotel as their husbands. Instead they had alternative accommodation in another hotel and Peter Alliss described their departure each evening as being 'like leaving a hospital after visiting hour'.

Though Rees's telephone did not stop

ringing until well after midnight as the Press continued to chase the story of the day, he diplomatically refused to be drawn on the whole unseemly episode while the match was still in progress, although he later gave his version in his official report to the PGA. Weetman was then called before the disciplinary committee and suspended from PGA-sponsored tournaments for a year. Some months later the sentence was reduced at the instigation of Rees.

In a curious way this whole unfortunate business may have united the British team, and they came out with guns blazing in the singles, no one more so than Brown, the hard man of the team. It was he who led the counter attack, relishing the opportunity of taking on the quick-tempered Bolt and beating him by four and three. It was a hard match in which much metaphorical blood was spilt, and when they shook hands Bolt was alleged to have said: 'I guess you won, but I did not enjoy it a bit.' To which Brown is said to have replied: 'And nor would I have done after the licking I have just given you.'

Bolt was so angry that he broke a club in his frustration and in the locker room vent even more wrath on the crowd which, he claimed, was the worst in the world. 'They roared when their guys won, cheered when I missed a putt and sat on their hands if I played a good shot. Good relations, hell! Don't make me sick.' Though Ed Furgol tried to calm him down, Bolt was unrepentant and it was alleged that he was one of three Americans who did not attend the prize-giving.

Harry Moffitt, then president of the American PGA, was not in support of Bolt. He said later that when Bolt's remarks got around, 'several of the team came to me and said the crowd had been very fair. It had applauded their good shots as well as those of their opponents.' The general opinion was that the crowd had simply and understandably been louder in their support of the British than they had been of the Americans. Nevertheless crowd behaviour and their partisanship were widely discussed and drew a letter from Lord Brabazon to *The Times*, in which he wrote:

> I have great sympathy with Bolt, but what is a crowd to do when their hero wins a hole by virtue of the 'enemy' missing a putt? Let us take the case of the Cup's fate being dependent on one last match, both balls about six feet from the hole. The Englishman misses his, the American misses. Is the crowd to remain mute for fear of cheering a missed putt and being dubbed unsporting? Surely it is straining human nature too much.

One way and another therefore, several sour tastes were left in the mouth after what should have been a glorious occasion. The Americans did not know what had hit them in the singles but Mr Moffitt was generous enough to say that the result had been a tonic for the Ryder Cup and in his opinion it would now go on for 'years and years'. Nevertheless, organization of the match did come in for criticism from Henry Longhurst, who suggested that the Lindrick clubhouse had been quite unsuitable for an occasion of this magnitude. 'Nor do I think that a normally commercial hotel bang on the tramlines of an industrial city is the place to house a visiting Ryder Cup team,' he added.

This year the British team was selected entirely from a new points system, only the Match-play champion (Christy O'Connor) getting in automatically. If this worked out pretty well, only the immensely promising David Thomas failing to get in when otherwise he might well have been selected, the Americans did end up short of Ben Hogan, Sam Snead, Jimmy Demaret and Cary Middlecoff, which drew from Leonard Crawley the comment that no team without that quartet could be described as 'fully representative'. Bernard Darwin, writing in *The Times*, took a different stance, commenting: 'The argument that America's best players were left behind does not ring true. No place can be gained in their team without constant proof of great ability. It is true that the team did not contain famous names, but reputation is no guarantee of success.'

Nor did it look other than a very familiar story on the first day, for at lunch the United States were up in three matches and square in the other. As so often, the Americans came out of the trap the quicker, both Doug Ford and Dow Finsterwald and, behind them, Art Wall and Fred Hawkins, beginning with birdies at the first two holes. It was nevertheless not entirely reflective of their golf as a whole, for Ford and Finsterwald, against Alliss and Bernard Hunt, missed an awful lot of fairways, although they got away with it.

At one point the Americans, out in 32, were four up, but slowly the holes came back and at the eighteenth Hunt had a chance to square − only to miss not his first

short putt of the day. It was a fine opportunity lost and when the Americans began the afternoon 4, 4, 2, 4, 3, 3 they were back to four up and out of reach.

The solitary British point came from Rees and Bousfield, who were quite unperturbed by the 3, 3, start from Wall and Hawkins. Still two down at the turn, they won back the tenth, halved the next seven holes and then went into lunch all square when Rees made up for a poor tee shot from Bousfield at the par three eighteenth by holing a putt of 12 feet. Rees continued to be the strong man in the afternoon, but it was two errors by Hawkins, first when he underclubbed into a bunker at the tenth and then when he fluffed a chip at the eleventh, that opened the door. In a trice the British pair had gone from one down to one up, and from that point they grew steadily in strength.

Ken Bousfield extricates himself from a very awkward lie at Lindrick

Ken Bousfield holes out to beat Lionel Hebert on Lindrick's 15th green and, though he was unaware of it at that moment, this was the putt that won the Ryder Cup

Burke, the American captain, was a player of glorious style and with Ted Kroll very efficient they mostly had the upper hand in the morning against Weetman, who was none too happy driving to narrow fairways, and Faulkner. But somehow the Americans could not break clear, constantly either one up or all square. When they did, immediately after lunch, it was emphatic. In eight holes they went from one up to four up and were scarcely seen again.

Dick Mayer, the American Open champion, and Bolt played the most unanswerable golf, being round in 67 to stand three up on Brown and O'Connor, neither of whom could drive to save their lives. They missed eight of the first nine greens, although they scrambled heroically. However, that sort of

thing could not go on and Mayer and Bolt, out again in the afternoon in 32 and then starting for home 5, 3, 3, 3, won very much at a canter.

For all the headlines in the morning papers about the supposed row between Weetman and his captain, Rees detected a certain resilience about his team over breakfast. On reaching the course, he found that the wind had switched overnight, making it an entirely different proposition, the first hole now requiring a much longer club for the second shot than on the first day. It made all the difference, for there was no doubt that the Americans' short game deserted them on greens that had suddenly become quite quick.

To an extent they had probably contributed to their own defeat by their earlier decision to play the smaller British ball. This measured 1.62 inches as opposed to the 'American-sized' ball of 1.68. For many years the latter's adoption in this country was bitterly opposed, but now the game worldwide is played almost exclusively with the bigger ball. Leonard Crawley was a strong advocate of this, pointing out that the larger ball was 'far more responsive to a delicate touch near the hole and it is strange to reflect that the world's greatest professionals can be tempted by the thought of a few paltry yards of additional length [the smaller ball could be hit further] to foresake a ball with which at home they earn their daily bread'.

At all events, five of the Americans took three putts on the first green, including Burke, whom Rees allowed to come in as substitute for Kroll who had been taken ill. The match could have been claimed as a walk-over, but Rees felt that such would never have been in the true spirit of the Ryder Cup, even though it did mean Peter Mills, a newcomer, unexpectedly having to face the class golfer of the American team.

Far from being overawed, Mills, whose classic swing was deserving of more than just this one Ryder Cup appearance, rose to the occasion − though it has to be admitted that Burke was some way below his best, round in 77 and five down at lunch. Furthermore, Bousfield was five up on Lionel Hebert, Brown four up on Bolt, Rees four up on Furgol, Hunt one up on Ford, O'Connor square with Finsterwald and only Alliss and Bradshaw down, both by one hole, to Hawkins and Mayer. By the time Rees went out, three of the four British players ahead of him were up, and by winning three of the first six they made sure in double-quick time that technically their side was ahead. Rees's 33 to the turn was the best of the morning as he stormed clear, anxious to finish his match as soon as possible so that he could get out on the course to urge on his troops. He duly obliged by

seven and six, by which time Brown and Mills had already put paid to Bolt and Burke.

Alliss admittedly went down to Hawkins, but that was still 4−4 and the Americans were now in disarray, almost like a cricket team losing a whole succession of wickets. It was as if every roar going up from different parts of the golf course were sending shivers down the spines of the visitors and soon there was Hunt, out in 32, polishing off Ford by six and five, and then O'Connor winning six of the first eight holes in the afternoon to leave Finsterwald far behind.

Only one point was needed now but Bousfield, at one stage seven up on Lionel Hebert, suddenly lost three holes in a row and briefly there was the prospect of an unthinkable collapse. There were few scoreboards out on the course to tell Bousfield the overall picture, but soon Rees and Faulkner came charging through the bushes and when he halved the fifteenth in four to win by four and three, it was all over. The magic seventh point had been gained.

GREAT BRITAIN		UNITED STATES
Foursomes		
P. Alliss & B.J. Hunt	lost to	D. Ford & D. Finsterwald 2 & 1
K. Bousfield & D.J. Rees 3 & 2	beat	A. Wall & F. Hawkins
M. Faulkner & H. Weetman	lost to	T. Kroll & J. Burke 4 & 3
C. O'Connor & E.C. Brown	lost to	R. Mayer & T. Bolt 7 & 5
Singles		
Brown 4 & 3	beat	Bolt
R.P. Mills 5 & 3	beat	Burke
Alliss	lost to	Hawkins 2 & 1
Bousfield 4 & 3	beat	L. Hebert
Rees 7 & 6	beat	E. Furgol
Hunt 6 & 5	beat	Ford
O'Connor 7 & 6	beat	Finsterwald
H. Bradshaw	halved with	Mayer

Great Britain 7½ − United States 4½

United States 8½ – Great Britain 3½

Played at Eldorado Country Club, California, 6, 7 November 1959

The twenty-nine passengers who had boarded the charter flight from Los Angeles to Palm Springs for the thirteenth Ryder Cup match at Eldorado in 1959 were to call it the 'Long Drop Club'. The 150 miles or so should have taken them forty minutes, just a short hop across the San Jacinto mountains. Instead it became for the British team and their various camp followers an hour and a half of sheer terror as they were tossed around by a violent storm until many thought the end had come. It brought back all too vividly the memories of February 1958 when the aircraft carrying home Manchester United players after a European Cup tie crashed at Munich with the loss of twenty-one lives, seven of them members of a young and brilliant team known as the 'Busby Babes' after their manager, Matt Busby.

On board, covering the Ryder Cup match for the *Daily Express*, was their golf correspondent Ronald Heager, whose story made the front-page lead the following day, the first time golf had reached such vaunted heights. 'We were tossed around like a cocktail in a shaker....From our flying height of 13,000 feet we dropped like a stone to 9000 feet. It was like falling in a giant lift when the cable had snapped. Only...your stomach stayed on the 10th storey. It was the Big Dipper – without the laughs,' read part of his cable.

Later, in the 1977 Ryder Cup programme, Heager wrote:

> The date carved indelibly in our minds was October 29 1959 – seven days before the team was due on the tee against the United States under Sam Snead. Behind them was a planned acclimatisation after landing in New York [on the *Queen Elizabeth*]. Golf in Atlantic City, Washington and Atlanta and that morning the big hop from Atlanta to Los Angeles. Next there were just 140 miles and a brief flight to the air-conditioned comfort of the Desi Arnaz Hotel at Palm Desert. That was what we thought as we filed into the plane.

> The reality proved to be the nightmare none of the 29 passengers would forget. 'Keep your seat belts fastened. There may be a little rough weather ahead,' our captain warned us. Rough? A little? A few minutes away as we approached the jagged peaks of the San Jacinto Mountains the plane began to toss like a cork as we met the storm that lit the vivid purple skies.

> The bumps were mild at first but sufficient to turn bronzed golfers ashen. Heads ducked down between knees. Collars were loosened. In the eye of the storm the jolts increased in frequency and violence. We were trapped in a big lift racing up and down, berserk. The climax was still to come.

> It arrived with a new dimension of violence. There was a sickening downward plunge. We were a stone dropped into a well. Anything not strapped down took off and floated to the roof of the plane. Weightless. A grinding, crunching agonised sound of metal on metal heightened the horror. We didn't know it then but this was the brink of calamity. From that robots' wrestling match of sound we inched back from the edge of disaster. The metallic judderings of the aircraft were beautiful noises to the grappling pilot. He had regained command of the ship. He had won his battle with the furies of the elements.

He turned back for Los Angeles, announcing that he would try again later. But, as the team filed off the aircraft, several of them falling to their knees and kissing the ground with relief, Dai Rees, the captain, stated firmly that on no account would the team fly again that night. The journey was made instead by Greyhound bus.

The 1959 British team which did its best but failed to keep the Ryder Cup, losing 8½–3½ at Eldorado in California. Left to right; Peter Alliss, Eric Brown, Ken Bousfield, Dai Rees, Harry Weetman, Dave Thomas, Bernard Hunt, Peter Mills, Norman Drew, Christy O'Connor

Later, there were memories: of the stewardess standing in the aisle and being grabbed by Peter Mills as she took off for the roof; of Bernard Hunt's camera being stuck to the ceiling of the aircraft and his idly wondering how he would ever get it down again; of Lou Freedman, a vice-president of the PGA, almost pleading 'let it crash and be done with, I can't stand this any longer'; of Frank Pennink, then of the *Daily Mail* and subsequently a golf-course architect of repute, sitting apparently quite unperturbed and gazing out of the window; of Harry Weetman saying 'I bloody near messed my pants,' and getting the reply from whomever, 'I've got news for you, Harry. I did!'

Thus was formed, at the instigation of John Letters, of the Letters Golf Company, the 'Long Drop Club'. Among its members was one of the American players, Doug Ford, who had hitched a lift. But one of the British team who did not qualify was John Panton. He had flown out on his own after an SOS from Commander Roe, the PGA secretary, to cover for Mills, who had been complaining of back trouble. As it happened, Panton did not get a game; and nor did Mills for that matter. The two newcomers to the side were Norman Drew, an Ulsterman – the first to play for Britain in both the Walker Cup and Ryder Cup – and David Thomas. The big Welshman did not get into the team automatically but was selected ahead of David Snell, which meant that for the first time the reigning Matchplay champion failed to make the Ryder Cup team.

Meanwhile the Americans, hell-bent on revenge after their defeat at Lindrick, brought in, for the second time under the captaincy of Sam Snead, Julius Boros, who had missed the 1957 match because of a broken leg, Jay Hebert, Bob Rosburg, the PGA champion, and the big-hitting Mike Souchak. It was the inevitable strong-looking team, but even so there were some glaring absentees, such as Billy Casper, who had that summer won the US Open at Winged Foot, Arnold Palmer, the 1958 Masters champion, Ken Venturi and Gene Littler, none of them having yet completed their probationary period before becoming full members of the American PGA. Rules were as strictly applied then as they are today.

Despite these omissions the Americans had little difficulty in regaining the Ryder Cup, this time by 8½−3½ on another desert course just four years old and only a short distance from Thunderbird, where the match had been played four years earlier. Dotted with imported palm and citrus trees, it bore the hand of the same architect, Lawrence Hughes, and contained seven artificial lakes, which was fast becoming the means of defending a modern golf course. Indeed, it was the two close by the green at the eighteenth, which at 470 yards Henry Longhurst described as one of the finest finishing holes in the world, that were to play a crucial part in the match as Britain for once almost held their own in the four-somes. They lost them by 2½−1½ but it was within a touch of being 2−2, and though half a point may not make a lot of difference in scoring terms, it almost certainly did psy-chologically.

It was Harry Weetman who was the culprit. He and Thomas had been one down at lunch to the vastly experienced Snead and Middlecoff, but they had held on and with three holes to play they were one up. At the seventeenth Thomas, who had holed out well all day, faced a putt of five feet for the match. Though he missed it, there was still every chance that the day would still end at 2−2 for at the eighteenth the big Welshman unleashed a corking drive while Middlecoff, whose nerves were invariably on edge, hooked into the rough.

It was therefore a make-or-break situation for Snead and he had to go for the green. He hit a good one, but not good enough, and there was, for the watching members of the British party, the cheering sight of the Americans' ball dropping into the water to the left of the green. They could therefore − other than chipping in − now do no better than make five and all the British pair needed was a five themselves for the match. In the circumstances all Weetman had to do was lay up with an eight or nine iron. Instead, all foolish bravado, he took out his five iron and went into the water on the right. Both sides had to pick out under penalty and inevitably there was only one outcome after that. The Americans, Snead holing from 10 feet, got their five, the British did not and the match was halved. 'Why didn't I play safe? I never do. It's not my game. I just didn't hit the right shot,' said a forlorn Weetman afterwards.

By contrast Dow Finsterwald had found himself in very much the same situation a short time earlier as he and Boros, of America, also came to the last one up on Rees and Ken Bousfield. Boros similarly hit a good drive and Finsterwald actually pulled out a four wood for the second shot. But at the last moment common sense prevailed as he put it back and played instead a safe four iron. Bousfield, knowing the hole had to be won, had no alternative but to go for the green, found the same water hazard on the right and the British pair lost, two down.

Britain did have some encouragement, for Peter Alliss and Christy O'Connor, who returned a 63 in one practice round, were scarcely any less efficient in the 'real thing', three up at lunch on Art Wall, that year's Masters champion, and Doug Ford and four under fours for the 34 holes it took them to win. It was a particular relief to Alliss, who had a record of nought out of four in his two previous Ryder Cup matches. However, the top foursome was always going America's way, Souchak and Rosburg being round in 68 in the morning and six up on Eric Brown and a none too fit Bernard Hunt, who was fighting an attack of influenza for most of the week. Beaten by five and four, Hunt gave way to Drew in the singles.

If some thought that Drew would be out of his depth, particularly when he was put out top in the singles, they were proved emphatically wrong. Though at one point four down to Ford, he wormed his way back to be only one behind at lunch, a position that was unchanged when they came to the eighteenth. Here Drew bravely took a spoon for his second, hit the middle of the green and earned a halved match.

However, for the most part it was again a case of the Americans making the faster starts. Moreover they were between them fourteen under fours in the morning against the opposition's eight over. Only one British player, Brown, won the first hole and by completing his morning round in 68 he was three up on Middlecoff, ultimately winning by four and three. The Scot's remarkable singles record was therefore maintained as he added another scalp to those already collected: Lloyd Mangrum, Jerry Barber and Tommy Bolt. Not that it had any bearing on the destination of the Ryder Cup, for it had been abundantly obvious after 18 holes that the Americans were home and dry, up in six of the eight singles. Other than Middlecoff, only Jay Hebert was down, by one to Alliss.

In the end this game ended in another half, Alliss putting like a demon which he had to do since he played the short holes thoroughly badly, making threes only twice all day as he fought a hook. Still one down coming to the last, Alliss's task was made easier when Hebert found the water on the right, though that was no guarantee that the American would not get a chip-and-putt five. So Alliss decided that he had to get a four to be safe, struck a glorious three iron to the heart of the green and was therefore the only British player that year to emerge unbeaten.

Elsewhere there were occasional flashes of revival, especially from the lion-hearted Rees, who got back from six down to all square against Finsterwald. Then Rees went two down again, won the seventeenth with an eagle three and was only denied at the

Sam Snead negotiates a chip shot against Dave Thomas in the 1959 Ryder Cup at Palm Desert. Snead won by six and five

Harry Weetman gets his side out of trouble at Palm Desert in 1959. In partnership with Dave Thomas, they halved with Sam Snead and Cary Middlecoff

last where Finsterwald chipped stone dead from the back of the green. An outgunned Bousfield, with an outward half of 32 in the afternoon, also got back to two down against the much longer Souchak, but Weetman, Thomas and O'Connor could make nothing of Rosburg, Snead and Wall and that was it.

This was to prove the last time a visiting British Ryder Cup team made the journey by sea. Ahead lay the days of increasingly fast airliners, jets and then Concorde. Leonard Crawley wrote in the *Daily Telegraph*:

I regard it as essential that the British party should fly out one week beforehand and get

rid of the present two weeks' unnecessary preliminaries wandering about the United States and tiring themselves out like the Children of Israel in the desert before getting to the promised land. Travelling, and the kindest hospitality, is all great fun but it is nevertheless frightfully exhausting.

It was also to prove the last time the match was played over 36 holes of foursomes and singles. Changes were afoot, though Henry Cotton, writing in *Golf Illustrated*, said quite firmly:

I do not like the idea of making the Ryder Cup match singles, foursomes and fourballs as is suggested, but we may be forced to it for economic reasons. Sponsors would be easier to get for a 'three-day show' − this is the American angle − for when Bob Hudson drops out of his self-imposed role, there is no one to take over.

UNITED STATES		GREAT BRITAIN
	Foursomes	
B. Rosburg & M. Souchak 5 & 4	beat	B.J. Hunt & E.C. Brown
J. Boros & D. Finsterwald 2 holes	beat	D.J. Rees & K. Bousfield
A. Wall & D. Ford	lost to	C. O'Connor & P. Alliss 3 & 2
S. Snead & C. Middlecoff	halved with	H. Weetman & D.C. Thomas
	Singles	
Ford	halved with	N. Drew
Souchak 3 & 2	beat	Bousfield
Rosburg 6 & 5	beat	Weetman
Snead 6 & 5	beat	Thomas
Wall 7 & 6	beat	O'Connor
Finsterwald 1 hole	beat	Rees
J. Hebert	halved with	Alliss
Middlecoff 4 & 3	lost to	Brown

United States 8½ − Great Britain 3½

Great Britain 9½ — United States 14½
Played at Royal Lytham and St Anne's, 13, 14 October 1961

Less than a month before the United States team was due to leave for the 1961 Ryder Cup at Royal Lytham and St Anne's, Sam Snead, who at forty-nine was due to make his eighth consecutive appearance in the match, innocently teed up his ball in the Losantiville Pro–Am Golf Championship in Cincinnati. But the moment he struck his opening drive he was to put an unsuspected noose around his neck and was subsequently to be withdrawn from the American team.

'Snead kicked out of Ryder Cup' made headlines all over the world, for here was one of the greatest players the game has known, the man who as captain at Eldorado two years earlier had led America to victory, disgraced by his breach of the PGA's strict rules that forbade a professional to play in any event that conflicted with an official PGA Tour event — in this case the Portland, Oregon Open.

Snead had already decided to take some

The American team about to board the train to Liverpool (presumably changing the way) prior to the 1961 match at Royal Lytham. Left to right: Jerry Barber, Bill Collins, Gene Littler, Doug Ford, Arnold Palmer, Jay Hebert, Mike Souchak, Dow Finsterwald, Billy Casper, Art Wall

time off before leaving for England and three weeks earlier he had written to the tournament officials in Oregon stating that he would not be playing. But then, unaware that he would be in breach of the rules, he decided to have some fun and play in the Pro−Am Championship, a 36-hole better-ball scratch event in which he was partnering his old friend, the Walker Cup player Ed Tutwiler. They were considered strong contenders to take the title away from the holders, Bob Kepler, the Ohio state coach, and a young amateur by the name of Jack Nicklaus.

According to John M. Olman, a contributor to the *Cincinnati Enquirer*:

> When Snead arrived in Cincinatti, he was reminded that certain touring pros, including tournament winners and other 'name players', needed sponsor approval from a PGA-sanctioned tournament in order to compete in another event being held at the same time. Snead, winner of the 1961 Tournament of Champions, was one of these players but he did not think the Pro−Am was covered by PGA policy.
>
> 'I figured it wasn't anything more than a glorified exhibition,' Snead later explained. 'Five minutes before I'm set to tee off, someone tells me I'd better get permission from the Portland sponsors, so I sent off a wire right away. When I finish 18 holes, I come into the clubhouse and there's the answer. Permission not granted.'
>
> A short while later Snead received another telegram − this time from the PGA − which informed him that he was being fined $500 and would be suspended from tournament play for six months. The suspension also meant that he would have to relinquish his place on the American Ryder Cup team.

This was in spite of the fact that Snead had immediately withdrawn from the Pro−Am after the first round in the hope that the executive committee would be sympathetic towards him. But three days later he received official confirmation that he was out of the Ryder Cup and that his place would be taken by Doug Ford, who had been eleventh in the points standings for the ten-man team. Fortunately, as it happened, the two men were the same size and Ford, who had played in the previous three matches, was able to wear Snead's official uniform.

'This is the worst slap in the face I have ever had,' stormed Snead. 'I went out of my way to enter enough tournaments to qualify for the Ryder Cup and I won't take it sitting down.' He added that he would get a good lawyer and lodge an official appeal. The appeal was heard at the PGA's annual meeting after the Ryder Cup and the suspension was reduced to 45 days. Snead none the less never appeared in the Ryder Cup again, though he was made non-playing captain in 1969. In seven singles he had been beaten only once.

At least one group of British supporters was said to have immediately cancelled their hotel accommodation when they heard that Snead was not playing, but even so it remained a powerful American team with places at last for Billy Casper, Arnold Palmer and Gene Littler, the last three American Open champions who had by then served their PGA apprenticeship.

The 1961 match was the first to be played by two sets of 18-hole foursomes and singles, which doubled the number of points from 12 to 24. The move had been proposed by Lord Brabazon, president of the British PGA, at an executive meeting in March 1960. An alteration to Sam Ryder's original Trust Deed for 36-hole matches was necessary, but it was unanimously agreed to approach the American PGA for their approval, which was granted. In September 1960 a tournament players' sub-committee made a further recommendation for the match to be extended to three days, the extra day to include fourball matches. They were told that the format for 1961 had already been agreed, but at the same time they were assured that fourball matches would be introduced in 1963.

Jerry Barber, whose short game was one of the very best

These 18-hole 'sprint matches', as they were sometimes called, restored the game of golf's traditional format. In theory they gave the British a better chance, since the shorter the distance the more evenly matched two players can be; and on all sides the move was greeted as a great success, not least by the public. It did not make any difference to the overall result, America winning 14½–9½, though with three of the eight foursomes and seven of the sixteen singles going to the last hole, it would not have taken much to tip the scales.

Perhaps the only disadvantage to the new format was that it imposed too much responsibility on the two captains, Dai Rees, who was leading Britain for the fourth consecutive time, and Jerry Barber, both of whom were also playing. Wrote Henry Longhurst:

If we are to have 18-hole matches, which I most devoutly hope, then either the order of both morning and afternoon matches must be announced overnight, or we must have a non-playing captain, or the captain must not play himself in the morning, or the captain, if he plays in the morning, must have a sort of assistant-cum-adviser with whom to consult at lunchtime regarding the team for the afternoon.

In the foursomes Rees had hardly got in when the first match was due to go out in the afternoon, and this threw an impossible burden of selection upon him. He could have seen nothing of the other players; he had only minutes to decide; and he had to get his own lunch and rest. He thus made what most critics deemed an error of selection [keeping faith with Bernard Hunt and John Panton who were consequently heavily beaten a second time] which he later defended on the grounds that the players concerned 'could hardly play so badly twice running'.

They not only could, but did!

Barber, on the other hand, left himself out of the morning foursomes and though the American captain did play twice in the singles (losing them both), the message got across. This was the last time Britain were to appoint a playing captain and there was only one more occasion when the Americans did so, Palmer leading the side two years later at East Lake, Atlanta.

Unaccustomed though the Americans were to 18-hole match-play (even that last bastion, the US PGA, had in 1958 turned to stroke-play), it did not make any difference to their coming out of the trap the quicker of the two sides. As Tom Scott pointed out in *Golf Illustrated*, 'It's the old story. Our men regard the match as something so special that they are unable to play their regular golf at the start and when they come to their senses, their opponents are one or two holes to the good.'

So it proved again, for in the foursomes on a heavenly morning of bright sunshine reflecting off the heavy dew, the Americans, after only three holes, were two up, one up, one up and three up. Ford and Littler, in the top match, were even given the present of winning the short first hole in a bogey four, though Peter Alliss and Christy O'Connor did wake themselves up after an awful 5, 5, 5 start to win almost resoundingly, by four and three. Alliss was the man responsible, for he had begun the recovery with a glorious second shot right into the middle of the sixth green to set up a birdie four, and it inspired him. Again and again he sank crucial putts. 'I do not think he has ever played better, or a more decisive part, under the greatest possible pressure,' wrote Leonard Crawley in the *Daily Telegraph*.

However, this was Britain's only point of the morning. In the second match Hunt and Panton had a miserable time on the greens. They were four down after seven holes to Art Wall and Jay Hebert and soon lost without trace, while that reliable combination of Rees and Ken Bousfield probably never got over the seventh hole, where they had looked like getting back to all square against Palmer and Casper but instead went two down when the Americans pitched in from the rough for a birdie four.

A third American point from Mike Souchak and a newcomer to the match, Bill Collins, was less easily gained than it had looked like being after they had won the first three holes in 2, 4, 4 against two British newcomers, Neil Coles and Tom Haliburton. By the eleventh the match was square, but birdies by the Americans at the next two holes restored a lead to which they clung by the skin of their teeth.

Having built their bridge the Americans then crossed it, also winning the second series of foursomes 3−1 for an overall advantage of 6−2. This time it was Rees, who was to win three of his four matches at the age of forty-nine − twenty-four years after his first Ryder Cup match, and Bousfield who alone came up trumps. They beat Collins and Souchak by four and two,

assisted as they were by the Americans having two sixes and a seven in their first nine holes. Neither Hunt nor Panton could regain their excellent form on the practice days, losing by five and four to Palmer and Casper, but both the other foursomes went all the way.

Alliss was again the strong man as he and O'Connor held Wall and Hebert for seventeen holes when they were still all square. Both sides hit fine drives at the eighteenth and O'Connor then followed with an even better one to the middle of the green. Wall followed him, but though his shot finished slightly further from the flag, Hebert, typically, sank the putt for a birdie three and that was something Alliss was unable to match. There was a brave effort, too, from Coles and Haliburton for they had been four down to Barber and Dow Finsterwald with only seven to play. But threes at the twelfth and, more rarely, at the fifteenth and seventeenth swiftly narrowed the gap before time ran out.

There was always the wishful thought that there could be another 'Lindrick comeback' in the singles. Harry Weetman, brought in to open the batting, almost got the better of Ford, losing only on the last hole where he had a putt to win but missed it, just as he did an even shorter one for the half and therefore lost. That was a double blow, for at that moment the British lost what little impetus they had. Whereas this first series of singles might have been shared, the Americans took it 4−2 with two halved, one of the latter being a delightful encounter between Alliss and Palmer. There was never more than a hole between them and the spirit of the Ryder Cup was perfectly reflected when Palmer conceded his opponent's two-foot putt at the last for a four, just as, in turn, Alliss immediately did Palmer's.

It was the ever-reliable Rees, against Hebert, and a revived Hunt, against Barber, who brought home the only two British points, Coles nevertheless doing splendidly

The British team in 1961. Left to right: (standing) John Panton, Ralph Moffitt, Bernard Hunt, Harry Weetman, Christy O'Connor; (seated) Ken Bousfield, Neil Coles, Dai Rees, Tom Haliburton, Peter Alliss

in halving with Littler — and very nearly beating him, since the American Open champion had to make a three at the last to save his neck. So that was 10–4 to the Americans and it was all over bar the shouting, of which there was still some since the British did at least take the final series of singles by 4½–3½ to make the overall margin presentable.

Again it was up to Weetman, out first, to keep Britain's head above water if he could, but though he went out in 33, Wall was even better, out in 31 and two up. There was really very little that Weetman could do about that, and America's victory was formally sealed when Souchak, one down at the turn to Hunt, proceeded to play the next eight holes in three threes and five fours to win by two and one. Palmer, given something of a fright by Haliburton who had two

twos in his first five holes, duly pulled away for a third American point, but Alliss, in another elegant match, this time against Collins, again had something significant to say for himself. Rees, Bousfield, Coles and O'Connor, with three and a half points between them, 'mopped up the tail' to close the gap to presentable proportions.

Afterwards the *Daily Mail* produced a statistical analysis of the play and it indicated that technically there was very little to choose between the two teams. In the 399 holes Britain had hit the most fairways (234 against 214) but fewer greens (153 against 157). The short holes were 'halved', with both sides on the green 67 times and off it 29 times. Britain had the more single putts (117 against 110), but that was balanced by their three-putting seven times against the Americans' four and also by their having been in more bunkers (27 against 22). Perhaps it was the eighteenth that told the most significant story. Of the ten games that went the full distance, America won three times, halved six times and lost only once.

GREAT BRITAIN		UNITED STATES
Foursomes (a.m.)		
C. O'Connor & P. Alliss	lost to	D. Ford & G. Littler 4 & 3
J. Panton & B.J. Hunt	lost to	A. Wall & J. Hebert 4 & 3
D.J. Rees & K. Bousfield	lost to	W. Casper & A. Palmer 2 & 1
T.B. Haliburton & N.C. Coles	lost to	W. Collins & M. Souchak 1 hole
Foursomes (p.m.)		
O'Connor & Alliss	lost to	Wall & Hebert 1 hole
Panton & Hunt	lost to	Casper & Palmer 5 & 4
Rees & Bousfield	beat	Collins & Souchak 4 & 2
Haliburton & Coles	lost to	J. Barber & D. Finsterwald 1 hole

GREAT BRITAIN		UNITED STATES
Singles (a.m.)		
H. Weetman	lost to	Ford 1 hole
R.L. Moffitt	lost to	Souchak 5 & 4
Alliss	halved with	Palmer
Bousfield	lost to	Casper 5 & 3
Rees	beat	Hebert
2 & 1		
Coles	halved with	Littler
Hunt	beat	Barber
5 & 4		
O'Connor	lost to	Finsterwald 2 & 1
Singles (p.m.)		
Weetman	lost to	Wall 1 hole
Alliss	beat	Collins
3 & 2		
Hunt	lost to	Souchak 2 & 1
Haliburton	lost to	Palmer 2 & 1
Rees	beat	Ford
4 & 3		
Bousfield	beat	Barber
1 hole		
Coles	beat	Finsterwald
1 hole		
O'Connor	halved with	Littler

Great Britain 9½ — United States 14½

United States 23 – Great Britain 9

Played at East Lake, Atlanta, 11, 12, 13 October 1963

Britain had learnt two lessons from the previous two Ryder Cup matches by the time the team set forth for the 1963 match at East Lake, Atlanta. Neither did them much immediate good, but at least there were steps in the right direction. The first was that it was now impractical, with 18-hole matches and fourballs as well as foursomes and singles over three days, to have a playing captain. Dai Rees, who had led the side with such distinction since 1955, was consequently replaced by John Fallon, whose only appearance as a player had been in 1955. The second was that in previous visits to the States altogether too much time had been spent stooging around before getting down to the serious business of the match. Now that for the first time the journey was being made by air rather than by sea (other, that is, than by Neil Coles, who had then and still has an aversion to flying), it was decided that there should be a cut-back on the social engagements with arrival delayed until the previous week-end.

Perhaps intrigued by this novel mode of travel, it was also initially agreed at an executive committee meeting in December 1962 that for the first time an official PGA party should accompany the team as opposed to just the manager. This would comprise the president of the PGA, any vice-presidents, the captain of the PGA, the chairman and secretary of the PGA and the wives of both players and officials. They would travel first class, the return air fare being £321.10s. However, these were not yet the years of bounty and at the next executive committee meeting it was decided that by travelling tourist there would be a saving of £2000. In addition, the wives, though still welcome, would have to pay for themselves.

It was once again a case of travelling more in hope than in expectation, for there was no doubt that this was going to be another formidable American team, captained as it was by Arnold Palmer, the most respected golfer in the world at that time. He had by then won the Masters three times, the US Open once and then endeared himself to the British by renewing American interest in the Open championship, which he had won both at Royal Birkdale in 1961 and at Troon (now Royal Troon) the following year. Palmer had under him Bob Rosburg and four newcomers to the match in Tony Lema, Billy Maxwell, Johnny Pott and Dave Ragan, and he said unhesitatingly before a ball had even been hit at East Lake that this team 'would beat the rest of the world combined'.

Whether or not this was an exaggeration, they certainly proved much too strong for the British for whom Brian Huggett, George Will and Geoffrey Hunt were making first appearances. The younger Hunt therefore joined his brother Bernard, which revived memories of the days when the Whitcombe brothers had played for Britain. The margin was 20–6, with six games halved. 'All things considered, it seemed just about right,' commented Henry Longhurst afterwards. 'Though there were one or two points lost which might have come our way, there were others which did come our way and might not have done. Any team which gets twenty-five per cent in America is doing quite well.'

Henry Cotton was of like mind. He wrote in *Golf Illustrated*:

I repeat what I have often said, that we cannot win this match in America. Despite the advantage we have in playing our own small-sized golf ball on these short visits to play in international encounters, we were again outclassed. We know, and have known all along, since the game of golf got under way in America in the twenties, that good players were in great numbers there, and with the sun throughout the year, practice facilities and huge rewards, we were up against an insoluble problem. The present top home players, by no means poor performers, are leagues outside the tough American ones.

There were, though, two passages in the match when the British star twinkled quite brightly. On the first morning they shared the foursomes 2−2 and that was something that had never been done in America before. And then, in the first series of singles on the third day, they did even better, taking them by 4½−3½. What happened in between and then on the final afternoon bore no comparison. America swept the board in the second series of foursomes, then took the fourball games by 6−2 and the last eight singles by 7½−½.

Fallon's one moment of inspiration was to put two of his new boys, Huggett and Will, out top on the first morning, even though he might have had second thoughts when he found them up against Palmer, partnered by what transpired to be a rather nervous Pott. Will hit a screamer down the first fairway and there they were, one up right away. It was a lead they defended with the utmost resolution. Though the Americans caught them by the thirteenth, Huggett played the telling shots at all the right moments, the end coming swiftly and deservedly since the Americans were heading for something like a 78 when they went down by three and two.

Nor was the golf any too bright behind.

In the days when they still dressed for dinner. The 1963 British team which lost at East Lake, Atlanta. Left to right: (standing) Neil Coles, Christy O'Connor, Peter Alliss, Dave Thomas, Guy Hunt, George Will; (seated) Tom Haliburton, Bernard Hunt, John Fallon (capt), Brian Huggett, Harry Weetman

The British team, with wives, wave farewell en route to East Lake in 1963. At the head of the steps is Geoffrey Hunt and below him George Will, Dave Thomas, Brian Huggett, Bernard Hunt, Christy O'Connor, Tom Haliburton, Harry Weetman, John Fallon and Peter Alliss

Peter Alliss and Christy O'Connor did not even break 80 and yet lost to Ragan and Billy Casper by only a single hole. By contrast Harry Weetman and Dave Thomas, at one point two down, played beautifully, coming home to gain a half against Dow Finsterwald and Gene Littler. Again, their play on the eighteenth could not have been bettered when, one down, Thomas almost knocked the flag out of the hole with his tee shot, Finsterwald splashed dead from a bunker, but Weetman fearlessly holed the putt for a two.

Similarly Bernard Hunt and Neil Coles, who had also been two down, came back heroically, their reward coming at the last gasp when they won the eighteenth to halve with Lema and the bear-like Julius Boros, of whom an American remarked, 'He never goes into the rough unless it is to get a Coke!' On this occasion a par three at the eighteenth was good enough, Lema missing the green at a hole measuring 230 yards and

then the subsequent putt as well. Coles and Hunt had played really well coming home and were on cloud nine, not only with their own performance but with the fact that Britain had actually emerged from the foursomes level-pegging. 'We were as chuffed as anything as we ate lunch,' recalls Coles, 'and then up comes Johnny Fallon and says "you boys played so well this morning, I'm going to split you up this afternoon, Neil to play with Geoff Hunt and Bernard with Tom Haliburton." We couldn't believe our ears. We just sat and gaped.'

Consequently a partnership for whom the adrenalin was in full flow was disarmed, and the price was paid in full as in the afternoon the United States made a clean sweep of the foursomes, Maxwell and Goalby, Palmer and Casper and Littler and Finsterwald (against Coles and Geoff Hunt) all winning with varying degrees of comfort. Indeed, only the last foursome got as far as the eighteenth, Bernard Hunt and Haliburton being all square against Boros and Lema. But Hunt hooked his tee shot and then, after Haliburton had played a difficult chip just about as well as anyone could have done to the fiercely sloping green, Hunt narrowly missed the saving putt.

The Americans were always likely to come into their own in the fourballs, for it provided them with the ideal stage on which to show off their considerable skills. No one revelled in it more than Palmer, and he was four under par off his own bat when he and Finsterwald saw off Huggett and Thomas by five and four in the top match. But it was not entirely a disastrous morning for the British. Alliss and Bernard Hunt rose to the occasion with a better-ball of 67 to halve with Littler and Boros, Alliss again doing his stuff by holing the crucial and eminently missable putt on the final green. By then Weetman and Will had been overwhelmed by Casper and Maxwell, particularly Casper, but Coles and O'Connor, out in 33, had a real dog-fight with Goalby and Ragan and also came to the final hole all square. It was still touch and go after the tee shots, and most of the British onlookers were praying that O'Connor would lay his treacherous putt of 30 feet or so close enough to get a half. Instead he holed it for a two, and there was no American answer to that.

The afternoon tale was a much sorrier one, albeit tantalizingly so with two games going to the last, a third to the seventeenth and the other to the sixteenth. The pattern was set straight away for Finsterwald, again partnering Palmer, hooked violently off the first tee, played out and then pitched in for a three! Somehow it was always the Americans who did this sort of thing. This time the Americans' better-ball score was 29 and

Coles and O'Connor were dead and buried. In 23 consecutive holes Palmer and Finsterwald had between them recorded fourteen birdies. Nor was there much reprieve in the other games, the only piece of salvaging being done by Huggett and Thomas, who eventually appeared through the semi-darkness long after everyone else, reporting that they had halved with Goalby and Ragan.

Though there were sixteen singles to come, Britain had little chance since they were already eight points behind. But there was a spark of life still in them, as on the last morning they came away with 4½ points − 3½, the particular hero being Alliss who, in his opponent's own back yard, beat

Peter Alliss splashes out of a sand trap at the 12th hole at Atlanta in 1963, going on to beat Arnold Palmer by one hole − one of a number of distinguished performances

Palmer in a sort of 'replay' to their halved match at Royal Lytham two years earlier. It was another fine match and came to its climax at the seventeenth as Alliss still clung to his one-hole lead. However, Palmer was never more dangerous than when seemingly cornered and typically he played a brilliant second shot so close that a birdie was inevitable. Yet Alliss, from 12 feet, holed his putt for a three as well and then at the last laid an even longer putt dead, forcing Palmer, with a courteous little bow, to admit defeat.

Weetman, too, scaled new heights with his defeat of Boros, the reigning US Open champion, in another game that went all the way. Weetman, out in 35, was two up but Boros came back to square before, with a birdie at the sixteenth, Weetman went ahead again. This time he did not weaken and with a perfect tee shot at the last, he was home. And then, hot on his heels, came Bernard Hunt, swapping punch for punch with Finsterwald for nine holes and then profiting by the American taking a couple of unexpected and untidy sixes. The door was open, and Hunt was through it in a flash.

Huggett, a real little bulldog, had already accounted for the nervous Pott, and Coles, two down and two to play against Casper, salvaged a half as he holed an almost embarrassing number of freak putts, not the least of them at the eighteenth, though all he got from the former American champion at the end was a terse: 'Good putting round, Neil.' O'Connor, always suspect around the hole, could have done with some of that for with it he might well have beaten Littler, but neither Geoffrey Hunt nor Thomas could handle their respective opponents of Lema and Goalby.

America were therefore left needing only a point from the last eight singles. It duly arrived from Littler, who was altogether too hot for the ageing Haliburton, winning by six and five. When the cause was already so obviously lost, no one quite understood why Haliburton, then forty-eight and obviously

at the end of his Ryder Cup career, should have been preferred to the much younger Geoffrey Hunt, who could have done with the experience.

Indeed, the curtain came down like a dark veil as Britain managed only half a point and that from Alliss, who after his sorry debut in the 1953 match was now regarded as the king pin. This time he held that fine stylist Lema, but at least one observer lamented how little Alliss was ever seen on the practice ground.

Certainly Palmer, in a post-match interview, said that he thought the British did not practise enough. Fallon thought the difference lay around the greens, and Hunt believed it was on them. Coles was perhaps the most realistic. His assessment was that the Americans were simply two or three shots better.

UNITED STATES		GREAT BRITAIN
Foursomes (a.m.)		
A. Palmer & J. Pott	lost to	B. Huggett & G. Will 3 & 2
W. Casper & D. Ragan 1 hole	beat	P. Alliss & C. O'Connor
G. Littler & D. Finsterwald	halved with	D.C. Thomas & H. Weetman
J. Boros & A. Lema	halved with	N.C. Coles & B.J. Hunt
Foursomes (p.m.)		
W. Maxwell & R. Goalby 4 & 3	beat	Thomas & Weetman
Palmer & Casper 5 & 4	beat	Huggett & Will
Littler & Finsterwald 2 & 1	beat	Coles & G.M. Hunt
Boros & Lema 1 hole	beat	T.B. Haliburton & B.J. Hunt
Fourballs (a.m.)		
Palmer & Finsterwald 5 & 4	beat	Huggett & Thomas
Littler & Boros	halved with	Alliss & B.J. Hunt
Casper & Maxwell 3 & 2	beat	Weetman & Will
Goalby & Ragan	lost to	Coles & O'Connor 1 hole

UNITED STATES		GREAT BRITAIN

Fourballs (p.m.)

UNITED STATES		GREAT BRITAIN
Palmer & Finsterwald 3 & 2	beat	Coles & O'Connor
Lema & Pott 1 hole	beat	Alliss & B.J. Hunt
Casper & Maxwell 2 & 1	beat	Haliburton & G.M. Hunt
Goalby & Ragan	halved with	Huggett & Thomas

Singles (a.m.)

Lema 5 & 3	beat	G.M. Hunt
Pott	lost to	Huggett 3 & 1
Palmer	lost to	Alliss 1 hole
Casper	halved with	Coles
Goalby 3 & 2	beat	Thomas
Littler 1 hole	beat	O'Connor
Boros	lost to	Weetman 1 hole
Finsterwald	lost to	B.J. Hunt 2 holes

Singles (p.m.)

Palmer 3 & 2	beat	Will
Ragan 2 & 1	beat	Coles
Lema	halved with	Alliss
Littler 6 & 5	beat	Haliburton
Boros 2 & 1	beat	Weetman
Maxwell 2 & 1	beat	O'Connor
Finsterwald 4 & 3	beat	Thomas
Goalby 2 & 1	beat	B.J. Hunt

United States 23 — Great Britain 9

Great Britain 12½ – United States 19½

Played at Royal Birkdale, 7, 8, 9 October 1965

If the 1965 Ryder Cup at Royal Birkdale had been played over 9 holes rather than 18, Great Britain would have won it by 15 matches to 12 with five halved. Instead the United States completed their thirteenth victory by 18–11 with three halved, and behind that one brief analysis lay the whole story after three days of probably the finest and most exhilarating golf that had ever been seen in Britain. When their backs were to the wall the Americans had the deeper reserves on which to call, both in stamina and terms of the killer instinct. It was this that made all the difference on a golf course that, by its very nature, played right into their hands.

Royal Birkdale, set among some glorious natural duneland on the outskirts of Southport, is highly regarded by the professionals and though the Americans had not played very well there that summer in the Open championship (Tony Lema, the defending champion, having the highest finish, joint fifth as Peter Thomson won the title for a fifth time), they put all that behind them when it was national rather than individual pride that was at stake.

No less than four of the last six holes at Birkdale, the thirteenth, fifteenth, seventeenth and eighteenth, were then played as par fives, though the eighteenth has since been reduced to a long par four. It was here that the Americans had the advantage, for these holes were mostly out of reach in two strokes and had therefore to be played with a driver, long iron or wood and then a pitch. It was the Americans' expertise with the wedge that marked their superiority.

Much was understandably made of two critical fourball games on the second morning when Dave Thomas and George Will were four up and seven to play and lost, and Lionel Platts and Peter Butler, who were four up and four to play, only halved. Had both these games been won, Britain would certainly have been ahead and a different story might have been told. Yet it was Will's conviction that the match was lost not then but at the fifteenth, seventeenth and eighteenth, where so many games hinged. He said later:

At none of these holes was it possible to reach the green in two and players were faced with approach shots of 50 or 60 yards. It was on these little strokes at these three holes that Britain lost the Ryder Cup. The real difference was that while the British players tried to lob the ball into the air and fairly well up to the stick, the Americans flew the ball in low, checked it on the bounce and then let it run up to the hole. This difference in technique made all the difference to the pitch. With the lob shot that we were playing, sometimes the ball would go shooting on way past the hole and on other occasions it would check too quickly and finish well short. The Americans were pitching the ball consistently, time after time, so that they could judge accurately where to pitch it on the green and how much roll it would take to run up to the flag.

I noted that the Americans played this shot with their wedges much more stiff-wristed than our team. This produced the low flight, the quick check and then roll. Perhaps one reason why the Americans excel at this shot is that they invariably play on well-watered greens, whereas we play on a different type of course each week – sometimes fast-running and sometimes soft. Birkdale was in really magnificent condition but the rain prior to the match had made it ideal from the American point of view.

Both Henry Cotton and Byron Nelson, America's non-playing captain, were in broad agreement with this observation,

Harold Wilson, the former Labour Prime Minister, finds the 1965 match at Royal Birkdale rather more amusing than Henry Cotton, who is on his right

Cotton believing that the superior American pitching technique developed from the use in the States of the 1.68 inch ball (though at Birkdale the Americans again opted for the smaller British ball), Nelson adding that any team which between them had won four million dollars 'must be more used to holing pressure putts on the big occasion'.

And very much a big occasion it was, for the staging of this Ryder Cup eclipsed all the previous matches in either Britain or America and set a prototype for the future. It was acclaimed on all sides and was due very much to the vision of Brian Park, both a vice-president of the PGA and a member of Royal Birkdale, who produced £11,000 out of his own pocket to promote the match.

Gone were the days of a few dirty old marquees, toilets that were little more than four pieces of torn hessian, and an apology of a programme. Instead there was a large tented village, a trade exhibition and hospitality pavilions, a 160-page programme so bulky that the lady club members selling them could carry only ten at a time, and Mini Mokes driven by well-known women golfers such as Frances Smith, a former British champion, carrying scoreboards giving not only the position of the individual matches but the state of play overall.

It was against this almost fairground atmosphere that the Americans arrived, bearing four fresh faces in Tommy Jacobs, Don January, Dave Marr and Ken Venturi, whose victory in the US Open the previous year had had emotional overtones. Not only had Venturi come back from a debilitating back injury that almost forced him to quit the game altogether but, in his finest hour at Congressional, Washington, he was for the whole of his final round — 36 holes on one day then being played for the last time — on the point of collapse with heat exhaustion in extreme humidity and had to be accompanied by a doctor. Early in 1965 Venturi had then developed circulatory problems in his hands, which required surgery — and indeed he wore gloves on both hands at Birkdale. This may partially have explained his three defeats in four games.

The United States were further handicapped because Johnny Pott had ruptured a muscle in his side during practice and could not play. An offer by Harry Weetman, who had been made British captain on a split vote ahead of Eric Brown, for the Americans to send out a replacement was rejected; and in any case there was always, in an emergency, Byron Nelson, who might have been fifty-three but was still mightily impressive when joining his team for the practice rounds.

Britain's newcomers to a team still chosen entirely off the order of merit (the points allocation none the less having been changed again and weighted more towards winners) were Lionel Platts, Peter Butler, Jimmy Martin and Jimmy Hitchcock and, with two years in which to have forgotten the last defeat, optimism was as high as ever. It was fuelled to an extent by the fact that only a matter of weeks earlier Britain's amateurs had gone to Baltimore and tied for the Walker Cup, an unprecedented performance by any visiting international team in America. Weetman immediately sent a cable to Joe Carr, the British captain: 'Great golf. Well done. Don't destroy the recipe. Keep it for me.'

Measured against most of the previous Ryder Cups, the British start was for once encouraging, the first series of four-somes being shared 2−2 and this then being repeated in the afternoon, making the teams level at 4−4. The particular heroes in the morning were Will and Dave Thomas, for they were up against Marr and the great Arnold Palmer and thumped them six and five after making birdies at each of the first three holes. There was no holding them after that, Thomas outdriving Marr by a country mile and even going for, and making, the carry over the cross-bunker at the sixth which was not far short of being 300 yards distant.

Peter Alliss and Christy O'Connor were similarly away to a flier, winning three of the first four holes in birdies and seeing off Venturi and January, whose golf, it has to be said, was rather indifferent for they were well over par when they conceded defeat by five and four. The roar that greeted this win came wafting across the course just as Butler, in the top match, was about to putt on the final green and he had to reorganize himself before holing out to another shout that could conceivably have saved his and Platts' neck after a disastrous start in which they had lost the first three holes to Julius Boros and Lema. It was only the twenty-second putt of the round for the British pair, which tells something of the poorer quality of the rest of their game, but Boros was equal to the demands of the moment and in went his putt as well, for a much narrower win than the Americans had anticipated. Quickly there then came news of a second American point as Billy Casper and Gene Littler, after a slow start, duly polished off the tried and trusted partnership of Neil Coles and Bernard Hunt.

If all the talk at lunch had been about the performance of Thomas and Will, they rapidly came down to earth in the afternoon when, as luck would have it, they again drew Palmer and Marr, who had shown they meant business by spending a good deal of the luncheon interval on the practice ground. And what golf the Americans played: six consecutive threes from the

Left: Tony Jacklin (left) peeps round Sandy Lyle as they watch their opponents putt at The Greenbrier in 1979. They halved with Lee Trevino and Gil Morgan

Jack Nicklaus at Royal Lytham in 1977, the last time the match was between Britain and the United States

Tony Jacklin chips at Muirfield in 1973. This was the year Britain led after the first day, were level at the end of the second but collapsed on the third

Left: Jack Nicklaus and (right) Tom Watson put their combined heads together over a putt at Walton Heath in 1981. They were just part of what was said to have been the strongest American team ever

Above: It also rains in America. Craig Stadler and (right) Lanny Wadkins at PGA National in 1983

Left: One of Tony Jacklin's gambles in the 1983 Ryder Cup at the PGA National was to partner the great Severiano Ballesteros with the team's youngest member, Paul Way, seen here on the right discussing the fall of the green. They partnered one another four times and were beaten only once

Left: Sam Torrance gets a soaking but, more importantly, he also gets the ball out of the stream in front of the eighth green at the Belfry in 1985

Below: Jerry Pate and (right) Ben Crenshaw adopt an unusual pose at Walton Heath in 1981

Above: All smiles at The Belfry. Left to right (back): Jose Rivero, Bernhard Langer, Nick Faldo, Sam Torrance, Tony Jacklin, Nick Faldo, Paul Way, Ken Brown, Severiano Ballesteros. (front) Howard Clark, Ian Woosnam, Jose-Maria Canizares, Manuel Pinero

Above: As players, Jack Nicklaus (right) mostly got the better of Tony Jacklin. But as respective non playing captains at Muirfield Village in 1987, the roles were reversed

Right: For once the Europeans' holing out was much better than that of the Americans at The Belfry in 1985 and here Ian Woosnam celebrates another putt finding its mark

Above: A sign of the times as rival supporters wave the flag at Muirfield Village in 1987

Above: Relief on the faces of Calvin Peete, Jack Nicklaus and Bob Gilder after America's narrow escape at PGA National in 1983

Right: Hale Irwin and (right) Tom Kite won twice together in the fourballs at The Greenbrier in 1979

Above: Jose-Maria Olazabal pitches up to the green at Muirfield Village. Note the absence of grandstands but still a perfect view for thousands on the grassy banks

Left: Nick Faldo (right) and Bernhard Langer (second from left) congratulate one another after they had defeated Tom Watson and Jay Haas in the opening foursomes at the PGA National in 1983. Tommy Horton is on the left and Tony Jacklin between the two players

Bernhard Langer can hardly believe it as he holes a chip shot at Muirfield Village's tenth hole in 1987

The Belfry, 1989: Payne Stewart (right) gives directions to Curtis Strange close to the seventeenth green in the fourball matches. They lost their match to Mark James and Howard Clark

Above: Payne Stewart has another heave at his ball in the water. It took him three attempts to get out and he lost to Jose-Maria Olazabal

A moment the O'Connors will treasure all their lives as Ann hugs Christy after his defeat of Fred Couples

An aerial view of The Belfry during the 1989 match and clearly showing the size of the tented village, the largest ever to be assembled at a sporting event in Britain

The American team is all smiles after their victory in 1965 at Royal Birkdale. Left to right: (standing) Tommy Jacobs, Johnny Pott, Ken Venturi, Billy Casper, Arnold Palmer, Julius Boros, Don January, Tony Lema; (kneeling) Gene Littler, Byron Nelson (non playing captain), Dave Marr

second, an outward half in just 30 strokes and a complete reversal of the morning's result as they exacted revenge by six and five. Palmer was like an enraged tiger. Such golf, particularly at foursomes, had never been seen before.

But behind them Casper and Littler caught a fairly similar onslaught from Alliss and O'Connor, four model players all at the top of their games. The British pair were out in 31 and yet only one up amid the barrage of birdies from both sides. Then the Americans drew level with a birdie at the long thirteenth, but they could not quite manage them at the fifteenth and seven-

teenth and it was the fours the two Britons made here that were decisive. Then the States edged ahead again, Boros and Lema three under par when they saw off Hitchcock and Martin by five and four, only for Coles and Hunt to wipe clear the deficit, four under par when they accounted for Venturi and January by three and two.

The closeness of the eight fourball matches on the second day is best illustrated by the fact that seven of them went to the eighteenth green. They will always be remembered, however, for the wonderful opportunities lost by both Thomas and Will and then Platts and Butler. The former were four up with eight to play but dropped their guard when neither could make a three at either the twelfth or fourteenth, two short holes. January and Tommy Jacobs did, and furthermore, with a run of 4, 3, 4 at the fifteenth, sixteenth and seventeenth, all of them birdies, snatched victory when defeat had seemed inevitable.

Hardly had this sunk home than even worse was to follow, for behind them Platts and Butler, four up and four to play, could only halve with Casper and Littler. Butler, after two tremendous shots to the fifteenth green, had in fact two putts for the match. Instead he took three to get down and it was Littler who took full toll, holing two long putts for birdies at the sixteenth and seventeenth and then pitching dead for another at the last.

The other two games were shared, Palmer and Marr winning for America and Coles and Hunt (a combination that for pronunciation Henry Longhurst once drily observed was the commentator's nightmare!) for Britain. So that was the United States ahead by a point overall, and by nightfall they were two clear with another 2½ points against 1½. Again, however, it might have been so different, for after nine holes in the afternoon Britain were, in order, one up, all square, two up and two up. Yet only Alliss and O'Connor managed to hang on in the top match, Alliss summoning a brilliant winning stroke against Palmer and Marr as he toed in his four wood and let rip just to reach the eighteenth green, which was out of range to the others. There were no such heroics from Thomas and Will, for they had fallen two down after birdies by January and Jacobs at the tenth and eleventh and, try as they might, they could get only one of these holes back.

Next came Casper and Littler as, for the second time that day, they got a half out of Platts and Butler, drawing level with a two at the twelfth and a birdie four at the fifteenth, falling behind again at the sixteenth but winning the seventeenth and very nearly

the eighteenth too, Platts saving the day by getting down in two from a bunker 70 yards short of the green to match Casper's four. And then, to make matters even worse for Britain, Venturi and Lema made birdies at the tenth and eleventh to draw level with Hunt and Coles, edged ahead with a two at the fourteenth and stayed there.

If it had all been very tight to that point, it was much less so in the singles. Led by Palmer, who carried far too many big guns for Hitchcock, the Americans ensconced themselves even more firmly by winning the morning session 5½–2½, the other points coming from Boros, Lema, Marr and Jacobs with January adding the half. Only Hunt, against Littler, and Alliss, against Casper, won for Britain, the latter holing out manfully on the last green from five feet (left hand below right, incidentally) after his opponent had first drawn attention to the fact that Alliss's ball was resting on a spike mark, which could in those days be repaired, though whether this was through sportsmanship or gamesmanship is open to speculation.

In the afternoon, therefore, the Americans needed but two more points for victory and they came immediately, Lema played brilliantly, six under par when he put away O'Connor by six and four. Boros soon followed him into the winners' enclosure, having disposed of poor Hitchcock who could not find his game at all, and the rest was academic.

It was appropriate that one of the knockout blows should have been delivered by Lema, who had enchanted so many not only this week but the year before when he had won the Open at St Andrews. Shortly after the Ryder Cup he was also to leave his mark on the Piccadilly World Match-play championship when he lost to Gary Player after being seven up and seventeen to play. Lema, a great stylist, seldom did anything by halves. But he was never to be seen in Britain again. Early in 1966 he was killed in an air crash.

GREAT BRITAIN		UNITED STATES
Foursomes (a.m.)		
L. Platts & P.J. Butler	lost to	J. Boros & A. Lema 1 hole
D.C. Thomas & G. Will 6 & 5	beat	A. Palmer & D. Marr
B.J. Hunt & N.C. Coles	lost to	W. Casper & G. Littler 2 & 1
P. Alliss & C. O'Connor 5 & 4	beat	K. Venturi & D. January
Foursomes (p.m.)		
Thomas & Will	lost to	Palmer & Marr 6 & 5
Alliss & O'Connor 2 & 1	beat	Casper & Littler
J. Martin & J. Hitchcock	lost to	Boros & Lema 5 & 4
Hunt & Coles 3 & 2	beat	Venturi & January
Fourballs (a.m.)		
Thomas & Will	lost to	January & T. Jacobs 1 hole
Platts & Butler	halved with	Casper & Littler
Alliss & O'Connor	lost to	Palmer & Marr 6 & 4
Hunt & Coles 1 hole	beat	Boros & Lema
Fourballs (p.m.)		
Alliss & O'Connor 2 holes	beat	Palmer & Marr
Thomas & Will	lost to	January & Jacobs 1 hole
Platts & Butler	halved with	Casper & Littler
Hunt & Coles	lost to	Venturi & Lema 1 hole

GREAT BRITAIN		UNITED STATES
Singles (a.m.)		
Hitchcock	lost to	Palmer 3 & 2
Platts	lost to	Boros 4 & 2
Butler	lost to	Lema 1 hole
Coles	lost to	Marr 2 holes
Hunt 2 holes	beat	Littler
Thomas	lost to	Jacobs 2 & 1
Alliss 1 hole	beat	Casper
Will	halved with	January
Singles (p.m.)		
O'Connor	lost to	Lema 6 & 4
Hitchcock	lost to	Boros 2 & 1
Butler	lost to	Palmer 2 holes
Alliss 3 & 1	beat	Venturi
Coles 3 & 2	beat	Casper
Will	lost to	Littler 2 & 1
Hunt	lost to	Marr 1 hole
Platts 1 hole	beat	Jacobs

Great Britain 12½ — United States 19½

United States 23½ – Great Britain 8½

Played at Houston, Texas, 20, 21, 22 October 1967

Though Arnold Palmer's greatest years were now behind him, he was still, going into the 1967 Ryder Cup match at Houston, regarded as the Emperor. He was close to becoming the first golfer in history with tournament winnings of over one million dollars – the landmark was reached the following year – and, as a qualified pilot, he now flew his own aircraft to many of the tournaments in which he competed. Back at his Pennsylvania home in Latrobe his office contains models of everything he has ever flown, from a lunar module to a Boeing 747. More spectators, it was often said, were prepared to stand and watch Palmer unload his clubs from the trunk of his car than would be attracted by a lesser mortal completing a round of 67. In a word, he had charisma.

Perhaps only one man was not in awe of Palmer and that was Ben Hogan, who at the age of fifty-five was recalled to captain a team which was to record its biggest victory yet, by 23½–8½. The best example of this came in the exchange they had in the locker room at the Champions' course at Houston, which proved to be the last occasion on which the choice of the 1.68 inch or the 1.62 inch ball was permitted. By the time he breezed into the locker room for his first practice round, news had reached Palmer's ears of Hogan's surprising decision to play the smaller ball and, spying his captain at its far end, he called out, 'Say, Ben, is that right we are going to play the small ball?' There were a few moments of pregnant silence before Hogan replied tersely, 'That's what I said.' Undeterred, Palmer, warming to the rebuff, retorted, 'Well, supposing I haven't got any small balls?' To which Hogan gave him perhaps the ultimate answer: 'Who said you're playing, Palmer? And by the way, are you sure you've brought your clubs, or would you like to borrow those as well?'

No doubt it was all said in good clean fun, but in a few short and well-chosen words Hogan had made it implicitly clear who was captain, with no outward regard for a man who himself had captained the side only four years earlier. Hogan was the master, too, at the gala presentation dinner before the match, as Peter Alliss recalls in the second volume of his autobiography.

> The teams were introduced individually to the audience by their captains. Dai Rees, our captain, made rather a meal of it, going on about the things each of us had won and done. As we stood up in turn, there were polite ripples of applause. Hogan then stood up and asked the audience to reserve its applause to the end. When he had finished, he introduced his team individually by name only and then, when they were all standing, said, 'Ladies and gentlemen, the United States Ryder Cup team – the finest golfers in the world.' Storm of applause, and the British ten down before a ball had been hit.

A note of disharmony had been struck before the British team left for America. Harry Weetman, who had captained the team two years earlier, had been included among the six representatives of the PGA's official party led by the president, Lord Derby. However, Weetman refused to sign an undertaking that he would be under the full control of Rees and his name was consequently withdrawn. 'I see no reason why Weetman should refuse,' said Brian Park, who had by then become executive director of the PGA. 'Everybody else has signed.' Clearly the rift between Rees and Weetman all those years earlier during the 1957 match at Lindrick had never fully healed.

Nor was the atmosphere improved by noises being made behind the scenes that it was time the British team should be streng-

Britain clearly expected some bad weather for the 1967 match at Champions in Houston judging by their rain gear. Left to right: (back row) Tony Jacklin, Peter Alliss, Dave Thomas, Bernard Hunt, George Will, Christy O'Connor; (front row) Malcolm Gregson, Hugh Boyle, Dai Rees, Brian Huggett, Neil Coles

thened by the inclusion of golfers from the Commonwealth, or even the rest of the world, the argument gaining force from the fact that the big American television companies had expressed no interest in covering the match. Tony Jacklin, in his *Champion's Story*, even claimed that there were suggestions that this could be the last Ryder Cup, and in the circumstances he was full of praise for Rees.

[He] did a great job in making us believe in ourselves against all the odds. . . . Dai, aware of the criticisms and the threat to the continuation of the matches which, apart from all else, do the finances of our PGA a power of good, whipped us into a mood of more than cautious optimism and after he had finished with us, we felt that we had at least an outside chance. What an inspiring little man he is!

The date of the match had twice been switched, first from June — because it was too hot — to September, and then to October. It proved to be merely the delay of the inevitable, for so sweeping was the American victory that it was abundantly clear that the gap in ability between the British and American professionals was as wide as, if not wider than, it had ever been.

As Rees nevertheless pointed out, seventeen of the thirty-two matches went to the seventeenth or eighteenth greens, and he singled out for particular praise Dave Thomas and Jacklin, who was only just beginning to make his mark on the game and winning instant fame when, in the Dunlop Masters at Royal St George's that year, he not only took the title but scored the first hole in one to be recorded on

British television. 'They played the sort of golf,' wrote Rees in *Thirty Years of Championship Golf*, 'I have always dreamed that British teams might produce against Americans one day: powerful, aggressive, going boldly for every chip and putt.'

Jacklin, having clinched the last place by finishing tenth in the Ryder Cup points table, was one of three newcomers in the British team along with Malcolm Gregson and Hugh Boyle. He won two and halved one of his three matches, all of them with Thomas as they took both their foursomes and then half a point in one of their fourballs. Thomas was nevertheless the leading points scorer, for in five outings he was beaten only once. This compared with five out of five for Palmer and also Gardner Dickinson who, with Doug Sanders, Gay Brewer, Bobby Nichols and Al Geiberger, was making his first appearance. Note that there was still no place for Jack Nicklaus, even though he had by then won the US Open for a second time, the Masters three times, the PGA once and the Open once. He had still not completed his five-year probation as a member of the PGA.

For all the closeness of some of the matches, the only time that Britain were remotely in the hunt was in the opening series of foursomes in which they held the United States to 2½−1½. Indeed, there could not have been a better start, Brian Huggett and George Will winning the first two holes against Billy Casper and Julius Boros in the top match and staying ahead through the first twelve holes. However, Will bunkered his side's second to the thirteenth, caught a tree with his drive at the next and suddenly they were one down. But then Huggett cut loose with a big drive down the sixteenth and Will made the most of it with a delicate pitch to set up a birdie. Back on terms again, they held on for the half they deserved.

Having been all square at the turn, Alliss and Christy O'Connor subsided to defeat against Palmer and Dickinson, while Bernard Hunt and Neil Coles, a tried and trusted partnership, took quite a pasting from Nichols and Johnny Pott, which may not, in a small way, have been surprising. Coles still remembers Hunt turning to him on the first fairway, studying the second shot and then saying, 'You know, I don't think I can hit it!' This was Hunt's seventh Ryder Cup, yet here he was still as nervous as a kitten. Playing for your country does strange things.

Jacklin, too, admitted to being very much on edge, but he took great comfort from the company of the genial Thomas, who he knew could be relied upon to hit the longer ball against Sanders and Brewer. Out in 35, they were two up and, with neither American anywhere near his best, they cruised home very comfortably by four and three.

Rees dropped Hunt and Coles in the afternoon, bringing in Gregson and Boyle, but they were no match for Palmer and Dickinson who hit them with 32 to the turn. Ahead of them Huggett and Will had another tremendous game with Casper and Boros, being round in 69 but this time losing one down. Nevertheless it was only one hole that separated them in two rounds of golf all day.

With Alliss and O'Connor on the receiving end again, this time from Nichols and Pott, it was therefore left to Jacklin and Thomas to salvage what they could. Life was again made easier for them since Littler and Geiberger struck a bad patch on the inward half, losing three holes to par and the match by three and two.

Already three points down, Britain were sunk without trace in the fourballs for all they could get out of the eight matches was half a point. It was as miserable a day as anyone could remember, even if four of the games did go to the eighteenth. Coles and Hunt, very much back in form, lost by a hole to Nichols and Pott, and so did Jacklin and Thomas to Littler and Geiberger, the short putt Thomas missed at the seventeenth, with Jacklin already out of the hole since he had driven out of bounds, being crucial. This clash was repeated in the afternoon and this time Jacklin and Thomas managed a half to avoid a complete whitewash. The other three games were all lost, even that played by Will and Boyle, who had been four up at the turn but then collapsed and lost by one down to Palmer, who had not played in the morning, and Boros. Ahead now by 13−3, the Americans could hardly fail − and nor did they.

Of the four singles Britain won, two of them were delivered by Coles as he each time beat Sanders by two and one. He remembers that it did not exactly look like happening when he was plugged in a bunker late in their second encounter, and what stung him was Sanders' remark that 'one game each would be about right'. Coles promptly gritted his teeth, got up and down from the very difficult lie and, instead of losing, won again.

Huggett, with a fine win over Boros, and Alliss, who stirred himself at last in beating Brewer, provided other faint rays of sunshine, but the brutal fact of the matter was that the last series of singles was immaterial since the United States were already home and dry. Such had been their superiority,

Brian Huggett recovers from sand at Houston's ninth hole in 1969, he and George Will halving the opening foursome against Billy Casper and Julius Boros

particularly since the war, that there must have been a case for discontinuing the match, so one-sided had it become. Yet no one spoke more vehemently for its continuation than the Americans themselves, notably the United States PGA president, Leo Fraser, who said:

> The reasons are simple. For the American players this is the one occasion when they are playing for something bigger than money. They get nothing, apart from very moderate expenses. But to them this is the greatest honour in golf. And if you think playing in the Ryder Cup does not affect them, let me tell you I have known players who will stand over a four-foot putt that may be worth $50,000 to them, looking as though they have stepped right out of the ice-box. Not a trace of nerves. Yet I have seen these same players in a Ryder Cup match get so tensed up that they have asked to be rested.

Rees had no doubt about what had to be done, making three main points almost as soon as the last putt had been holed. They were:

1 We need more tournaments to toughen up the mental approach of our players.
2 We have got to water our greens and let the grass grow on them so that we can master the only department of the game in which the Americans consistently beat us. If we do that we might decide to go absolutely for the bigger ball.
3 We have got to learn to hit the ball high and down the flagstick − and get rid of that outdated pitch-and-run shot which our golf courses at present demand.

The sentiment was echoed at the same time by Leonard Crawley in the *Daily Telegraph*.

> We must face facts and admit that American golfers are superior to our own in every department of the game. The big ball, upon which they are brought up, requires more control and a better method of striking and they are far superior on and around the green.

It cannot be said too often that it is easy to go from the big to little ball, but to go from the little to the big one requires months of hard work and experience.

Meanwhile, back in England, P.B. 'Laddie' Lucas wrote to the *Daily Express* in wholehearted support of Rees's blueprint.

> Dai Rees has given a lead, now let the PGA plead with the Royal and Ancient, the National Golf Unions and the manufacturers that there is at the moment only one practical policy for Britain's survival as a first-class golfing power. Play the big ball exclusively in an agreed list of selected tournaments, championships and international matches in this country. Have we the leadership, the resolve and the strength to pursue this path?

Thankfully these ingredients were there, and in 1968 it was agreed, despite strong opposition from the manufacturers who had a monopoly of the small-ball market worldwide, to introduce the 1.68 inch ball in professional tournaments for an experimental three-year period. From that moment golf in Britain, Europe and elsewhere turned its most decisive corner. After the darkest night in Houston, a new dawn was about to break.

UNITED STATES		GREAT BRITAIN
Foursomes (a.m.)		
W. Casper & J. Boros	halved with	B.G.C. Huggett & G. Will
A. Palmer & G. Dickinson 2 & 1	beat	P. Alliss & C. O'Connor
D. Sanders & G. Brewer	lost to	A. Jacklin & D.C. Thomas 4 & 3
R. Nichols & J. Pott 6 & 5	beat	B.J. Hunt & N.C. Coles
Foursomes (p.m.)		
Casper & Boros 1 hole	beat	Huggett & Will
Palmer & Dickinson 5 & 4	beat	M. Gregson & H. Boyle
G. Littler & A. Geiberger	lost to	Jacklin & Thomas 3 & 2
Nichols & Pott 2 & 1	beat	Alliss & O'Connor
Foursomes (a.m.)		
Casper & Brewer 3 & 2	beat	Alliss & O'Connor
Nichols & Pott 1 hole	beat	Hunt & Coles
Littler & Geiberger 1 hole	beat	Jacklin & Thomas
Dickinson & Sanders 3 & 2	beat	Huggett & Will
Fourballs (a.m.)		
Casper & Brewer 5 & 3	beat	Hunt & Coles
Dickinson & Sanders 3 & 2	beat	Alliss & Gregson
Palmer & Boros 1 hole	beat	Will & Boyle
Littler & Geiberger	halved with	Jacklin & Thomas

UNITED STATES		GREAT BRITAIN
Singles (a.m.)		
Brewer 4 & 3	beat	Boyle
Casper 2 & 1	beat	Alliss
Palmer 3 & 2	beat	Jacklin
Boros 1 hole	lost to	Huggett
Sanders 2 & 1	lost to	Coles
Geiberger 4 & 2	beat	Gregson
Littler	halved with	Thomas
Nichols	halved with	Hunt
Singles (p.m.)		
Palmer 5 & 3	beat	Huggett
Brewer	lost to	Alliss 2 & 1
Dickinson 3 & 2	beat	Jacklin
Nichols 3 & 2	beat	O'Connor
Pott 3 & 1	beat	Will
Geiberger 2 & 1	beat	Gregson
Boros	halved with	Hunt
Sanders	lost to	Coles 2 & 1

United States 23½ — Great Britain 8½

Great Britain 16 — United States 16
Played at Royal Birkdale, 18, 19, 20 September 1969

Ten thousand people and more crammed every vantage point they could find around Royal Birkdale's eighteenth hole in the grey, fading light of a damp September evening, their necks craned for a glimpse of the two principal figures on what to them was the loneliest stage in the world. No script could have been more dramatically written: Great Britain and the United States level at 15½ matches each, and now Tony Jacklin and Jack Nicklaus, the only two players left on the course, all square, one to play. Nor were there two better men to fill the leading roles: Jacklin, who earlier that summer had become the first British golfer to win the Open championship in eighteen years, and Nicklaus, the greatest golfer of his time, already winner of three Masters, two US Opens, one PGA and one British Open, yet playing now in his first Ryder Cup match. Upon these two did everything hinge.

As they descended the red shale path from the eighteenth tee, Jacklin was some yards ahead, lost in concentration when suddenly Nicklaus called his name. Jacklin paused and waited.

'How do you feel, Tony?' asked Nicklaus as he moved alongside.

'Bloody awful,' replied Jacklin with absolute honesty.

'I thought you might,' replied Nicklaus, 'but if it's any consolation, so do I. A bugger isn't it?!'

With this mutual understanding of the pressure they were both under, they went their separate ways, Jacklin left of centre of the fairway but a little way ahead of Nicklaus. It was the American who had to play first and he hit his second to the 'fat' of the green, perhaps 10 yards right of the flag. Jacklin followed bravely over the left-hand bunker. His ball ran to the back of the green

and he had to putt first.

Barely a sound could be heard as lips were pursed, nails bitten and brows mopped. Jacklin took his time. He got the right line, but the putt was always just short and came to rest less than 18 inches from the hole. Nicklaus, 'going to school' on what he had seen, went boldly across the damp turf for what would have been an eagle three and victory not only for him but for the United States as well. His ball ran three or four feet past, and now he had to putt again.

Hunched in that characteristic manner of his, Nicklaus holed for his four. Now it was Jacklin's turn, but even as he stepped forward, so Nicklaus stooped, picked up his opponent's marker and with a grin offered his hand. Their game was halved and the match was tied. 'I am sure you would have holed,' said Nicklaus, 'but I was not prepared to see you miss.' Thus ended with one supreme gesture a match that will for ever stand as a memorial to all that is best about the Ryder Cup.

Perhaps some minds went back to the short putt Syd Easterbrook had, in similar circumstances, holed for outright victory on the eighteenth green at Southport and Ainsdale, only just down the road from Birkdale, thirty-six years earlier — but that was in the early days of the Ryder Cup and long before the American monopoly had set in. Furthermore, it was the second time in this summer of 1969 that British golf had received a major uplift. Still fresh in the memory was Jacklin's victory in the Open at Royal Lytham, his play then of the last hole, when two strokes ahead of Bob Charles, being right out of the same top drawer. If Severiano Ballesteros, Sandy Lyle, Nick Faldo and Bernhard Langer have all since played considerable parts in Europe's standing in the golfing world today, there is certainly no doubt that the man who initially lit the fuse was Jacklin.

In addition to the use of the big ball being made compulsory and the match being commercially sponsored for the first time (by Senior Service), another essential difference from preceding years was that there were now twelve players on each side instead of ten. This had to make sense, for it not only gave the two captains, Eric Brown and Sam Snead, greater room in which to manipulate, but it put less of a demand on the players – unless, of course, your name happened to be Jacklin. He alone played in all six games in three days, a total of 104 holes out of a possible 108, and, befitting this new-born star, he was unbeaten, winning four and halving two.

Snead's disadvantage was that he had no less than ten newcomers in his side, the only two who had played before being Gene Littler and Billy Casper. However, Nicklaus's introduction to the match along with Lee Trevino, who had won the US Open the year before, and other fine players such as Dave Hill, who was to play a critical role in the match, Raymond Floyd, Frank Beard and Tommy Aaron, who had been in the same American Walker Cup side as Nicklaus in 1959, hardly made it a team lacking in golfing experience.

Brown on the other hand, had five newcomers: Bernard Gallacher, who at twenty was the youngest player to have represented Britain in the Ryder Cup, Alex Caygill, Maurice Bembridge, Peter Townsend and Brian Barnes. Neil Coles still thinks Brown was the best captain under whom he played, and he was full of fighting talk long before the team had even assembled. 'An idea has got round that I hate Americans,' said Brown. 'I don't – off the course. But on the course I do hate them. I want to massacre them in a golf sense and that's the spirit I want to get through to my side, especially the younger ones. To support us I want the biggest crowd ever seen in this country and I want every man, woman

Dave Hill, who was involved in some heated games in the tied match at Royal Birkdale in 1969

and child to be roaring us on.'

It was also true that in a team talk beforehand, Brown told his players not to look for the American balls in the rough, which was quite thick. However, Gallacher says that the real reason behind this was never fully explained. 'Eric only made the point not to be unhelpful to the Americans, but this was because, if in looking for a ball we accidentally trod on it, we could lose the hole,' he explains.

Sadly for a match that will always be remembered for its epic finish, it also had its moments of rancour, most of them centring around Hill and, more particularly, Ken Still. As early as the foursomes on the first morning, Bembridge had to ask Still on the thirteenth tee to move because the American was in the corner of his eye as he addressed the ball. Still responded theatrically by moving everyone – caddies, players and officials – from their customary places beside the tee box. At the same hole Trevino bunkered the Americans' second shot under the lip and when Still tried to explode, the ball rebounded and hit him on the shoulder. 'It hit you, didn't it?' queried Trevino. There was no reply. 'Pick it up,' Trevino said, and strode on to the next tee.

Still did not play that afternoon nor the following morning in the first of the four-balls, but he did in the afternoon in partnership with Hill against Gallacher again, this time with Brian Huggett. It was an ugly match from as early as the first green, Hill having to be asked to stand still while Huggett putted. Then it was Still's turn to be asked to move, because he was almost breathing down Huggett's neck on the green. 'I want you behind me from now on,' said Huggett, never one to mince words. At the next, just as Gallacher was about to putt after a long succession of waggles, Still suddenly called out to his caddie, who was attending the flag: 'I don't want you to do that. Bernard's caddie should be doing it.'

It all came to a climax at the short seventh where, with Gallacher some three feet from the hole, Still putted up just inside him and then holed out. 'You can't do that,' protested the British pair. 'You've played out of turn.' Their intention was for the ball to be re-marked, but even as David Melville, the professional from La Moye who was acting as referee, was furiously delving into the rule book for the correct procedure, Still snatched up Gallacher's marker and snorted: 'You can have the hole and the goddam Cup.'

Nor was even that the end of it, for Gallacher recalls that at the eighth Still protested when Gallacher conceded him a meaningless putt for a four because it was on the same (but shorter) line as the putt Hill faced – and in fact holed – for a birdie three. But by then the two captains had arrived hot-foot, and together with Lord Derby, president of the PGA, they managed to cool things down, not only among the four players but also in the increasingly incensed crowd. 'Still got very erratic after that,' remembers Gallacher, 'but it seemed to inspire Hill and it was he who beat us.'

Huggett provides the sequel, for at the Prince of Wales Hotel in Southport that evening he and Hill had another argument in the corridor outside the restaurant. 'But that was the end of it,' says Huggett, 'and when immediately after the Ryder Cup we all flew to America for the Alcan tournament, Hill came down the aisle and said to me, "How about a practice round together?" It was nice peace offering.'

Unfortunate though this undercurrent was, it was from the beginning the most gripping match, Britain for once making the sort of fast start that had so often eluded them. They all but made a clean sweep of the opening series of foursomes, winning the top three games and halving the other, though typically the Americans came back at them in the afternoon and closed the gap at the end of the day to 4½–3½.

The particular heroes were Jacklin and Townsend for they won twice, first against Hill and Aaron and then against Casper and Beard. Dark of hair, slim of build, they almost gave the appearance of being young brothers, with total confidence in one another and straight into their stride in the morning with birdies at each of the first three holes, to lead two up. When they won by three and one they were seven under par, and there was no better stroke with which to finish it than Townsend's three wood to the seventeenth. It came to rest six feet from the flag and Jacklin holed for the eagle.

In the afternoon they were not quite as brilliant and were even a shade fortunate to hang on to Casper, who made a few telling mistakes at crucial times, and Beard. Indeed, it was not until the seventeenth that the young Britons at last got their noses ahead and then stayed there, as Townsend played a brilliant little pitch over a bunker at the eighteenth for a half in four. How well, once again, Townsend had played.

Though both Coles and Huggett, and behind them Gallacher and Bembridge, had

Brian Huggett breaks down after halving with Billy Casper and mistakenly believing Britain had won the 1969 Ryder Cup at Royal Birkdale. In fact one game was still going on and when Tony Jacklin and Jack Nicklaus halved as well, the whole match was tied

won in the morning, they both lost in the afternoon by one down, the former having a ragged game against Hill and Aaron, too many holes being won in fives and in one case even a six. Gallacher and Bembridge did reach the eighteenth all square against Trevino and Littler, but they never looked like making a four which the Americans did, thanks to a delightful chip right by the hole from Littler. And straight on top of that came a sad finish from Hunt and Butler against Nicklaus and Sikes, who were allowed to get away with a half in six at the seventeenth and then took the eighteenth with a four to win one up.

A measure of the closeness of the fourballs on the second day was that seven of the eight games went to the eighteenth, the one exception being that ill-tempered match of Hill and Still against Gallacher and Huggett, the Americans winning by two and one. 'We must remember,' wrote Leonard Crawley, 'that all four are born fighters who are not prepared to bow the knee to anyone.'

Britain in fact took the morning session by 2½–1½ to extend their overall lead, Jacklin and Townsend again doing their stuff

though not this time in partnership. Boldly, even rashly, Eric Brown switched them, Townsend to play with O'Connor and Jacklin with Coles, the latter taking the considerable scalps of Nicklaus and Dan Sikes. Coles has never forgotten their winning hole – the seventeenth – for he was the only one who could get a four, but just as he was about to putt, Jacklin whispered to him not to leave it short. 'That was the last thing I wanted to hear at that point,' recalls Coles, 'but anyway I didn't and we won.'

Just as on the first day, Britain enjoyed a better morning than they did afternoon for in the second session the Americans won two games and halved the other two, and that left the two sides level at 8–8, sixteen singles to come and everything to play for. By lunch on the last day the prize was there for the taking, for Britain won 5–3 to creep ahead once more. It was the tail that swung the pendulum, for after Trevino, Hill and Casper had won three of the first four games for America, O'Connor, Bembridge, Butler and Jacklin (four and three against Nicklaus)

Jack Nicklaus shakes hands with Tony Jacklin after conceding him the putt that tied the 1969 match at Royal Birkdale

Leo Fraser of the American PGA hands over the Ryder Cup to Lord Derby, president of the British PGA, for a year's safe-keeping after the famous tie in 1969

took the last four. At the press conference before the players went out again, Eric Brown was almost incoherent with excitement.

Yet once again it was the Americans who came out fighting for their lives, Hill, Barber, Sikes and Littler bringing home the points against two for Britain from the audaciously brilliant Gallacher, who beat Trevino by four and three, and the ever reliable Butler, who took good care of Douglass. So again the two sides were level, and only two games out on the course.

Huggett recalls as if it were yesterday

coming to the last all square with Casper and mistakenly believing that behind him Jacklin was one up on Nicklaus. In fact Jacklin had lost the sixteenth to go back to one down and when, just as Huggett was about to putt on the eighteenth green, a tremendous shout went up from the seventeenth, he was convinced that it could only mean that Jacklin had won. What the Open champion had done instead was hole a huge putt for an eagle three to draw level again. In his ignorance Huggett therefore thought that he had this putt of a yard or so not just to halve with Casper but to win the Ryder

Cup. In it went and, tears pouring down his face, he half collapsed into the arms of his captain. It was only after he had recovered that he learned the true situation, and by then Jacklin and Nicklaus were advancing down the eighteenth fairway, both of them feeling like nothing on earth.

GREAT BRITAIN		UNITED STATES
Foursomes (a.m.)		
N.C. Coles & B.G.C. Huggett 3 & 2	beat	M. Barber & R. Floyd
B. Gallacher & M. Bembridge 2 & 1	beat	L. Trevino & K. Still
A. Jacklin & P. Townsend 3 & 1	beat	D. Hill & T. Aaron
C. O'Connor & P. Alliss	halved with	W. Casper & F. Beard
Foursomes (p.m.)		
Coles & Huggett	lost to	Hill & Aaron 1 hole
Gallacher & Bembridge	lost to	Trevino & G. Littler 1 hole
Jacklin & Townsend 1 hole	beat	Casper & Beard
P.J. Butler & B.J. Hunt	lost to	Nicklaus & D. Sikes 1 hole
Fourballs (a.m.)		
O'Connor & Townsend 1 hole	beat	Hill & D. Douglass
Huggett & A. Caygill	halved with	Floyd & Barber
B. Barnes & Alliss	lost to	Trevino & Littler 1 hole
Jacklin & Coles 1 hole	beat	Nicklaus & Sikes

GREAT BRITAIN		UNITED STATES
Fourballs (p.m.)		
Butler & Townsend	lost to	Casper & Beard 2 holes
Huggett & Gallacher	lost to	Hill & Still 2 & 1
Bembridge & Hunt	halved with	Aaron & Floyd
Jacklin & Coles	halved with	Trevino & Barber
Singles (a.m.)		
Alliss	lost to	Trevino 2 & 1
Townsend	lost to	Hill 5 & 4
Coles 1 hole	beat	Aaron
Barnes	lost to	Casper 1 hole
O'Connor 5 & 4	beat	Beard
Bembridge 1 hole	beat	Still
Butler 1 hole	beat	Floyd
Jacklin 4 & 3	beat	Nicklaus
Singles (p.m.)		
Barnes	lost to	Hill 4 & 2
Gallacher 4 & 3	beat	Trevino
Bembridge	lost to	Barber 7 & 6
Butler 3 & 2	beat	Douglass
Coles	lost to	Sikes 4 & 3
O'Connor	lost to	Littler 2 & 1
Huggett	halved with	Casper
Jacklin	halved with	Nicklaus

Great Britain 16 — United States 16

United States 18½ – Great Britain 13½

Played at Old Warson, St Louis, 16, 17, 18 September 1971

If 1969 had been an unforgettable year for Tony Jacklin, first winning the Open championship and then playing a major part in the tied Ryder Cup match at Royal Birkdale, 1970 did not fall far short. It was then that he became the first British golfer since Ted Ray in 1920 to take the US Open at Hazeltine in Chaska, Minnesota. Nor was there any doubt about it as he dominated the championship from first to last, striding further and further ahead of the field and finishing no less than seven strokes clear of Dave

Hill, whose temperamental outburst revived swift memories of Royal Birkdale and the Ryder Cup.

On a golf course so difficult to some that in the first round Arnold Palmer took 79, Gary Player 80 and Jack Nicklaus 81, Hill, when asked what he thought the golf course lacked, replied, 'Eighty acres of corn and a few cows. They ruined a good farm when they built this course.' Such verbal abuse cost him a fine of $150, and in any case Jacklin proved how playable it was with

The British team fly out to St Louis for the 1971 match. John Garner is at the top of the steps with Christy O'Connor, Peter Butler, Harry Bannerman, Tony Jacklin and Brian Huggett below him. Still with their feet on the ground are, left to right, Eric Brown, the captain, Maurice Bembridge, Bernard Gallacher, Peter Oosterhuis, Brian Barnes and Peter Townsend

rounds of 71, 70, 70, 70, each one therefore under the par of 72.

Before he went out in the last round, Jacklin found a note pinned to his locker containing one word: 'Tempo'. It had been put there by his good friend Bert Yancey, who knew only too well the value of swinging the club as slowly as possible. It is worth noting that this friendship had come about as a result of Jacklin having become the first British professional to appreciate the value of playing extensively in America – indeed, he had won one other US Tour event before the Open, the Greater Jacksonville in 1968 (a title he was to regain in 1972).

At a time of a greater awareness of tournament golf and the appointment of John Jacobs as the PGA's first Tournament Director General, it became clear that others would almost certainly follow Jacklin's lead and it was for this reason that in 1971, for the match at Old Warson, the method of selecting the British team was changed. Six came straight off the order of merit, while the other six were chosen by a selection committee comprising Eric Brown, who had been re-elected captain, Dai Rees and Neil Coles. It was a safeguard against someone like Jacklin, because of his commitments abroad, not accumulating enough points to get in automatically. In an amended version this selection process is still in operation today. As it happened, the selectors opted for the first nine in the order of merit, added to them without too much thought Jacklin and Christy O'Connor, who had missed a number of tournaments because of injury, and after longer debate, John Garner. He was one of three newcomers, Peter Oosterhuis and Harry Bannerman being the others.

The Americans, on the other hand, were sticking to their two-year method of selection. Jay Hebert was the new captain and the fresh faces Dave Stockton, Charles Coody, Mason Rudolph and J.C. 'Jesse' Snead, nephew of Sam. There were some early doubts about Lee Trevino since he had suffered an appendicitis, while Billy Casper was nursing a broken toe incurred when groping around in the dark trying to find his hotel bathroom. Casper did not in fact play in either of the singles, but Trevino bounced back full of energy, losing only one of his five games.

For the first time the British team was accompanied by the British Golf Supporters Association, 186 strong, who chartered a Boeing 707. This also kept the PGA's costs down, and Brian Huggett made it his business to speak to every one of them on the flight into the cauldron of heat that was awaiting them on arrival in Missouri. Some days the temperature rose to over 100 degrees; fortunately, there was a five-day acclimatization period.

Coles's abiding memory is of being told by Brown that he would partner O'Connor in the opening foursome. It was then a matter of who would drive the odds, but when Coles first raised the matter on the eve of the match O'Connor replied that there was plenty of time and that he would think about it. By breakfast he was still apparently thinking, and when Coles pressed him again on the practice ground before the start (which because of rain was delayed an hour, with the opening ceremony washed out), the Irishman had still not made up his mind. The matter was raised, again without avail, on the practice green and by the time they got to the tee, still no decision had been made. By now Coles was on the point of tearing out what little hair he had, but O'Connor had his master plan. 'I tell you what we'll do, we'll toss for it,' Coles recalls him saying. 'And we did!'

Furthermore, it worked. Not only did Coles and O'Connor beat Casper and Miller Barber, but on a morning of unprecedented success in America, Britain led 3–1 and were still ahead at the end of the day, although admittedly less comfortably at 4½–3½. Thanks were due in the end to Jacklin as, blessed still with magic in his hands, he chipped in at the last in the afternoon to snatch the all-important half in

No wonder Peter Oosterhuis is smiling. He had just beaten Arnold Palmer by three and two

partnership with Huggett against Trevino and Rudolph.

Ironically, perhaps the best golf of the day had been played by Oosterhuis and Peter Townsend and yet they lost each time, by two holes to Arnold Palmer and Gardner Dickinson in the morning and by one hole to the same pair in the afternoon. Oosterhuis fell into Ryder Cup golf as if he had been playing it all his life; with his first putt, one of 20 yards, he holed it for a birdie three.

One of the more alarming moments had come when Maurice Bembridge and Peter Butler had gone through the turn three up on Coody and Frank Beard and then returned 5, 6, 4, 5 — two double bogeys and a

bogey — to go back to all square. However, the rocking ship was steadied and when Coody drove into the rough at the last, it was Butler who holed for the winning four.

The British team therefore slept more hopefully in America than they had ever done, the Royal Birkdale tie still fresh in their minds and now a one-point lead away from home. But such a state of near euphoria was rapidly dashed. Elsewhere in the hotel the Americans were steeling themselves for the fourball backlash — and what a backlash it was. They won the morning play 4−0 and the afternoon 2½−1½, and everything was changed right around, the United States now ahead by 10−6.

On arrival in America the British had put forward a proposition that rather than play all the foursomes on the first day and all fourballs on the second, they should instead be split. This was rejected because it was too late to change the arrangements, but there would seem little doubt that the enormously long day that was inevitable with two series of fourballs had some effect on the British players, particularly in that heat. They breakfasted at 5.45 a.m., the last putt did not go in until after 6 p.m. and the only relief they got was on the monorail they were able to board to negotiate the steep incline between the twelfth tee and thirteenth green. In fact, the recommended change to the format was adopted two years later.

One incident transcended all else on this bleak day for the British, and that was when in the third match in the morning Bernard Gallacher and Oosterhuis forfeited the seventh hole to Palmer and Dickinson on an unusual technicality. The circumstances were that the Americans had just won the sixth, a par five where Palmer had had a birdie four, to go one up and they therefore had the honour on the next tee, a short hole of 207 yards.

Palmer hit such a fine-looking ball to the green that Gallacher's caddie, an American club golfer by the name of Jack McLeod, was completely in awe of it and he blurted out, 'Great shot, what did you hit?' Palmer replied, 'A five iron.' Gallacher was in fact unaware of this exchange and, not being as strong a player anyway, had to hit a three iron. Both sides made three, but before they left the green Gallacher was caught by surprise when Palmer and Dickinson were seen to go into consultation with the referee, the professional golfer John Conley, who announced that the Americans had in fact won the hole because the British pair had infringed the rule which forbids the asking of advice. Rule 9a, as it was then, stated: 'A player may give advice to, or ask advice from only his partner or either of their caddies.' Further, under Rule 37−2 of that time, 'For any breach of that rule by his caddie the player incurs the relative penalty' − which in this case was loss of the hole.

The referee consulted Joe Dey, who was then Commissioner of the United States PGA Tournament Players' Division, and Joe Black, a PGA rules official. Dey later explained that Conley could not have acted otherwise when he recognized a clear breach of the Rules of Golf. Nor was he entitled to turn a deaf ear, either at the time of the incident or when the matter was subsequently drawn to his attention.

Certainly the hole was played out, and through the mists of time Gallacher remains convinced that the initiative came from the American players, though at least one account states that Palmer, 'greatly to his credit, and in the true spirit in which such matches ought to be played, appealed against the decision'. Whether this reporter was actually on the spot and heard the whole exchange or picked it up second hand is less certain. But Gallacher certainly was there and it is his lasting impression that this was 'a bit of gamesmanship. Off camera Palmer could be a very lethal weapon, and I must say that my high regard for him has never been quite the same again.'

Brown, the British captain, was quickly on the scene and his words at the time were that 'this is a lousy ruling. If the Americans want to play it this way, we certainly won't.' Neverthless the facts are that the exchange, however inadvertent, did take place and the referee had no option but to take the steps he did.

The whole affair had a disastrous effect on the British pair and, now two down, they subsided to defeat by five and four. The tide also ran against them in the other games as Trevino and Rudolph, Beard and Snead, and Nicklaus and Littler all won by two and one to ease their country ahead. It was closer in the afternoon, and typically Gallacher put the morning traumas behind him as he teamed up with Oosterhuis to record

Britain's only win of the day, against Trevino and Casper.

It was Oosterhuis, however, who was largely responsible, for it was he who had most of the birdies in putting his side ahead, although it was Gallacher's four at the last that kept them there when it mattered most. The half point was provided by Coles and O'Connor, and a fine fighting effort it was too, since they were four down after only five holes to Coody and Beard. Remarkably they then took the next four with one birdie by O'Connor at the sixth and then three in a row from Coles. But in no time at all they were two down again, only for Coles to make winning birdies at the sixteenth and seventeenth; and there it stayed. The disappointment was the defeat of Jacklin and Huggett by Littler and Snead, but against that Townsend and Bannerman very nearly held the mighty combination of Nicklaus and Palmer, Nicklaus having to hole from 15 feet at the last for a birdie to win. It gave the Americans a better − ball score of 64 against the Britons' 65.

Again, therefore, the Americans were in a commanding position going into the singles and any lingering doubts they may have had were quickly dispersed when Trevino, who was to prove a constant thorn in the side to the career of Jacklin, won four of the first five holes. Jacklin got four of them back, but not the fifth. Indeed, the only British winners in the morning were Brian Barnes, against Rudolph, and Oosterhuis, who made surprisingly short work of Littler, it proving to be the beginnings of his fine record in Ryder Cup singles. Halves were gained by Coles against Beard, Gallacher against Stockton and, most memorably of all, by Bannerman against Palmer. He was in his element and I can see him now striding up the eighteenth fairway, a cigar in his mouth, relishing every moment of it.

This left America needing only two more points from the last series of singles. One of them came swiftly, Trevino demolishing Huggett by seven and six, and it was left to

Snead to provide the knock-out punch when he beat Jacklin on the last green. Some hope had still stirred when Jacklin holed a massive putt for a birdie on the seventeenth green to square, but he rather duffed his pitch to the last and that was it.

The remaining games consequently became rather meaningless except to the players themselves, though Britain did at least come out of this final series at 4−4. A closer analysis of the results reveals that in the foursomes and singles the two teams tied 12−12. But America took the fourballs 6½−1½ and there was no answer to that. Even so, it was Britain's best performance to date in the States which, together with the tie at Royal Birkdale, was something from which Eric Brown, the captain, could extract satisfaction. On the flight back to Britain his wife, Joan, took the microphone from a stewardess and sang: 'They did it my way.'

UNITED STATES		GREAT BRITAIN
Foursomes (a.m.)		
W. Casper & M. Barber	lost to	N.C. Coles & C. O'Connor 2 & 1
A. Palmer & G. Dickinson 2 holes	beat	P. Townsend & P. Oosterhuis
J. Nicklaus & D. Stockton	lost to	B.G.C. Huggett & A. Jacklin 3 & 2
C. Coody & F. Beard	lost to	M. Bembridge & P.J. Butler 1 hole
Foursomes (p.m.)		
Casper & Barber	lost to	H. Bannerman & B. Gallacher 2 & 1
Palmer & Dickinson 1 hole	beat	Townsend & Oosterhuis
L. Trevino & M. Rudolph	halved with	Huggett & Jacklin
Nicklaus & J.C. Snead 5 & 3	beat	Bembridge & Butler

UNITED STATES		GREAT BRITAIN
Fourballs (a.m.)		
Trevino & Rudolph 2 & 1	beat	O'Connor & Barnes
Beard & Snead 2 & 1	beat	Coles & J. Garner
Palmer & Dickinson 5 & 4	beat	Oosterhuis & Gallacher
Nicklaus & G. Littler 2 & 1	beat	Townsend & Bannerman
Fourballs (p.m.)		
Trevino & Casper	lost to	Gallacher & Oosterhuis 1 hole
Littler & Snead 2 & 1	beat	Jacklin & Huggett
Palmer & Nicklaus 1 hole	beat	Townsend & Bannerman
Coody & Beard	halved with	Coles & O'Connor
Singles (a.m.)		
Trevino 1 hole	beat	Jacklin
Stockton	halved with	Gallacher
Rudolph	lost to	Barnes 1 hole
Littler	lost to	Oosterhuis 4 & 3
Nicklaus 3 & 2	beat	Townsend
Dickinson 5 & 4	beat	O'Connor
Palmer	halved with	Bannerman
Beard	halved with	Coles
Singles (p.m.)		
Trevino 7 & 6	beat	Huggett
Snead 1 hole	beat	Jacklin
Barber	lost to	Barnes 2 & 1
Stockton 1 hole	beat	Townsend
Coody	lost to	Gallacher 2 & 1
Nicklaus 5 & 3	beat	Coles
Palmer	lost to	Oosterhuis 3 & 2
Dickinson	lost to	Bannerman 2 & 1

United States 18½ — Great Britain 13½

Great Britain and Ireland 13 – United States 19

Played at Muirfield, 20, 21, 22 September 1973

It was at about two o'clock on the morning of 21 September that Britain's high hopes of winning the 1973 Ryder Cup match took a decided turn for the worse. It was then that Bernard Gallacher woke in his North Berwick hotel room in a cold sweat, feeling both sick and dizzy. Something he had eaten over a quiet team dinner a few hours earlier had violently disagreed with him. Far from getting it out of his system, Gallacher became worse. Between 4 and 5 a.m. his wife, Lesley, had to summon a doctor, who diagnosed food poisoning, and by seven o'clock Bernard Hunt, Britain's captain, knew that one of the aces in his hand of few high cards was out of that day's play. It could not have come at a worse moment.

In this, the first and still the only Ryder Cup match to have been played in Scotland, at the home of the Honourable Company of Edinburgh Golfers at Muirfield, Gallacher and Brian Barnes had been the inspiration behind Britain's 5½–2½ lead after the first day, first by one hole in the foursomes against Lee Trevino and Billy Casper and then by five and four in the fourballs against Tommy Aaron and Gay Brewer. The latter was the biggest winning margin a British pair had had at fourball play, and each time they had been given the responsibility of playing top.

The following morning the two Scots were due to go out top again, this time against Jack Nicklaus and Tom Weiskopf, a wonderfully talented golfer who earlier that summer had at long last realized his potential by winning the Open championship at Royal Troon. Gallacher in particular could not wait to get at them, and he remembers sitting in the restaurant watching Jackie Burke, the American captain, Nicklaus and

Arnold Palmer deep in consultation long after their meal was finished, pondering the crisis that was staring them in the face.

But within a matter of hours Gallacher was a stricken man and Hunt had to regroup his forces. Barnes recalls his chin dropping when he heard the news, and the morale of the whole team suffered a blow. 'Some of them looked upon it as a bad omen,' says Barnes, who was not exactly over the moon himself when Hunt told him that his new partner would be Peter Butler, who had been summoned from his bed at 8 a.m. and told he was due on the tee at 9.30. 'I thought I ought to have played with someone with a more attacking game than dear old Pete,' he says, 'someone younger and less conservative.' At all events, they lost both in the morning in the foursomes – when Butler nevertheless holed in one at the sixteenth – and again in the afternoon fourballs. Consequently the Americans, having tied this pre-lunch series 2–2 and then won the next 3½–½, drew level at 8–8. They had made good their escape and though Gallacher, rather to his surprise since he was still very weak and receiving injections, came back for both the singles, the damage had been done. The United States finished much more comfortable winners than had once seemed likely.

No one was more relieved than Burke, who had been captain of the losing team at Lindrick in 1957. One defeat could be put down to bad luck, but two might have looked like carelessness! Weiskopf was not the only newcomer to the team. Homero Blancas, Lou Graham and Chi Chi Rodriguez were the others, while for Nicklaus it was a sentimental return to Muirfield. It was here that he had been a member of the 1959 American

Jack Burke junior is lifted shoulder high after America's victory at Muirfield in 1973. Left to right: Lee Trevino, Lou Graham, Dave Hill, Arnold Palmer, Billy Casper, Tommy Aaron (half hidden), Jack Nicklaus and J.C.Snead

Walker Cup team and here as well that he had won his first Open championship in 1966. Such, indeed, was his attachment to the place that when he built his first golf course at Columbus, Ohio he called it Muirfield Village, the club's emblem being an outline of the Open championship trophy.

Having earlier that year won his fourteenth major championship to beat the record of Bobby Jones, Nicklaus was very much the superstar and caused something of a stir by failing to make the journey from Washington with the rest of the American team – because, it was said, he wanted to see a football game in Miami. In fact he arrived only a few hours late, but it did not stop Lee Trevino from remarking in one of the pre-match press interviews that he would have liked to have stayed behind for an even better reason in that his wife had only recently been delivered of a baby girl.

No doubt more was made of this than was necessary, for Nicklaus has always been a strong supporter of the Ryder Cup. In his book, *Jack Nicklaus On and Off the Fairway*, he wrote:

> For me, and I think a lot of other golfers who've been fortunate to participate in them, international team contests are the most enjoyable events in golf. If the game has one drawback, it is its individuality, its self-concernedness – its selfishness, to be blunt about the matter. Playing for a team, and particularly for your country in someone else's country, really brings a group of guys together.

What was made less public was a remark by Trevino, who also had a strong attachment to Muirfield since he had won the Open there the year before, that if he could not beat Peter Oosterhuis in the singles he 'would kiss the American team's asses!' In fact he halved, and there is in circulation, so it is said, a photograph of the American team with their trousers around their knees awaiting his unfulfilled promise!

For a match now sponsored by Sun Alliance, Great Britain & Ireland, as the team was now officially called, once more changed their method of selection, theoretically taking the first eight players off the Ryder Cup points table and then adding four more at the discretion of the selectors, Hunt, and captain, Dai Rees and Oosterhuis. The latter's swift promotion to the role of selector in what was only his second Ryder Cup campaign was due to a clause which stated that the leader of the order of merit should have a say in the team. In fact the selectors stuck exactly to the merit table, John Garner, Eddie Polland, Clive Clark and Brian Huggett, who were lying respectively ninth, tenth, eleventh and twelfth in the table, getting the nod of approval since there was not a sufficiently strong case for promoting anyone else above them. Yet, having chosen Garner and then been caught a man short because of Gallacher's illness, Hunt still did not give him a game. In two Ryder Cups, therefore, at St Louis in 1971 and now at Muirfield, Garner went to the first tee only once.

There was no disguising the fact that even in the early 1970s when Tony Jacklin was still very much a force in the game and Oosterhuis, who that spring had led by three strokes going into the last round of the Masters only to be beaten, was threatening to become one, Britain still possessed something of a cricket team's batting 'tail'. In other words they could field perhaps half a dozen players quite capable of holding their own, but after that they were decidedly suspect.

That was why it was always important to get off on the right foot. They had done so at Royal Birkdale in 1969, again at St Louis in 1971, and now they did so once more at Muirfield: 2½–1½ in the morning foursomes, 3–1 in the fourball and straight away three points clear. In more than forty years of the Ryder Cup there had been nothing to touch it, and it all emanated from Barnes, a large and reassuring figure with a pipe in-

Peter Butler in high glee after holing in one at the 16th during the 1973 match at Muirfield

variably clamped between his teeth, and Gallacher.

Uncharacteristically, Trevino and Casper began by taking three putts at the first and two in a bunker at the second. But by the sixteenth they were back to all square and though they lost the seventeenth to a birdie four, the odds were on a half when Gallacher drove into a bunker at the last. However, he made up for it with a fine pitch and Barnes rolled the putt firmly home.

With Polland and Maurice Bembridge on to something of a hiding against Palmer and Nicklaus at the bottom since they were five down at the turn, attention switched to the middle-order games. It was the old warriors

Neil Coles and Christy O'Connor who came up trumps, O'Connor in particular playing some telling strokes with both his sand wedge and putter to turn the tables on Weiskopf and J.C. Snead. So there was another point in the bag, and now it was up to Jacklin and Oosterhuis to widen the gap, one up straight away and then halving eleven consecutive holes.

Rather unexpectedly they hit a bad patch, Oosterhuis bunkered at the thirteenth, Jacklin fluffing a pitch at the next, and they were one down. However, Graham let them off the hook with a timid approach putt at the sixteenth and the British pair looked likely to take the seventeenth as well until

Rodriguez holed a monster putt after Graham's pitch had got a fortunate kick off the bank.

This was enough to earn the Americans a half, and if Jacklin and Oosterhuis were disappointed, they were unanswerable in the fourballs, making birdies at each of the first seven holes and going out in an astonishing better-ball of 28 to stand three up on Weiskopf and Casper. Oosterhuis started it all with birdies at each of the first three holes, then Jacklin made a two at the fourth, Oosterhuis a four at the fifth and Jacklin a three and then a two at the sixth and seventh. Yet the Americans were themselves out in 31 and with birdies at the twelfth and thirteenth they were back to only one down. That, however, was the end of their recovery, for Casper hooked and hooked again at the fifteenth, Weiskopf could not get down in two from the edge, and a par four was good enough to see the British juggernauts widen the gap again for the last time. It had been a marvellous exhibition from both sides.

If Gallacher had been the stronger man in the morning, it was Barnes who had all the shots in the afternoon. Three times, at the eighth, ninth and tenth, he played staggering strokes for birdies, the best of them undoubtedly being that from a bunker 150 yards short of the green at the eighth and then holing the putt for a three. Going down the eleventh they were therefore five up on Aaron and Brewer, and though the latter came back with two birdies of his own, Gallacher got in on the act with a two at the thirteenth and they were never under threat again.

Bembridge, having lost in the morning, did not expect to be playing in the afternoon and was half-way through a pint of beer when he was summoned to partner Brian Huggett against Nicklaus and Palmer. He was a different man, playing so well that Huggett, who had learnt that morning that he had become a father, had merely to do what he called the 'tidying up' in an unex-

pectedly comfortable victory by three and one. However, it was not all one-way traffic, for Trevino and Blancas, having been held to the turn by Coles and O'Connor, drew away on the inward half and here (in hindsight) was a very valuable point for the Americans.

The British rode the enforced absence of Gallacher fairly well in the foursomes on the second day. Though Barnes and Butler were beaten by Nicklaus and Weiskopf, they had, with the help of Butler's hole in one, made a match of it, while Huggett and Bembridge, two tough customers, made the most of some very ragged golf by Graham and Rodriguez, who were something like eight over par when they lost.

Another British point swiftly followed as Jacklin and Oosterhuis won on the home green against Palmer and Dave Hill, by all accounts something of a reluctant participant and playing, indeed, his only game. Having been three up, perhaps they ought to have settled things earlier, but they could not and in the end they got home only when Palmer, of all people, failed to get out of a bunker at the eighteenth. In the bottom match Trevino and Casper made no such mistakes against the tiring Coles and O'Connor.

America had therefore stopped the rot and in the afternoon they made a clean sweep of the fourballs to draw level at 8—8, exactly as it had been at Royal Birkdale four years earlier. The one British pocket of resistance was found in Bembridge and Huggett, Trevino fending them off time and time again and Blancas contributing here and there. A one-hole lead after 13 holes was short-lived, but Huggett raised hopes again with a soaring four wood to the final green. He had a putt to win but it stayed on the lip and the game, perhaps rightly, was halved.

Barnes was the heroic figure in the top match, seemingly often playing Palmer and Snead single-handed and bowing only at the seventeenth where he just failed to get up

The British team are dressed more like touring cricketers than golfers at Muirfield in 1973. Left to right: (standing) Peter Oosterhuis, Peter Butler, Tony Jacklin, Eddie Polland, Brian Barnes, John Garner; (seated) Maurice Bembridge, Christy O'Connor, Bernard Gallacher, Bernard Hunt (captain), Clive Clark, Neil Coles, Brian Huggett

and down from the right-hand bunker, thus also failing to match Snead's two memorable shots, a drive and two iron to the front of the green. So that was the Americans one up, and Palmer stepped in to make absolutely sure at the last, holing from five yards for a birdie three.

Nor could Jacklin and Oosterhuis recapture their form of the previous day, the latter beginning the slide with a bad error at the twelfth and Brewer, in partnership with Casper, punishing it with a two at the thirteenth and a three out of sand at the fourteenth. Predictably the remaining match was always safely in American control, Nicklaus and Weiskopf having too much heavy artillery for the small-arms fire of Polland and Clark.

By comparison with the last day at Birkdale, this final day was very much of an anti-climax. Justifiably Hunt made Oosterhuis his anchor-man in case of a tight finish, but surprisingly he 'hid' Jacklin at number four in the order instead of putting him out top where he could have been an inspirational figure, leading the rest by example. As it was, America ran away with the first three matches as Casper, Weiskopf and Blancas took good care of Barnes, Gallacher and Butler. Jacklin managed the only full point, beating Aaron. Certainly honours were shared between Coles and Brewer, Bembridge and Nicklaus, and Oosterhuis and Trevino. Who knows what might have happened had not Coles taken three putts at the last, or had Oosterhuis not topped his second at the seventeenth to let Trevino off the hook?

Arguably Hunt should not have played Gallacher again in the afternoon, since he was obviously still not himself after twenty-four hours in bed, still looking pale and drawn. Nor did the captain make use of Clark, Polland or Garner on this last day, thus highlighting Britain's lack of strength in the 'tail'. By mid-afternoon it was all over, for though Huggett came out fighting and beat Blancas comfortably, America's middle order fell like vultures on the staggering beast.

Afterwards Burke reflected that the near-disastrous opening day had been the making of the American team. 'We knew then that we had a fight on our hands,' he said, 'and it welded us together.' He thought that for once it was not the Americans' putting that was decisive but their driving, which he regarded as phenomenal. 'It's becoming a big man's game,' he reflected. 'They just keep hitting the ball further and further. Sooner or later it is going to get the other man down.' Burke believed that reputation counted for a great deal. 'I remember,' he recalled, 'that I never liked playing Ben Hogan. You sort of know you've lost before you start, and in some cases I think that was true this week.'

GREAT BRITAIN AND IRELAND		UNITED STATES
Foursomes (a.m.)		
B.W. Barnes & B.J. Gallacher 1 hole	beat	L. Trevino & W.J. Casper
C. O'Connor & N.C. Coles 3 & 2	beat	T. Weiskopf & J.C. Snead
A. Jacklin & P.A. Oosterhuis	halved with	J. Rodriguez & L. Graham
M.E. Bembridge & E. Polland	lost to	J.W. Nicklaus & A. Palmer 6 & 5
Fourballs (p.m.)		
Barnes & Gallacher 5 & 4	beat	T. Aaron & G. Brewer
Bembridge & B.G.C. Huggett 3 & 1	beat	Palmer & Nicklaus
Jacklin & Oosterhuis 3 & 1	beat	Weiskopf & Casper
O'Connor & Coles	lost to	Trevino & H. Blancas 2 & 1
Foursomes (a.m.)		
Barnes & P.J. Butler	lost to	Nicklaus & Weiskopf 1 hole
Oosterhuis & Jacklin 2 holes	beat	Palmer & D. Hill
Bembridge & Huggett 5 & 4	beat	Rodriguez & Graham
Coles & O'Connor	lost to	Trevino & Casper 2 & 1
Fourballs (p.m.)		
Barnes & Butler	lost to	Palmer & Snead 2 holes
Jacklin & Oosterhuis	lost to	Brewer & Casper 3 & 2
C. Clark & Polland	lost to	Nicklaus & Weiskopf 3 & 2
Bembridge & Huggett	halved with	Trevino & Blancas

GREAT BRITAIN AND IRELAND		UNITED STATES
Singles (a.m.)		
Barnes	lost to	Casper 2 & 1
Gallacher	lost to	Weiskopf 3 & 1
Butler	lost to	Blancas 5 & 4
Jacklin 2 & 1	beat	Aaron
Coles	halved with	Brewer
O'Connor	lost to	Snead 1 hole
Bembridge	halved with	Nicklaus
Oosterhuis	halved with	Trevino
	Singles (p.m.)	
Huggett 4 & 2	beat	Blancas
Barnes	lost to	Snead 3 & 1
Gallacher 6 & 5	lost to	Brewer
Jacklin	lost to	Casper 2 & 1
Coles	lost to	Trevino 6 & 5
O'Connor	halved with	Weiskopf
Bembridge	lost to	Nicklaus 2 holes
Oosterhuis 4 & 2	beat	Palmer

Great Britain and Ireland 13 — United States 19

United States 21 —
Great Britain & Ireland 11

Played at Laurel Valley, Pennsylvania, 19, 20, 21 September 1975

Whenever one looks back on 1975, it is probably true to say that nothing stands out more in golfing terms than Jack Nicklaus's fifth victory in the Masters. It was memorable not only for its pulsating finish but also for the quality of its contenders, as the two men he beat by a stroke, Johnny Miller and Tom Weiskopf, were then the two most serious pretenders to his throne, both thrilling golfers in their own right and in that week particularly Miller, whose last two rounds of 65 and 66 all but caught the great

man. Asked later if he had seen the huge and, as it proved, decisive putt Nicklaus holed for a birdie two across the sixteenth green, Miller, who was at the time partnering Weiskopf and waiting on the tee, made the memorable remark: 'No, but I certainly found the bear prints on the green' — as Nicklaus, club aloft, leaped exultantly into the air. Even then, both Weiskopf and Miller came to the last hole facing reasonable putts with which to tie. Both missed.

In September, the week-end before the

The 1975 British team at Laurel Valley. Left to right: Guy Hunt, Brian Huggett, Maurice Bembridge, Peter Townsend, Tommy Horton, Tony Jacklin, Bernard Hunt (captain), Christy O'Connor junior, Norman Wood, Eamonn Darcy, John O'Leary, Brian Barnes, Peter Oosterhuis

Ryder Cup at Laurel Valley, Nicklaus, who by then had added a fourth PGA championship to his collection of major titles, won his fifth tournament of the year, the so-called 'World Open' at Pinehurst. Indeed, he went so far as to say that he was now playing the best golf of his life, even though there were other years when he had won more titles. For a man not inclined to exaggerate, that was quite something.

Nicklaus had won that one by another stroke from Weiskopf and Billy Casper, and with eight members of the British Ryder Cup team all finishing nowhere, the inevitable mountain they knew they would have to climb at Laurel Valley looked, and indeed was, as insurmountable as ever. Just a glance at the two teams beforehand proved that. Nicklaus, Miller (who with Hale Irwin was making his first appearance in the match), Weiskopf, Casper, Lee Trevino, Gene Littler, Al Geiberger, Ray Floyd and Lou Graham had between them won twenty-eight majors. Indeed, the only two who had not taken a major championship were Bob Murphy and J.C. Snead. Ranged against that, on the British side, was just Tony Jacklin with one British Open and one US Open; and he was no longer the force he had been, after having moved to Jersey where he was finding both his will to win and his form to be elusive.

David and Goliath; lambs to the slaughter; any similar cliché you care to name fitted the bill, and sure enough the match took its predicted pattern, the Americans taking their opponents by the throat as early as the first series of four-somes, of which they made a clean sweep before running out the most comfortable of winners by 21−11, the only minimal consolation to the British being that it was not as bad as the 23½−8½ margin at Houston eight years earlier.

And yet out of all this wreckage there emerged one shining British knight in armour, for whenever the match is recalled the first name that comes to mind is not that

Two minds are sometimes better than one as Peter Oosterhuis, with putter, and Tony Jacklin try and work out the contours of the 12th green at Laurel Valley in 1975. They lost, by three and one, to Al Geiberger and Johnny Miller

of any of the Americans but instead that of Brian Barnes who, twice on the same day, beat Nicklaus in the singles, winning by four and two in the morning and by two and one in the afternoon. No one is now more dismissive of that performance than Barnes himself.

I still, all these years on, have difficulty in getting away from it. Whenever I attend a company day or dinner I am introduced as the man who twice beat Nicklaus head to head. But you know, I never did consider it as that fantastic. Certainly I enjoyed it at the time, but in my own mind I soon forgot it.

Eighteen holes of match-play is not a lot different to sudden death, and two wins like that do not mean as much to a professional as they would to an amateur.

Furthermore, Barnes was at the time the first to point out that Nicklaus was nowhere near his best − five or six over par for the 33 holes they played and a long way from being the heroic figure Barnes had always felt him to be. What Barnes does remember is how well Nicklaus took his two defeats.

I know how bloody mad he was, but he never showed it and congratulated me very warmly. We talked fishing a lot of the way round, and you know, it was Jack who was responsible for re-matching us again in the afternoon. America had won the Ryder Cup by then and it was he who suggested to Arnold Palmer, their captain, that the order of play should be fiddled so that we met again. It gave the crowd something to watch and I remember Jack saying to me on the first tee: 'You've beaten me once but there ain't no way you're going to beat me again.' And then he started − birdie, birdie, and I didn't think I would. But I did.

The fact that the contest was all over when there were still eight singles to play brought the Ryder Cup closer to the point of crisis. It was the Americans' seventeenth victory in twenty-one meetings, and Palmer, whose appointment as non-playing captain was only natural since he had been playing − professional at Laurel Valley throughout his career and lived only fifteen minutes away at Latrobe, conceded that some sort of overhaul was needed. He was nevertheless firmly of the opinion that the Ryder Cup was very much worth preserving.

There are occasions even in professional sport when who wins by how much isn't everything, and the Ryder Cup is most certainly one of them. I do not think it should be dropped just because the Americans usually win. There

has never been a punch pulled yet in the Ryder Cup.

While not finally committing himself, Palmer's thoughts, which had the backing of all twenty-four players, were that next time there should be only one round a day instead of two, keeping it at twelve a side but having five fourball matches on the first day, ten singles on the second and then some sort of stroke-play competition. He also suggested, with greater conviction, that the British PGA should widen its selection to include Commonwealth players. This was hardly surprising since Dale Hayes, of South Africa, was that year the clear winner of the order of merit, while Bob Shearer, of Australia, was second and other members of the Commonwealth such as Hugh Biocchi, Jack Newton and Graham Marsh were all in the top twelve. (What no one noticed particularly was that twenty-sixth place was taken by an eighteen-year-old Spaniard, Severiano Ballesteros − but then his second place in the Open championship at Royal Birkdale was still the best part of twelve months away, the flagship of the Spanish golfing armada not yet under full sail.)

By now the British team was being selected straight off the money list rather than an order of merit points table and, because so many overseas players were in full cry, the selectors, who were still empowered to choose four in addition to the top eight who got in automatically, went down to fifteenth place in their nomination of Tommy Horton. He was one of six newcomers, Eamonn Darcy, Norman Wood, Guy Hunt, John O'Leary and Christy O'Connor Junior being the others. Neil Coles had declared himself unavailable because the sea crossing would have left him insufficient time in which to acclimatize.

Selecting most of the team on the basis of money was not widely welcomed as a procedure. It was done largely at the instigation of John Jacobs, the Tournament Director General who, only a month before the Ryder Cup, had been successful in negotiating the formation of a fully autonomous Tournament Players' Division of the PGA. Indeed, at a subsequent players' meeting, nine out of ten voted in favour of the old points system. But the objection came too late, and subsequent events have proved Jacobs to have been right in his judgement.

The Americans, with only three newcomers – Murphy, Miller and Irwin – had the greater Ryder Cup experience under their belts, and it was particularly welcome to see Gene Littler back in the team after recovery from an operation for cancer. Indeed, he had cancelled an invitation to play in England to be sure of his place in the team. That gave a further indication of the value the American players put on representing their country (although the absence of Casper from the flag-raising ceremony at the unearthly hour of 7.30 on the opening day did not endear him to his captain).

Heavy rain had left Laurel Valley playing every inch of its 7000 yards. Some of the practice rounds had to be curtailed because of flooding, and an 'exhibition' match between Palmer, Bernard Hunt (the British captain), Bob Hope and Perry Como was cancelled altogether. Play was therefore very much the 'target golf' at which the Americans are so adept, and as early as 9.15 on the first morning the pattern was set: America three up, two up, two up and one up in the four foursomes.

Nicklaus and Weiskopf duly went on to beat Barnes and Bernard Gallacher by five and four, Littler and Irwin got home by four and three against Wood and Maurice Bembridge, Miller and Geiberger by three and one against Jacklin and Oosterhuis, and Trevino and J.C. Snead by two and one against Horton and O'Leary. After the good starts enjoyed at Birkdale in 1969, at Old Warson in 1971 and then at Muirfield in 1973, this was for Britain very much a case of back to the bad old days.

Certainly the afternoon fourball matches

Brian Barnes, pipe and all, gets ready to putt in the 1975 match at Laurel Valley. He and Bernard Gallacher halved with Jack Nicklaus and Bob Murphy while in the singles Barnes beat Nicklaus both in the morning and afternoon

were closer, Jacklin and Oosterhuis picking up the first point when they beat Casper and Floyd, though neither for a time drove well and each kept putting the pressure on the other. However, Oosterhuis suddenly strung together a succession of birdies early on the second nine holes and they were home and drier than they were underfoot. Barnes and Gallacher, with a better-ball of 66, turned the heat on against Nicklaus and Murphy but could get only a half, while Horton and O'Leary required a four at the last for the same score and yet went down by two and one to Trevino and Irwin. Meanwhile Darcy and O'Connor Junior, two Irishmen making their first appearance, ran into an absolute onslaught from Weiskopf, who was out in 30 with his own ball and scarcely needed the presence of Graham, the Americans sailing serenely home by three and two.

The tally at the end of the first day was therefore 6½—1½. By lunch on the second it had become 9½—2½ and by nightfall 12½—3½. In the fourball play in the morning Jacklin and Oosterhuis managed a half against Casper and Miller and might have considered themselves slightly unlucky not to have won, in that Casper had to hole from about six feet on the last green after being bunkered. At the same time Jacklin, too, had found sand but exploded stone dead. Then along came Guy Hunt and Darcy, one down to Geiberger and Floyd, but Darcy hit a four wood to 12 feet and, as calm as you like, knocked in the putt for a birdie three and another halved game. Littler and Graham were heading for a 66 when they disposed of Barnes and Gallacher, while Horton and Wood, having held on well for ten holes against Nicklaus and Snead, were broken when the latter sank a bunker shot for a birdie at the eleventh.

In the afternoon foursomes there was no change to the general pattern. Jacklin and Brian Huggett had a sudden surge of birdies to beat Trevino and Murphy, but the heavy golf course was taking its toll. The best example of this was that each of the three winning American couples was over par and yet the closest of those games was the three and two by Geiberger and Graham. As Irwin said after he and Casper had beaten Oosterhuis and Bembridge, also by three and two: 'We ought to have been beaten six and four. But they played worse.'

The only question on that last day was whether the Americans could finish it all off before lunch and, as it were in cricketing terms, win by an innings. They did. Weiskopf, a giant in all respects against little Guy Hunt, landed the decisive blow in the seventh singles. He was quite merciless, six under par when he won by five and three. Ahead of him Murphy had beaten Jacklin, who could not play the short holes, Littler had beaten Huggett, Casper had beaten Darcy, Trevino had halved with Gallacher, Irwin had halved with Horton and that was

enough, the necessary 16½ points in the bag. It hardly mattered, therefore, that Britain won the final series of singles by the odd point, though there was naturally the small matter of individual pride.

Oosterhuis, for instance, seemed dead and buried at two down to Miller on the twelfth green and the American less than six feet from the flag. Yet it was Oosterhuis who holed much the longer putt, Miller who missed, and with that the big Englishman reeled off six threes in a row, four of them birdies, to preserve his unbeaten singles record. Then in the afternoon he beat Snead as well, and with 3½ points out of 6 he was the leading points scorer.

Gallacher, having met Trevino six times in the Ryder Cup and lost only once, proved again what a tough competitor he is, halving both with the Mexican and again with Geiberger in the afternoon. Horton was also unbeaten in the singles and that really was quite something, since first he was playing against the 1974 American Open champion Irwin, with whom he halved, and then Graham, the reigning champion, whom he beat. Wood also gained the notable scalp of Trevino, though the man of the hour, after closing time though it was, had to be Barnes.

At Houston, where the British had suffered their heaviest defeat in 1967, it had proved to be the darkest hour before the dawn, for immediately afterwards there had been the tie at Royal Birkdale. But the night which began at Laurel Valley was to prove a much longer one.

UNITED STATES		GREAT BRITAIN AND IRELAND
Foursomes (a.m.)		
J.W. Nicklaus & T. Weiskopf 5 & 4	beat	B.W. Barnes & B.J. Gallacher
G. Littler & H. Irwin 4 & 3	beat	N. Wood & M. Bembridge
A. Geiberger & J. Miller 3 & 1	beat	A. Jacklin & P.A. Oosterhuis
L. Trevino & J.C. Snead 2 & 1	beat	T. Horton & J. O'Leary
Fourballs (p.m.)		
W. Casper & R. Floyd	lost to	Jacklin & Oosterhuis 2 & 1
Weiskopf & L. Graham 3 & 2	beat	E. Darcy & C. O'Connor Jnr
Nicklaus & R. Murphy	halved with	Barnes & Gallacher
Trevino & Irwin 2 & 1	beat	Horton & O'Leary
Fourballs (a.m.)		
Casper & Miller	halved with	Jacklin & Oosterhuis
Nicklaus & Snead 4 & 2	beat	Horton & Wood
Littler & Graham 5 & 3	beat	Barnes & Gallacher
Geiberger & Floyd	halved with	Darcy & G.L. Hunt
Foursomes (p.m.)		
Trevino & Murphy	lost to	Jacklin & B.G.C. Huggett 3 & 2
Weiskopf & Miller 5 & 3	beat	O'Connor Jnr & O'Leary
Irwin & Casper 3 & 2	beat	Oosterhuis & Bembridge
Geiberger & Graham 3 & 2	beat	Darcy & Hunt

UNITED STATES		GREAT BRITAIN AND IRELAND
Singles (a.m.)		
Murphy 2 & 1	beat	Jacklin
Miller	lost to	Oosterhuis 2 holes
Trevino	halved with	Gallacher
Irwin	halved with	Horton
Littler 4 & 2	beat	Huggett
Casper 3 & 2	beat	Darcy
Weiskopf 5 & 4	beat	Hunt
Nicklaus	lost to	Barnes 4 & 2
Singles (p.m.)		
Floyd 1 hole	beat	Jacklin
Snead	lost to	Oosterhuis 3 & 2
Geiberger	halved with	Gallacher
Graham	lost to	Horton 2 & 1
Irwin 2 & 1	beat	O'Leary
Murphy 2 & 1	beat	Bembridge
Trevino	lost to	Wood 2 & 1
Nicklaus	lost to	Barnes 2 & 1

United States 21 — Great Britain and Ireland 11

Great Britain & Ireland 7½ – United States 12½

Played at Royal Lytham and St Anne's, 15, 16, 17 September 1977

It would be no exaggeration to say that the Golden Jubilee Ryder Cup match at Royal Lytham and St Anne's in 1977 struck new depths. After all the talk in the wake of Great Britain & Ireland's heavy defeat at Laurel Valley in 1975 and complaints from the players that they were having to play too much golf, the number of matches was reduced by roughly a third, from 32 points to a mere 20.

It was the third time there had been tinkering with the format, but it was so unsuccessful that it was never repeated. To recap: from 1927 until 1959 there were four 36-hole foursomes on the first day and eight 36-hole singles on the second. But in 1961, when by a coincidence the venue was also Royal Lytham, the tally was doubled to eight foursomes (four in the morning and four in the afternoon) and then two series of eight singles. That, however, was the last two-day match, for two years later, in 1963, two series of fourball matches were added. This meant a third day, raising the points total to 32, and other than the very minor switch in 1975 of alternating the foursomes and fourballs on the first two days, this continued until 1977. Then, with disastrous consequences, the PGAs of America and Britain agreed to play just five foursomes on the first day, five fourballs on the second and ten singles on the last.

It failed, not only because there proved to be too few matches for the public to watch on the first two days but also because of the ridiculous 45-minute intervals between starting times to accommodate television. This meant that there was as much as three hours between Bernard Gallacher and Brian Barnes driving off against Lanny Wadkins and Hale Irwin in the top foursome and, at the bottom, Tommy Horton and Mark James teeing up against Jack Nicklaus and Tom Watson. Consequently, with five matches spread all over the golf course, the essential spirit of the Ryder Cup was lost. Instead of the spectators being able to switch quickly from game to game according to the state of play, they were now poles apart. It also had the effect of the various games being played in a sort of vacuum, and the atmosphere was changed completely. Furthermore Colin Snape, who was then secretary of the PGA, recalls that play was so slow that television largely missed out as well.

Nor did the change of format in any way alter the pattern of recent events as the Americans continued their monopoly, 3½–1½ after the foursomes, 7½–2½ clear after the fourballs and then sharing the singles 5–5 for their eighteenth win in twenty-two meetings. It was the unhappiest three days there had been, not only from a British point of view but also for the Americans. They had had enough. Nine months later Don Padgett, president of the United States PGA, announced at The Greenbrier in West Virginia, where the 1979 match was to be played, that at the instigation if not insistence of the Americans, the Great Britain & Ireland side was to be extended to include continental Europeans and that the team would subsequently be known as 'Europe'.

It was a momentous step, and one that proved within the next decade to be not only the saving of the Ryder Cup but also the making of it. And if the credit for the move has to go to one man more than any other, it was Nicklaus – still, of course, a player but in all other respects an elder statesman – whose counsel was sought on

Brian Barnes sucks contentedly on his pipe while Bernard Gallacher waits to putt at Royal Lytham in 1977. They formed a regular partnership over a number of years

all aspects of golf. It was he who approached Lord Derby, president of the British PGA at Lytham, saying in effect that the fixture could not go on like this or it would surely die. Later he was to back up his words with a letter in which he stressed that 'it is vital to widen the selection procedures if the Ryder Cup is to continue to enjoy its past prestige'. Accordingly Ken Schofield, now executive director of the PGA European Tour, was summoned to Lord Derby's home at Knowsley and it was arranged for Brian Huggett, as the most recent captain, and Peter Butler, of the Ryder Cup committee, to complete the formalities at the 1978 Masters.

It was at about this time that a pictorial biography, *Jack Nicklaus On and Off the Fairway*, was on its way to the printers and one passage in it now makes compelling reading.

I've played in all five Ryder Cup matches since I became eligible for the US team in 1969, and I have greatly enjoyed both the camaraderie of the event and the relationships and goodwill that it promotes. However, I also happen to feel that as a golf contest pure and simple, it badly needs a change of format. As far as the American players are concerned, everyone wants and enjoys the honour of making the team but many find it difficult to get charged up for the matches themselves. By saying this, I'm not trying to put down my British friends, but the fact must be faced that British professional golf in recent years simply hasn't developed a sufficient depth of good players to make a true contest out of the event. Nor, from what I see, does there appear to be much likelihood of that situation changing in the foreseeable future.

I know national pride is involved, but at some point reality must prevail if the event isn't to decline into little more than an exhibition bout – and especially if it is to remain a vital part of the US golfing calendar. When you consider that the golfing population of the United States is roughly equivalent to that of the rest of the world, maybe a World versus the United States format would make the most sense. If that's too presumptuous, then the United States versus the English-speaking countries or even the United States versus Europe would seem viable formats.

Beneath this passage there is a footnote by the publishers, Stanley Paul, which reads: 'A change was made as we went to press, creating in effect a Europe vs USA format for future matches.'

There was still some reluctance on the part of the British PGA to make a change but, since their hand was being forced, there was one obvious road down which they were pointed. Not only had Severiano Ballesteros finished second in the 1976 Open championship at Royal Birkdale, but at the time of the Ryder Cup at Royal Lytham he was about to become for the first time the leading money-winner on the PGA European Tour, still known then as the European Tournament Players' Division. Furthermore, in 1976 and then at the end of 1977 Ballesteros partnered first Manuel Pinero and then Antonio Garrido to victory in the World Cup. As all three players were very much a part of the growing European family, it was therefore only logical for them to be a part of the Ryder Cup as well. Certainly the other players were unanimous in their approval; nor was there any objection from Mrs Joan Scarfe, daughter of Samuel Ryder who had donated the Cup.

If something of a veil has to be drawn over this last challenge by golfers exclusively drawn from Great Britain and Ireland, there was still a hint of the better times that lay ahead. Into the British team at the tender age of twenty came Nick Faldo and Ken Brown, together with Howard Clark (twenty-three), Mark James (twenty-three) and Peter Dawson (twenty-seven), the last-named still the only left-hander to have played in the Ryder Cup. This gave the team an average age of twenty-eight as opposed to the thirty-four of the Americans, their youngest being Wadkins (twenty-seven) and the oldest Don January (forty-seven). January, of course, had played before and the newcomers, in addition to Wadkins, were Hubert Green, that year's American Open champion, Jerry McGee, Ed Sneed and Tom Watson, very much the golfer of the year since he had won both the Masters and the Open in that historic confrontation with Nicklaus at Turnberry when, with a 65 on each of the last two days, he set a championship record of 268 for the four rounds.

In the years to come Brown and Clark were both to play significant Ryder Cup roles, but that week it was very much Faldo who emerged as the new prince. He won all his three games, two of them with Peter Oosterhuis and his single against Watson. Yet only two years earlier, when still an amateur, Faldo had had his entry for the Lytham Trophy returned because his handicap was too high! Three months later, and on the same course, he was crowned English champion.

Now, in only his second season as a professional, Faldo's picture was all over the front pages as he and Oosterhuis beat first Raymond Floyd and Lou Graham in the foursomes and then Floyd and Nicklaus in the fourballs. Yet, unknown to most, Faldo very nearly did not play at all. He had felt unwell the week before the Ryder Cup and had withdrawn from the Tournament Players' Championship at Foxhills. He saw a doctor who diagnosed glandular fever but kept it from him, informing only his parents. Then, on the first morning of the Ryder Cup, Faldo recalls waking up with a rash on his

Jack Nicklaus and Tom Watson have a look of confidence about them as they chalk up a foursomes win in the 1977 match at Royal Lytham

arms and some tenderness, which meant that it hurt to grip the club. Another doctor was called who also pronounced glandular fever, this time to Faldo himself. However, Brian Huggett, the British captain, was told that there was still no reason why Faldo should not play, and, to use his own description, 'Nick was tremendous.' For this part Faldo recalls Huggett being very secretive about his pairings and he felt that the only reason he partnered Oosterhuis was that they looked a pair, almost brothers, both well over six feet tall.

They could not have made a more discouraging start, Faldo missing a short putt for a three on the first green and the couple losing the first three holes to Floyd and Graham. With eight to play there was no change, but then the Americans made rather a mess of the eleventh and twelfth and with glorious second shots, first a wood by Faldo to the fourteenth and then a long iron by Oosterhuis to the fifteenth, they sneaked in front and, once leading, they were not shy of winning.

It was the only cheerful note on a day of might-have-beens. Dawson and Neil Coles, for instance, were two up and three to play on McGee and Dave Stockton but lost while Tony Jacklin and Eamonn Darcy, similarly two up and three to play, allowed Sneed and January to get away with a half. Stockton was largely responsible for this first American point. He holed from 8 yards at the sixteenth and 12 yards at the seventeenth to square the match, and then Coles presented them with the eighteenth when he drove into the left-hand bunker. Similarly Sneed holed a very missable putt to avoid going three down with three to play against Darcy and Jacklin, the former Open champion promptly being responsible for the loss of the sixteenth with a poor pitch and the seventeenth as well with a wild drive. That was 3½–1½ to the Americans, Wadkins and Hale Irwin making the most of Brian Barnes's apparent discomfort near the hole and winning three and one, while at the bottom Nicklaus and Watson were predictably too strong for James and Tommy Horton.

Normally the fourball matches are quite close affairs. In this instance they were not, making them even less of a spectacle for the undernourished spectators. Watson and Green beat Barnes and Horton by five and four, Sneed and Wadkins won by five and three against Coles and Dawson, and Stockton and Dave Hill were just as emphatic against Jacklin and Darcy. Irwin and Graham had less to spare, just one hole against James and Brown, who all but saved the day with the most exquisite of chips from behind the last green. It was therefore again left to Oosterhuis and Faldo to salvage some self-respect.

Faldo has a very clear memory of playing against Nicklaus, whom he had never met until that week. He had recently acquired a new graphite driver. 'I was hitting the ball miles,' he says, 'sometimes 30 yards past Nicklaus. I could feel his eyes boring into me but I never met his gaze and just kept looking straight ahead.' On an increasingly cold and blustery afternoon, nothing else seemed to matter. The milling crowd had eyes only for these two apparent boys in a man's world, each in turn inspiring the other so that when they won by three and one they had a better-ball of five under par, comfortably the best golf of the day.

Under the circumstances it was therefore strange to many that Huggett, facing a deficit of 2½ to 7½ going into the ten singles, should have kept his two trump cards up his sleeve. He put out Oosterhuis last and Faldo last but one in his order of play. Nor was this his only controversial decision, for he also left out Jacklin, still in many ways the darling of the British public and also on the course where he had won the Open eight years earlier. However, Huggett still vigorously defends himself on the grounds that Jacklin was not only playing badly, heading for a personal score in the mid 80s in the fourballs, but also appeared to be un-

Ken Brown goes through all manner of agonies as his chip from the back of the 18th green at Royal Lytham in 1977 just fails to go in. Conversely a spectator is totally unmoved

interested. He backs it up by saying that Dow Finsterwald, the American captain, said he would have done the same. 'In fact,' claims Huggett, 'none of my most experienced players did anything for me all week.'

For his part, Jacklin maintains that Huggett's personality did a complete U-turn. 'I was very disappointed with the way he handled the job and I doubted the wisdom of the way he did things. He didn't consult any of the players about pairings, he just did it in his room,' Jacklin wrote in *The Price of Success*. Nor was their relationship improved, claims Jacklin, when on walking out on to the course after lunch he was publicly dressed down by his captain for not having gone out earlier to support the rest of the team. 'So far as I was concerned Huggett was totally and utterly out of line.' Jacklin goes on: 'I went and took him to the other side of the fairway and told him that he was captain until the next evening and this wasn't Crystal Palace football team — it was twelve different individuals.' Shortly afterwards Huggett telephoned the former Open champion in his hotel room and said that he was sorry but Jacklin would not be playing the following day.

The shared singles lent some respectability to the final scoreline, but there was still no doubting the Americans' superiority. Wadkins won the top match as comfortably against Clark as Graham did against Coles behind him. Dawson, though slightly restricted in his movement because of a back that seized up on him, stemmed the flow by taking good care of January, and Barnes added another British point by just getting the better of Irwin. But, when Hill beat Horton on the fourteenth green the decisive American point was safely locked away.

Sadly, therefore, it was too late when Gallacher, who had had his putter stolen between the practice ground and the first tee, beat Nicklaus. He had to dive into the professional's shop where he bought a Ping instead of the Golden Goose he had always used and, after putting like a demon, he has

never used anything else since. There were more cheers, too, for Faldo as he added the considerable scalp of Watson, and also for Oosterhuis, who kept his hundred per cent singles record against McGee. But the Union Jack was already at half mast and it was never again to fly in isolation again against the Stars and Stripes at the Ryder Cup.

GREAT BRITAIN AND IRELAND		UNITED STATES
Foursomes		
B.J. Gallacher & B.W. Barnes	lost to	L. Wadkins & H. Irwin 3 & 1
N.C. Coles & P. Dawson	lost to	D. Stockton & J. McGee 1 hole
N. Faldo & P. Oosterhuis	beat	R. Floyd & L. Graham 2 & 1
E. Darcy & A. Jacklin	halved with	E. Sneed & D. January
T. Horton & M. James	lost to	J.W. Nicklaus & T. Watson 5 & 4
Fourballs		
Barnes & Horton	lost to	Watson & H. Green 5 & 4
Coles & Dawson	lost to	Sneed & Wadkins 5 & 3
Faldo & Oosterhuis	beat	Nicklaus & Floyd 3 & 1
Jacklin & Darcy	lost to	Stockton & D. Hill 5 & 3
James & K. Brown	lost to	Irwin & Graham 1 hole
Singles		
H. Clark	lost to	Wadkins 4 & 3
Coles	lost to	Graham 5 & 3
Dawson	beat	January 5 & 4
Barnes	beat	Irwin 1 hole
Horton	lost to	Hill 5 & 4
Gallacher	beat	Nicklaus 1 hole
Darcy	lost to	Green 1 hole
James	lost to	Floyd 2 & 1
Faldo	beat	Watson 1 hole
Oosterhuis	beat	McGee 2 holes

Great Britain and Ireland 7½ — United States 12½

United States 17 — Europe 11

Played at The Greenbrier, West Virginia, 14, 15, 16 September 1979

Having been instrumental in the formation of the PGA European Tour, John Jacobs, at the age of fifty-four, was given the honour of leading the first European Ryder Cup team for their mission to The Greenbrier, which for sheer grandeur was something of a cross between Buckingham Palace and The White House. He can have had little idea how difficult a task it was going to be, demanding every bit as much tact, diplomacy and firm-handedness as ever he had had to display in the political manoeuvrings that ultimately made the tournament players a separate body to that of the club professionals.

Yet it was not the two Spaniards, Severiano Ballesteros and Antonio Garrido,

who taxed his patience to the limits of endurance. It was instead the two young Britons Ken Brown and Mark James who marred the occasion, and to such an extent that, two months after their return home, Brown was fined £1000 and suspended from international team golf for a year while James was fined £1500, though he was not suspended. It is possible that they may even have cost Europe the match, for James, admittedly because of injury, played only once and Brown, because he wanted exclusively to partner James, only three times. Since only a point separated the two teams at 8½–7½ going into the singles, the United States might well have found themselves in greater difficulties than they already were.

For a time all was going nicely as Dai Rees (left), Lord Derby and Tony Jacklin share a joke

That they escaped to win by a fairly comfortable 17−11 was partially due to Jacobs having to turn a blind eye in another direction.

Though the disastrous format of 1977 had been abandoned and two sessions of foursomes and fourballs reinstated on the first two days, the points total was still less than it had been in the immediately − preceding years. For the first time all twelve players were due to compete in the singles, but this time only one round each, six in the morning and six in the afternoon, whereas in the past it had been two series of eight singles.

Because there was now no room for manoeuvre, some allowance consequently had to be made in case of injury or illness. Accordingly the two captains, Jacobs and Billy Casper, were asked at the end of the second day to put in a sealed envelope the name of the player they would stand down if for some reason the opposition was reduced to eleven men. The resultant 'pairing' would then be declared as having played a halved match. The whole procedure was discussed by the two captains with the Press before the match, and both men seemed absolutely clear on the matter.

As James had not played since the opening fourballs on the first morning, there was inevitably a large question mark against his being able to participate on the final day and it was during the preceding evening that Jacobs was approached by an embarrassed American PGA official with the request that Casper be allowed to change the name in his envelope. Though all sorts of American excuses were made at the time, Jacobs still believes that Casper had simply misunderstood the procedure and instead of naming his weakest player, in this case Gil Morgan who, because of a suspect shoulder, had played only one game, he had written down his strongest and most experienced, Lee Trevino.

It was, as P.B. 'Laddie' Lucas wrote in his biography of Jacobs, *The Man and his Methods*, 'a little like moving the goalposts in the middle of the match'. There were, as Lucas said, undoubtedly some former captains who would have raised two fingers. But not Jacobs. 'He played it straight down the middle. He put it to his team that, if they were going to win on the morrow, he did not want to lay the British and Europeans open to any suggestion of meanness, bad sportsmanship or worse.' Consequently he allowed the name to be changed. Morgan therefore duly went into the envelope, and Sandy Lyle found himself playing Trevino, who beat him. No one knows what would have happened had Jacobs insisted on the original pairing, but it did prove to be a second nail in the European coffin. The other had been self-inflicted.

When a Ryder Cup team is picked, certain rules are laid down. One of them is that the team travels in uniform. Jacobs smelled trouble as soon as his players assembled at Heathrow Airport. James arrived in anything but a uniform and looked, according to his captain, 'terrible'. Jacobs had grounds for sending him home but turned the other cheek, and there were times when he must have regretted it.

To a mere camp follower it appeared that James and Brown, already close friends, were in league with one another. Certainly, on one occasion when a team meeting was taking place, I met the pair of them 'window shopping' in the Greenbrier arcade, indifferent when reminded that they should have been somewhere else.

At the flag-raising they were, to put it mildly, a couple of very bored fidgets, and there were sufficient further incidents to lead Tony Jacklin to say now, looking back, that he would have told them both to pack their bags. Yet worst of all was Brown's reaction when, after he and James had lost their opening fourball, James withdrew with his genuine chest injury to be replaced by Des Smyth, the PGA Match-play champion, in the four-somes. Lucas, in his biography of Jacobs, describes Brown's conduct.

The consequences are writ in stone. Brown's behaviour towards his partner was, to say the least, uncivil. The two lost by seven and six and the captain was obliged to offer apologies all round for the Englishman's conduct. It was a humiliating affair. No 'bloody good talking to' or other psychological approach was going to change a man in Brown's mood. He was unpartnerable; the captain couldn't risk him, after the performance with Smyth, with either the toughest, no-nonsense character in the team or with the most tactful and resilient. The fact that Ken Brown, pursuing his young, idiosyncratic way, was eventually one of only three British and European winners in the singles only compounded the wretchedness of the whole affair.

Happily the rebellious streak in both these young men proved to be nothing more than a passing phase. They married, as Jacobs puts it, 'two corking girls' and have since served the professional game well. As Lucas summed up: 'Everyone makes mistakes but only fools make them twice.' Neither James nor Brown has proved himself to be a fool.

If the European team was, as a consequence, somewhat weakened, it has to be said however that so were the Americans. On the eve of the match Tom Watson, one of their main strengths as he was leading money-winner for the third successive year, withdrew from the team because his wife, Linda, was about to give birth to their first child, a daughter. It meant that Mark Hayes had to be called up at the last minute. He was one of no less than eight new 'caps', the others being Morgan, Larry Nelson, Fuzzy Zoeller, Andy Bean, Lee Elder, John Mahaffey and Tom Kite.

Apart from the two Spaniards, Europe's other newcomers were Smyth, Michael King and Sandy Lyle, who in only his second season had romped straight to the top of the European money list. The irony was that while Ballesteros, that year's British Open champion, and Garrido were brought in to strengthen the team, their contribution

Where did that one go? Des Smyth has to jump to find out

so far as points were concerned was almost negligible. They won one foursome together, but otherwise were beaten every time. This was particularly disappointing for Ballesteros, but he could not get away from Nelson. They met four times and Nelson, playing with absolute precision, won every one of them. Indeed, the American's five out of five was the outstanding performance of this particular Ryder Cup.

If in the past British teams had been overawed on the golf course, the European substitute had some excuse for being overawed off it. Set in 6500 acres of glorious rolling woodlands, the surrounding hills thick with oak, maple and pine, this West Virginian spa at The Greenbrier is recognized as being one of the most exclusive inland holiday resorts in the United States, almost daunting in its lofty magnificence. Inside the hotel there were 650 bedrooms, 10 marble-floored lobbies, 25 conference rooms, a dining room that held 1200 guests and a shopping arcade that might have come straight out of Piccadilly. Outside, black limousines waited to spirit guests away to various other pleasures: 20 tennis courts (five of them indoor), two swimming pools (one indoor), 250 miles of riding trails, a gun club for skeet and trap shooting, a theatre and a mountain lodge.

When a heavy downpour of rain delayed the start by forty minutes, no one even blinked as a mobile dryer appeared blowing hot air to dry the sodden greens. As usual the Americans were off to a flying start, winning the opening fourballs 3−1. The spearhead came from Nelson and Lanny Wadkins, who lost the first two holes to Ballesteros and Garrido but swiftly put matters to rights, ahead at the tenth and, mostly due to Nelson, never again under threat.

The best golf of the morning was nevertheless provided by Elder, the first black American to play in the match, and the mighty Bean. They were eight under par in beating Nick Faldo and Peter Oosterhuis, who for once was sadly out of form. With Trevino and Zoeller not exactly troubled by Brown and James, it was left to the tried and trusted partnership of Brian Barnes and Bernard Gallacher to salvage Europe's only point. Not that it looked that way when Hale Irwin and Mahaffey won three of the first six holes. But Gallacher steadied the ship and Barnes, with three twos, did the rest.

In the afternoon foursomes the Europeans did marginally better, Ballesteros and Garrido dovetailing well as they beat Zoeller and Hubert Green, while Jacklin and Lyle, who had not played in the morning, managed to hold Trevino and Morgan. However, Irwin and Kite slaughtered the tight-lipped Brown and perplexed Smyth and with Wadkins and Nelson too good for Barnes and Gallacher, the Americans went to bed well content, 5½−2½ ahead.

Yet for once it was not a case of it being the same old story. Jacklin and Lyle began the European recovery in the foursomes on the second morning, winning four of the first five holes against Elder and Mahaffey and scarcely playing a bad shot between them. Faldo and Oosterhuis were even more invincible against Bean and Kite, six up at the turn and home at a canter. Furthermore, behind them Barnes and Gallacher 'did it again', coming back this time from two down and seven to play as they took full toll of mistakes by Zoeller and Hayes. It was therefore only Wadkins and Nelson who made sure that America remained ahead. On greens as fast as most of the Europeans had ever seen, they putted Ballesteros and Garrido off the golf course.

This formidable American pair did the same thing again in the afternoon fourballs (out in a better-ball 28), but even so Europe very nearly drew level overall for in the other three games they were ahead in each coming down the finishing stretch. This was good enough to see Gallacher and Barnes, with eight birdies between them, home by three and two against Trevino and Zoeller, while Faldo, with a deft bunker shot at the last, just managed to protect the slender lead he and Oosterhuis had enjoyed throughout over Elder and Hayes.

The one European pair that could not hold on was Jacklin and Lyle, disappointing after their recovery from three down to one up and four to play against Irwin and Kite. If Lyle had got down in two from the back of the fifteenth they would have been two up, but it was the sixteenth that was their final undoing. First Jacklin dumped a seemingly straightforward pitch into the water and then Lyle, needing two putts for the half, three putted. At once Kite made a two at the seventeenth and though Lyle had a chance to save the match at the last, he

Ken Brown (left) was both fined and suspended and Mark James fined after bad behaviour during the 1979 match at The Greenbrier. Their expressions here seem to reflect their moods that week

missed from eight feet for the birdie.

Even so, that was 2—2 and still only a point between the two sides, 8½—7½ going into the singles — the closest it had ever been in America. However, it was to prove a false European dawn for, though in the top singles Bernard Gallacher, whose four wins in five games was another outstanding performance, inflicted on Wadkins his only defeat, all the other five morning singles went America's way. Three of them were nevertheless by just one hole, and the most crucial was probably that in which Jacklin failed to make the most of a three-hole lead after five holes against Kite. Had Jacklin holed from no more than a yard to go four up at the eighth, it could well have been a different tale. It must be said, however, that Kite played brilliantly after that for he had five birdies in the next ten holes. Garrido,

against Hayes, and Barnes, against Mahaffey, were the others to lose on the last green, Hayes making a birdie, but Michael King was outgunned by Bean while Ballesteros must have been sick to the death of the sight of Nelson, who beat him again.

The European cause was therefore just about hopeless in the afternoon, and though Faldo rose to his full height by beating Elder, the necessary American point came from Irwin with a comfortable victory over Smyth. Green also brought to an end Oosterhuis's unbeaten singles record; Trevino was too wily for Lyle, whose match-play record had never been as good as that in stroke-play, and the only other European point came from Brown against Zoeller. Afterwards Trevino predicted that the next match at Walton Health could be a hard one for the Americans. He was two years out.

Severiano Ballesteros about to play out of water at The Greenbrier. This was the first year Continentals played in the Ryder Cup

UNITED STATES		EUROPE
Foursomes (a.m.)		
Elder & Mahaffey	lost to	Lyle & Jacklin 5 & 4
Bean & Kite	lost to	Faldo & Oosterhuis 6 & 5
Zoeller & M. Hayes	lost to	Gallacher & Barnes 2 & 1
Wadkins & Nelson 3 & 2	beat	Ballesteros & Garrido
Fourballs (p.m.)		
Wadkins & Nelson 5 & 4	beat	Ballesteros & Garrido
Irwin & Kite 1 hole	beat	Lyle & Jacklin
Trevino & Zoeller	lost to	Gallacher & Barnes 3 & 2
Elder & Hayes	lost to	Faldo & Oosterhuis 1 hole
Singles		
Wadkins	lost to	Gallacher 3 & 2
Nelson 3 & 2	beat	Ballesteros
Kite 1 hole	beat	Jacklin
Hayes 1 hole	beat	Garrido
Bean 4 & 3	beat	M. King
Mahaffey 1 hole	beat	Barnes
Elder	lost to	Faldo 3 & 2
Irwin 5 & 3	beat	Smyth
Green 2 holes	beat	Oosterhuis
Zoeller	lost to	Brown 1 hole
Trevino 2 & 1	beat	Lyle
Morgan ½	(match not played)	James ½

United States 17 — Europe 11

UNITED STATES		EUROPE
Fourballs (a.m.)		
L. Wadkins & L. Nelson 2 & 1	beat	S. Ballesteros & A. Garrido
L. Trevino & F. Zoeller 3 & 2	beat	K. Brown & M. James
A. Bean & L. Elder 2 & 1	beat	N. Faldo & P. Oosterhuis
H. Irwin & J. Mahaffey	lost to	B. Gallacher & B. Barnes 2 & 1
Foursomes (p.m.)		
Irwin & T. Kite 7 & 6	beat	Brown & D. Smyth
Zoeller & H. Green	lost to	Ballesteros & Garrido 3 & 2
Trevino & G. Morgan	halved with	A.W.B. Lyle & A. Jacklin
Wadkins & Nelson 4 & 3	beat	Gallacher & Barnes

Europe 9½ — United States 18½
Played at Walton Heath, 18, 19, 20 September 1981

There have over the years been many extremely strong American Ryder Cup teams, but the one which came to Walton Health in 1981 still ranks as probably the finest of all. It was a positive *Debrett* of golf, including three of the current holders of the major championships in Tom Watson (Masters), Bill Rogers (British Open) and Larry Nelson, whose victory in the PGA championship at Atlanta only a month before the team flew to England meant that Howard Twitty, who had already been measured for his uniform, had to drop out. In support were Raymond Floyd, Hale Irwin, Johnny Miller, Jack Nicklaus, Jerry Pate and Lee Trevino, a formidable array of golfing talent which, between them, had accumulated no less than 36 major championships. Only Ben Crenshaw, Bruce Lietzke and Tom Kite had still to climb one of those particular rostra, and Crenshaw was to do so in the Masters three years later.

No team could therefore have been better equipped to meet the challenge of the Europeans now assembling to march into the better times of the eighties. And meet it they did. In thoroughly wet and miserable autumn weather they answered the every call of their captain, Dave Marr, and with some golf that was on occasions quite breathtaking for its excellence they swept to their biggest victory ever in Britain.

It is unlikely that even a team drawn from the rest of the world could have stopped this American onslaught, but the great irony was that, having enlisted the help of players from the Continent, this second European team went into the match lacking not only the ace in their pack, Severiano Ballesteros, but also Tony Jacklin who, while no longer perhaps exactly an ace, was still a pretty useful king. Both were available; neither was selected.

Looking back, this seems as absurd now as it did at the time, particularly since Ballesteros had by then not only won the 1979 Open championship but in 1980 his first Masters as well. Cause for celebration though both these victories were in Europe, having a star in their midst also led to problems. Accustomed as they were to being the poor relations, British and indeed European golf had for some time depended at its richer sponsored tournaments on attracting leading American players to boost the quality of the field. The only way they could do that was by offering financial inducements, otherwise known as appearance money. But now, by winning both the Open and the Masters, Ballesteros had proved that he was perhaps not so much the equal of such occasional American guests as Lee Trevino, Tom Weiskopf or Johnny Miller as even their superior. Consequently it was his belief that if Americans were entitled to appearance money, so was he. This, however, went very much against the grain of the European Tour and its secretary, Ken Schofield. An immovable object on the one hand therefore met head on an irresistible force on the other. Nor did Ballesteros stand in isolation. Among his supporters was John Jacobs, who was continuing as captain of the European team for a second term, and Jacklin, who had himself tasted the juiciest fruits in the game. In principle Jacobs was also opposed to appearance money, but only if it was across the board and therefore included Americans.

So strong was Ballesteros's conviction that in the season leading up to the Ryder Cup he played in only seven European tournaments, most of those on the Continent. For a time, indeed until August when the team was being chosen, he even refused to pay his membership fee of £50 to the European

Tour. Even when, reluctantly, he did re-join, his position with regard to the Ryder Cup team, ten of whom were coming straight off the money list and two by selection, remained very delicate.

Accordingly Jacobs rang Ballesteros in America, where he was spending most of his time, and asked him to make a gesture of goodwill by playing in the Carrolls Irish Open at Portmarnock and the Benson & Hedges at Fulford, after which event the team was being announced. 'I want you in the team, Seve,' said Jacobs, 'but there's little chance unless you are prepared to come over and play.' The Spaniard promised to think it over, but he did not play.

Before Jacobs sat down with the other two members of the selection committee, Neil Coles, the chairman, and Bernhard Langer, the leader of the money list, he tested which way the wind was blowing by asking the players he knew were going to be in the team whether or not they thought Ballesteros should be included. All, other than Bernard Gallacher, were against and even Gallacher qualified his opinion by saying that he would only want the Spaniard in if he were in Jacobs' shoes! The general feeling was that Ballesteros had not sup-ported the Tour sufficiently.

When the 1979 team for The Greenbrier had been chosen, Coles had been quite happy to leave the two choices entirely to Jacobs. This time he was not so disposed and said categorically that Ballesteros should be omitted. Jacobs still thought otherwise, and so the deciding vote was Langer's. As the new boy he understandably felt that he should go along with the sentiments of the rest of the team. Ballesteros was out.

The three selectors were, however, in broad agreement that one of the two 'special' places should go to Peter Ooster-huis, who had that year won the Canadian Open, and this left the remaining spot between Mark James, eleventh in the money list, and Jacklin, who had not helped his prospects by playing only moderately all

year and then poorly in the Benson & Hedges, particularly in the last round when arguably it mattered most. James got the vote, and Jacklin has never forgotten how hurt he was, 'after all I had done for the game in Europe' — and not forgetting the behaviour of James at The Greenbrier. To put it bluntly, he felt insulted.

Certainly Jacobs was man enough to ring Jacklin, saying how sorry he was but at the same time admitting that the decision was unanimous. The irony here was that on the flight back to England after the 1979 match Jacklin, on behalf of that team, had made a presentation to Jacobs of a cut-glass fruit bowl and matching glasses. 'John is the best captain I have played under and as far as I am concerned he can do the job for ever,' he had said at the time. Later he lobbied Lord Derby urging Jacobs' reappointment.

None the less the die was now cast, with four newcomers to the European team: Langer, a West German, two Spaniards in Jose-Maria Canizares and Manuel Pinero, and Sam Torrance. Slowly a team for the future was being built, and those who put faith in coincidences were quick to point out that twenty-four years had elapsed between the British victories in 1933 and 1957, and now another twenty-four years had passed since Lindrick. Furthermore Marr, the American captain, was a cousin of Jackie Burke, who had led that losing team.

Marr took it all in good part, saying that he had a submarine on stand-by for the return journey, just in case! Even so he had some cause for concern when on the first day Europe led 4½–3½, sharing the first foursomes 2–2 and then squeezing in front by the odd point in the fourballs. This was just what the doctor ordered and it also delighted Sun Alliance, the sponsors, whose chairman Lord Aldington had resisted rep-resentations from the PGA that the match should be played at the Association's new headquarters at The Belfry. He was con-vinced that the course was not yet ready and that Walton Health, just south of London

A mixture of hope and anxiety on the faces of Jerry Pate and (left) his wife, Soozi, sister Nancy and Ben Crenshaw's first wife, Polly, during the 1981 match at Walton Heath

and with a much deeper tradition, would be better appreciated by the Americans.

After two years of planning, both teams managed to arrive on the first tee wearing dark blue pullovers, though the confusion as to which team was which partially eased when the first of several heavy showers and thunderstorms promptly led to the donning of different coloured waterproofs. Quite what Sam Ryder would have thought had he known that the day would come when a German, Langer, and a Spaniard, Pinero, would head the challenge is a matter of some speculation, but again it was not the continental players who took the prominent role in Europe's encouraging start. Instead it was James and Sandy Lyle who were the heroes of the day, winning both morning and afternoon, as did Des Smyth, though in

his case with different partners – Bernard Gallacher in the morning and Canizares in the afternoon.

Three up after only five holes in the morning foursomes and four up after eleven, Lyle and James then became careless and lost three holes in a row to Rogers and Lietzke before the latter took the pressure off them with a swinging hook off the sixteenth tee. Another point quickly followed as Gallacher, aided by some inspired golf from Smyth, trampled all over Irwin and Floyd, seven under par for their sixteen holes.

The centres of attraction were nevertheless Oosterhuis and Nick Faldo, who had played so well together four years earlier at Royal Lytham, against Nicklaus and Watson. It looked for a time as if they were going to do it again, with two birdies in the first four holes and two up. But the Americans came back with three birdies in a row from the seventh and they rapidly distanced themselves as they turned for home. By then Trevino and Nelson had also won the top match—though only just, Nelson holing a monstrously long putt for a birdie on the final green after Langer and Pinero had twice come from behind to draw level.

So it was 2−2 and again it was Lyle and James who led the charge in the afternoon fourballs, Lyle putting like a demon from all over the shop. They were eight under par for the sixteen holes it took them to beat Crenshaw and Pate by three and two, which was better golf than Smyth and Canizares played in beating Rogers and Lietzke by six and five. They were six under, the American resistance crumbling as they conceded six holes out of seven, two of them to pars,

which is not often the case in fourball golf.

A European lead was guaranteed when Torrance and Howard Clark came back from two down to halve with Kite and Miller. Torrance had squared the match at the fourteenth with an eagle three, and very nearly snatched a victory, hitting the hole but staying out when putting for a birdie at the eighteenth. Irwin and Floyd were also under pressure from Gallacher and Darcy at all square and four to play but Floyd, watched now by the whole American team, was the man for the crisis with birdies at both the sixteenth and seventeenth, making six in all off his own bat.

As they had proved many times before, the Americans are never more dangerous than when in a tight corner and it was on the second morning that they took complete and utter control of the match. Of the remaining 20 points over the next two days

'My God, this British weather!', Dave Marr seems to be saying to himself as the Americans huddle for protection during a heavy shower at Walton Heath in 1981

they took 14, beginning with a 3−1 success in the fourballs. Despite jocular protests that he was now too old to play twice a day, Trevino answered the call to duty and, playing top each time with Pate, they trounced first Faldo and Torrance by seven and five and then in the foursomes Oosterhuis and Torrance by two and one.

It seemed at the time that the heart went out of the European team from the moment they lost the second fourball. Lyle and James were all square with Nelson and Kite standing on the seventeenth tee and when Lyle dropped his tee shot only inches from the flag, it looked as if they were about to go ahead. But Nelson holed a wonderful putt for a half in two and then, of all things, he did it again at the last for another birdie, to win one up. What a continuing thorn Nelson was proving to be in the European side!

Admittedly Langer and Pinero did get the better of Floyd and Irwin in the third game, but somehow that point snatched by Nelson and Kite was the spur the Americans needed. In some quite awful weather the whole team played brilliantly, the measure of it being that in the afternoon foursomes not one of the European pairs was over par and, indeed, some of them under, yet the United States made a clean sweep with only Trevino and Pate being taken as far as the seventeenth.

So at 10½−5½ the boot was very much back on the American foot. Public interest had also waned and on a now sodden golf course as bursts of heavy rain continued, the crowds were noticeably down, spirits sinking further as Trevino took only two hours and ten minutes to polish off Torrance by five and three and was back in the clubhouse even before Nicklaus, the last man, had driven off. The 20-minute intervals between each of the twelve matches again had their limitations.

Yet there was one match that is still talked about with awe, and that was the one in which Kite defeated Lyle by three and two. What golf it was, birdies and eagles

Larry Nelson could do no wrong at Walton Heath in 1981 and in goes another putt

flying in all directions, both six under par and all square through eleven holes. It was Lyle who wavered, but even so he was still six under par when he lost, Kite ten under. So that was a second point in the American bag, and though Gallacher halved with Rogers (he could have claimed the last hole when his opponent picked up a tiny putt without it being conceded, but very properly decided against), appropriately it was Nelson who gained the necessary American point. By defeating James by two holes he again emerged with a one hundred per cent record.

Some European crumbs were later collected by Pinero, Faldo and Clark − the last a notable one since he beat Watson − and finally the curtain came down as Nicklaus defeated Darcy. Since he was by then forty-one and already beginning to cut down on his commitments, there was a sixth sense that this was to be Nicklaus's last Ryder Cup as a player — and his last it was. He had gone out as everyone wanted to remember him, as a winner.

EUROPE		UNITED STATES
Foursomes (a.m.)		
B. Langer & M. Pinero	lost to	L. Trevino & L. Nelson 1 hole
A.W.B. Lyle & M. James 2 & 1	beat	W. Rogers & B. Lietzke
B. Gallacher & D. Smyth 3 & 2	beat	H. Irwin & R. Floyd
N. Faldo & P. Oosterhuis	lost to	J. Nicklaus & T. Watson 4 & 3
Fourballs (p.m.)		
S. Torrance & H. Clark	halved with	T. Kite & J. Miller
Lyle & James 3 & 2	beat	B. Crenshaw & J. Pate
Smyth & J.-M. Canizares 6 & 5	beat	Rogers & Lietzke
Gallacher & E. Darcy	lost to	Irwin & Floyd 2 & 1

EUROPE		UNITED STATES
Fourballs (a.m.)		
Faldo & Torrance	lost to	Trevino & Pate 7 & 5
Lyle & James	lost to	Nelson & Kite 1 hole
Langer & Pinero 2 & 1	beat	Floyd & Irwin
Canizares & Smyth	lost to	Nicklaus and Watson 3 & 2
Foursomes (p.m.)		
Oosterhuis & Torrance	lost to	Trevino & Pate 2 & 1
Langer & Pinero	lost to	Nicklaus & Watson 3 & 2
Lyle & James	lost to	Rogers & Floyd 3 & 2
Smyth & Gallacher	lost to	Kite & Nelson 3 & 2
Singles		
Torrance	lost to	Trevino 5 & 3
Lyle	lost to	Kite 3 & 2
Gallacher	halved with	Rogers
James	lost to	Nelson 2 holes
Smyth	lost to	Crenshaw 6 & 4
Langer	halved with	Lietzke
Pinero 4 & 2	beat	Pate
Canizares	lost to	Irwin 1 hole
Faldo 2 & 1	beat	Miller
Clark 4 & 3	beat	Watson
Oosterhuis	lost to	Floyd 1 hole
Darcy	lost to	Nicklaus 5 & 3

Europe 9½ — United States 18½

United States 14½ − Europe 13½

Played at PGA National, Florida, 14, 15, 16 October 1983

For three days the United States and Europe had been fighting neck and neck. Only fleetingly in the five sessions of play over the PGA National course in Florida had more than a point separated the two sides, Europe ahead after the first day, level at the end of the second and then a regular exchange of the lead, first to one side and then to the other all the way down the singles. How reminiscent it all was of that other great finish fourteen years earlier at Royal Birkdale when Jack Nicklaus and Tony Jacklin had come to the eighteenth dead level, with

the two teams also level, and then halved it for a tied match.

Now Nicklaus and Jacklin were there again, just as involved but this time helpless as rival non-playing captains, their every nerve at screaming point as they dashed hither and thither up and down the eighteenth fairway with first one game and then another. Team golf is cruel in some ways, for though every game is just as important as any other, in a tight finish the focus of attention must in the end centre on those still locked in combat when all the

Oh, the agony of it, as Tony Jacklin (left) and Bernard Gallacher can only watch and wait during the 1983 match at PGA National. Only a single point separated the two teams

others have long since done.

Thus it was that with the score at 13—13 and just two games still on the course, everything depended on Lanny Wadkins, one down playing the last against Jose-Maria Canizares, and Tom Watson, one up playing the seventeenth against Bernard Gallacher. It could not have been closer, and if Wadkins and Watson ultimately became the American heroes in this narrowest of all victories by 14½—13½, so too must a thought be spared for Canizares and Gallacher who, because of two slight errors when all depended on them, had to shoulder the responsibility of defeat when in fact others before them were equally guilty. For instance, Severiano Ballesteros, playing top, had been three up after only seven holes against a less than a hundred per cent fit Fuzzy Zoeller, but had only halved — and very nearly lost — and yet for all that, and not without justification, he is still looked upon as one of the heroes in the most desperate finish there had ever been in America as it breathed new life into the Ryder Cup.

Nevertheless it all began to go wrong so far as Europe was concerned as Canizares and Wadkins laid up their second shots short of the eighteenth, a par five of 578 yards, water leaking in from the right. Both teams were out on the fairway lending all the support they could, Ballesteros almost breathing down his fellow Spaniard's neck as he faced a high pitch over a guardian bunker. Agonizingly, Canizares misjudged it and came up short. Immediately Wadkins pounced with a breathtaking shot, almost pitching into the hole, and there was a halved game after all, Nicklaus sinking to his knees and kissing the spot from which Wadkins had played.

Now all rested on Watson and Gallacher, with the teams still level. Gallacher remembers it as if it were yesterday. He had not been feeling on top form all week, playing only in one foursome with Sandy Lyle which he had lost on the first morning,

and for much of the time he had trailed Watson, that year's British Open champion for a fifth time. But he had got back a hole and was only one down on the seventeenth tee, with the honour. It was a shot of 191 yards. He took a three iron, 'and when I hit it, I thought it was perfect,' Gallacher recalls. He continues:

> But perhaps the adrenalin was running and it was too big, bouncing through the green into a rotten lie. Then Tom missed the green on the right, though he had a good lie. I was convinced he was going to get a three from there and I knew I had to hit a very, very good chip to get a half. I tried to finesse it down the slope but it caught the grass just short of the green and stopped dead. Now I had to chip again and got the ball to four feet, and then Tom mucked up his chip as well. He got the next close to make sure of a four and so I had this four-footer for a half, and I still think to this day that I hit a good putt. There was a subtle break but I missed and that was it, two and one.

So, by the skin of their teeth, the Americans had survived and never had Jacklin felt such acute disappointment in all his life, not even when Lee Trevino had snatched the Open championship from his grasp at Muirfield in 1972. 'It was a hell of a let-down,' he says. 'We'd done everything right and now we had nothing to show for it.' Nor was it any consolation to him when Nicklaus, in offering his commiserations, admitted that 'it should have been another tie'.

But there was one thing Europe had got right, and that was that they had at last got the right captain, a man who had done it all in his time and was still close enough to the players to command their respect and loyalty. He got every last drop from them and instinctively one knew that a new dawn was about to break. Having been controversially left out of the 1979 team at Walton Heath, Jacklin's choice as captain was an inspired one that had come without any prior warning, the invitation being made

One of the greatest strokes of all time. Severiano Ballesteros watches the flight of his ball after taking a three wood out of a fairway bunker on the 18th hole at PGA National. With a chip and single putt he then halved with Fuzzy Zoeller

just as he was about to go out in the first round of the Car Care tournament at Sandmoor, Leeds the previous May. It was left to Ken Schofield, now executive director of the European Tour, to make the approach, which he did on the Sandmoor practice putting green.

Even though Jacklin was still bitter about his omission from the previous team and maintained in his book *The First Forty Years* that he did not accept immediately, Schofield remembers differently and, indeed, his version would seem to be correct. The appointment was announced only hours later, immediately after the first round at Sandmoor when Jacklin had a 65. He had nevertheless made one condition − that the team would travel first class. Now, backed

by sponsorship worth £300,000 over the next two years from Bell's scotch whisky, whom Colin Snape, secretary of the PGA, had approached on the departure of Sun Alliance, they did even better than that: they flew by Concorde. 'Too many times in the past,' wrote Jacklin, 'the Cup had been run, it seemed, more for the officials than for the players. Priorities had been in the wrong places. If I was to be captain it would be run and organised with the players in mind.' Not the least important factor was that for the first time the European team players were allowed, all expenses paid, their own caddies to accompany them.

What also influenced Jacklin's acceptance was the earlier appointment of Nicklaus as the American captain. It seemed right somehow that they should be in conflict again. The European team that year came straight off the money list, before Jacklin made his subsequent request for three nominations of his own. His most pressing problem was to make sure he had Ballesteros in his team, and after the Spaniard's omission from the previous match that was by no means a formality. It was during the Open championship at Royal Birkdale that Jacklin chose his moment, over breakfast in the Prince of Wales Hotel, Southport. He and Seve talked for half an hour, Ballesteros at first insisting that he did not want any part of the Ryder Cup but slowly weakening in the face of the solid arguments his captain put forward. Perhaps it was that they had the common bond of having been left out of the same team that did the trick. Ballesteros eventually agreed to think about it. Two weeks later he agreed to play.

There were four newcomers to the European team in Paul Way, who was only twenty, Gordon J. Brand, Brian Waites and Ian Woosnam; and five new Americans in Craig Stadler, Curtis Strange, Jay Haas, Calvin Peete and Bob Gilder. As Nicklaus pointed out beforehand in his prediction of a very close match, this gave the visitors the edge in experience, though it was neverthe-less one of the absurdities of the continuing two-year American selection process that their side did not include Larry Nelson, who had not only a hundred per cent record in the last two Ryder Cups but that year had won the American Open. No one could have had better qualifications than that, but the fact of the matter was that he had not collected enough points.

No one was more at home at West Palm Beach than Nicklaus, who lived only twenty minutes away from the course, and one evening he entertained both teams for dinner. For his part Jacklin and his wife, Vivien, had a suite in the sumptuous hotel right on the golf course and he made sure that his team, together with wives and girlfriends, regarded it as their suite, too; somewhere they could get away, relax and even eat privately. It was this attention to detail that particularly impressed Waites, at forty-three much the oldest member of the team, and he remembers too the specially absorbent shirts Jacklin ordered to counteract the humidity and the extra pairs of golf shoes because the course was so wet.

Indeed, both teams frequently had to pick and drop out of casual water in the steaming, stamina-sapping heat that soared well into the nineties. The opening four-somes were shared 2—2, Watson and Ben Crenshaw winning the top match very com-fortably for America since Gallacher and Sandy Lyle were palpably out of form, while at the bottom Peete and Tom Kite eventually broke Ballesteros and Way with twos at the fifteenth and seventeenth. However, Nick Faldo and Bernhard Langer were oozing as much confidence as they were water under their shoes and always had their match under control, beating Stadler and Lanny Wadkins by four and two. Immediately behind, Canizares and Sam Torrance had quickly won a couple of holes but Gilder and Ray Floyd had hauled them back at the turn, only to let it all slip again with a succession of mistakes, the most notable of which came at the 577-yard eleventh where Gilder at-tempted to lay up short of the water and instead hit the second shot into it!

All Jacklin's pairings had been planned way in advance, and quite the most daring was that of Ballesteros, whom he knew to be his key man, with Way. His belief was that the younger man would respond, and though they lost their first game together, a more awkward moment came when word arrived that Ballesteros was 'not very happy'. The Spaniard felt, he explained, as if he was 'acting like a father to Way and holding his hand'. Jacklin's reply was that this was exactly as he had intended it to be and, having been assured that the 'trouble' went no deeper, he persisted with the partnership. In their next three games together, Ballest-eros and Way won twice and halved the other.

In the afternoon fourballs Ballesteros and Way beat Floyd and Strange by one hole, but the real bonus came from Waites and Ken Brown, neither of whom had expected to play that day but who had been summoned from a few practice holes together to replace Gallacher and Lyle, who had asked to be dropped. They defeated Gil Morgan and Fuzzy Zoeller by two and one, and with Torrance, now partnered by Woosnam, getting a half against Crenshaw and Peete, Europe were ahead. The only partnership that lost that afternoon was Faldo and Langer, beaten two and one by Watson and Haas.

It had been noticeable how much longer the Europeans were off the tee, and Nicklaus admitted that his players had been 'killed on the par fives, which is most unusual for us'. Even so, Jacklin's message to his team as they relaxed later in their suite was 'to forget what happened today. You've got to do it all again tomorrow.' And another riveting day it was too, as Europe almost lost their grip in the morning's fourball play.

The first disappointment came when Waites and Brown, having earlier been three up, lost at the last to Wadkins and Stadler, who chipped in. Quickly there came news that Ballesteros and Way, having been one up, had lost the sixteenth and seventeenth to birdies from Morgan and Haas and were now one down. It was then that Ballesteros rose as only he can to such a crisis, hitting two immense wooden club shots to the back of the eighteenth green, chipping to a yard, holing the putt for a winning birdie four and getting the half.

To have lost that game as well would have been too much to bear, for though Faldo and Langer had done their bit again, Faldo playing particularly well, in beating Crenshaw and Peete, Torrance and Woosnam were lost without much trace against Watson and

Bernhard Langer gets a soaking but at least he got the ball out

Gilder. So that was 6—6 overall at lunch and at the end of the day the two teams were still locked at 8—8. Jacklin offered no respite to his trump partnerships, Faldo and Langer, and Ballesteros and Way, and out they went again in the foursomes. Nor did they let their captain down.

Ballesteros and Way, having made good their escape in the morning, won five of the first six holes against Watson and Gilder and though the Americans hit back with a late flurry of birdies, they could not close the gap. A similar pattern seemed to be set with Faldo and Langer three up on Floyd and Kite after five holes; but then they lost three in a row and almost four, Floyd missing a short putt for the win at the eighth. It was a crucial moment, but the Europeans steadied, regained the lead and then, just when they looked like going back to only one up at the sixteenth, instead won the hole and the match when Langer chipped in for a birdie three.

The Americans had nevertheless taken the other two games comfortably, Wadkins and Morgan by seven and five against Torrance and Canizares, and Strange and Haas by three and two against Brown and Waites. The strategies of the two captains for the singles were totally different. Nicklaus went for strength in depth at the bottom with Wadkins, Floyd and Watson; Jacklin for strength at the top with Ballesteros, Faldo and Langer.

In fact it was the American middle order which tipped the balance, for Gilder against G.J. Brand, Crenshaw against Lyle, Peete against Waites, and Stadler against Woosnam all won, the only defeat being suffered by Strange against the now rampant young Way. Indeed, it would not have been as close a finish as it was had not Torrance, trailing all afternoon to Kite and still one down playing the last, struck a wonderful pitch from out of the rough for a stone-cold winning birdie four to snatch a half.

This, together with the earlier victories of Faldo against Haas, Langer against Morgan

and, in the penultimate game, Brown against Floyd, breathed new life back into the match and how different it might have been had Ballesteros beaten Zoeller instead of only halving. Three up and seven to play looked safe enough, but suddenly Zoeller, despite a bad back, took four holes in a row before Ballesteros came again to win the sixteenth. Even then his cause seemed hopeless when at the eighteenth he hooked his drive into deep rough and recovered only as far as a fairway bunker, still 240 yards from the green. It was L-shaped, and with a stroke of absolute genius Ballesteros took a three wood, aiming up the stem as it were and then fading the ball so that it finished pin high in the fringe. Those at the firing rather than receiving end swear that it was the greatest shot, given the circumstances, they had ever seen, and with the seemingly inevitable chip and single putt, Ballesteros had escaped.

As the shadows lengthened and tension mounted to an almost unbearable level, it seemed that another tie was in prospect. But there was still Canizares left to play a pitch to the eighteenth and Gallacher to hit a tee shot to the seventeenth, and on those two strokes was one of the great Ryder Cups decided.

UNITED STATES		EUROPE
Foursomes (a.m.)		
T. Watson & B. Crenshaw 5 & 4	beat	B.J. Gallacher & A.W.B. Lyle
L. Wadkins & C. Stadler	lost to	N. Faldo & B. Langer 4 & 2
R. Floyd & B. Gilder	lost to	J.—M. Canizares & S. Torrance 4 & 3
T. Kite & C. Peete 2 & 1	beat	S. Ballesteros & P. Way
Fourballs (p.m.)		
G. Morgan & F. Zoeller	lost to	B. Waites & K. Brown 2 & 1
Watson & J. Haas 2 & 1	beat	Faldo & Langer
Floyd & C. Strange	lost to	Ballesteros & Way 1 hole
Crenshaw & Peete	halved with	Torrance & I. Woosnam
Fourballs (a.m.)		
Stadler & Wadkins 1 hole	beat	Waites & Brown
Peete & Crenshaw	lost to	Faldo & Langer 4 & 2
Morgan & Haas	halved with	Ballesteros & Way
Watson & Gilder 5 & 4	beat	Torrance & Woosnam
Foursomes (p.m.)		
Kite & Floyd	lost to	Faldo & Langer 3 & 2
Wadkins & Morgan 7 & 5	beat	Torrance & Canizares
Watson & Gilder	lost to	Ballesteros & Way 2 & 1
Haas & Strange 3 & 2	beat	Brown & Waites

UNITED STATES		EUROPE
Singles		
Zoeller	halved with	Ballesteros
Haas	lost to	Faldo 2 & 1
Morgan	lost to	Langer 2 holes
Gilder 2 holes	beat	G.J. Brand
Crenshaw 3 & 1	beat	Lyle
Peete 1 hole	beat	Waites
Strange	lost to	Way 2 & 1
Kite	halved with	Torrance
Stadler 3 & 2	beat	Woosnam
Wadkins	halved with	Canizares
Floyd	lost to	Brown 4 & 3
Watson 2 & 1	beat	Gallacher

United States 14½ — Europe 13½

Europe 16½ — United States 11½
Played at The Belfry, Sutton Coldfield, 13, 14, 15 September 1985

It was soon after four o'clock on the afternoon of 15 September 1985 that Sam Torrance, tears pouring down his cheeks, raised his arms aloft and stood in statuesque triumph on the eighteenth green at The Belfry. A split second beforehand he had watched his putt from six yards or more curl gently right to left and drop into the hole for a birdie three. He did not need a birdie to beat Andy North; a par would have done, even a bogey for that matter, but this was the moment for which so many had waited for so long as Europe at last won the Ryder Cup.

Twenty-eight years had passed since the last victory by the then Great Britain team and if now the numbers had been reinforced by continental players such as Severiano Ballesteros, Bernhard Langer, Manuel Pinero, Jose Rivero and Jose-Maria Canizares, no one cared. They were all 'one of us', and the taste of victory was no less sweet. As a thunderous roar went up from the crowds stacked high in the grandstands around the green and lining every inch of the fairway below, so Torrance was engulfed by his ecstatic fellow players led by Tony Jacklin, the captain. Not long afterwards the ground was trembling again, as twice Concorde passed low overhead, dipping its silver wings in salute, bringing yet another lump to the throat.

Here was a notable day not only for golf but for sport in general, and that the decisive putt should have been holed on the theatre of the eighteenth green with seemingly every man, woman and child in the country present could not have been better stage-managed. It was almost as if it had been pre-ordained, fate taking a hand when so easily it might have been Howard Clark who could have had the privilege of sinking the putt that won the Cup.

Even as Torrance was lining up his own, so was Clark, in much greater isolation, facing another to beat Mark O'Meara by two and one on the seventeenth. It was one of only four feet, but Clark missed it and seconds later, as he headed for the next tee, he did not need telling what had happened up ahead, that the match was all over. Clark did win his game by one hole, but it was Torrance to whom the crowd had been drawn because of the likelihood of a favourable result. They knew he had come back from three down with eight to play to stand all square on the eighteenth tee, and they knew too that the gangling North, that year's American Open champion, for the second time in his career, had cracked. He had ballooned his drive into the lake short of the fairway, whereas Torrance had hit a monster, so far that all he needed was a nine iron to the green at a hole measuring 474 yards. With North suffering a penalty stroke and taking four to reach the green, it was a triumphal march for Torrance all the way and with three for it, he finished in the best possible manner.

For Jacklin it was the fulfilment of his one remaining dream, something he would cherish as much as his victories in the Open championship in 1969 and in the US Open the following year. In some ways it meant even more to him for, as he said at the time, 'This was the day European golf came of age. The team was my inspiration and it shows the world how good we really are. We have so much talent, more perhaps than even we realize'. On a lesser scale it was also his revenge on Lee Trevino, now his opposing captain but earlier the man who had denied him a second Open championship at Muirfield and, on one other occasion, a possible World Match-play championship at Wentworth.

The putt that turned the 1985 Ryder Cup. Craig Stadler turns away in disbelief after missing a tiddler at The Belfry. America at this moment lost their lead and never regained it

Jacklin's reappointment as captain had been announced in January 1984. After the narrow defeat at the PGA National the previous autumn it was a formality, though the irony of that performance was that the team had been handed to him, all twelve players coming straight off the money list. This was a new departure but already Jacklin foresaw pitfalls, for with Ballesteros, Langer, Nick Faldo and Ken Brown playing more and more in America, he sensed the possibility of their not playing often enough in Europe to get into the team automatically.

His instinct was to have total control over the selection of the team. However, this was not approved and a compromise was reached whereby the leading nine players in the money list at the end of the 1985 Benson & Hedges would get their places by right and the other three would be chosen by Jacklin.

'It is not going to be easy to win,' he said, 'but if I have some control over the weaker end of the team − the top eight or nine should not be a problem − it might just tip the balance.' As it happened, both Ballesteros and Langer, who had that year won the Masters, played their way in and instead it was Faldo, Brown and Rivero who were hand-picked, the last a surprise choice though Jacklin described him as 'the sort of player who's got bottle'. He had not forgotten the putt Rivero had holed to win a tournament at The Belfry the previous year, believing also in 'horses for courses'.

The Americans had also made a slight change to their method of selection. In 1983 they had been without both Larry Nelson, their Open champion, and Hal Sutton, their PGA champion, the former because he had not accumulated enough points and the

Sam Torrance in his moment of triumph. He had sunk his birdie putt on the last green at The Belfry in 1985 and Europe had won the Ryder Cup

latter because he had not been a professional long enough. Now, provided they were US citizens, the champions of both these events got in automatically and North and Hubert Green duly took their places. It was North's first appearance in the match, the other newcomers being O'Meara, Sutton and Peter Jacobsen.

Europe's only player new to the Ryder Cup was Rivero, and the expectation weighing on the European team, nine of whom had been in the side which had lost so narrowly two years earlier, had one unfortunate repercussion. Record crowds in the region of 25,000 every day got rather carried away with the excitement of it all and there were complaints by some of the Americans that partisanship had gone too

far. It was, as mentioned in earlier chapters, nothing new, but it was of course a novel experience for this generation.

Even Jacobsen, normally the most imperturbable of men, said: 'Losing the Ryder Cup did not bother me as much as the behaviour of the galleries. All that cheering when we missed shots. I've never known anything like it before, especially not from a British crowd. You expect so much more from them.' There were also accusations of the American wives being 'hissed at', though this was almost certainly misinterpreted. Walking as they did inside the ropes, they were bound occasionally to obscure the view of the people who had paid to watch and the occasional 'Psst' was nothing more than a means of attracting their attention or asking them to crouch down.

Naturally the crowds were on Europe's side and if they cheered putts that won holes that was understandable. What the Americans found unacceptable was the occasional cheer when they missed a putt to lose a hole. Yet the result is the same, and to greet it in silent sympathy is alien to human nature, just as is the case in tennis when a crucial point is lost through an unforced error. Certainly Trevino did not complain and even went so far as to call his team 'a lot of cry-babies'.

After all the criticism of The Belfry in its formative years it must be said that the course had never been in better condition, while the on-site hotel made it an ideal location for the players, free as they were of the heavy traffic streaming up the motorways from north, south, east and west. Yet for a time they had little to cheer as the United States took the opening foursomes 3–1, though by the end of the day the prospects had substantially improved since Europe took the fourballs 2½–1½ to stand only a point behind at 3½–4½.

Much of this was due to Ballesteros and Pinero, who won twice together. In the morning they beat O'Meara, who was not at his best, and Curtis Strange. Ballesteros, on the other hand, was full of inspiration, driving the green for instance at that perilous water hole, the tenth, and holing several telling putts. Overall, however, the Americans played much the better golf, even if some of it was not all that great either. For instance, Lanny Wadkins and Raymond Floyd were out in 38 against Sandy Lyle, very much that year's hero since he had earlier won the Open championship at Royal St George's, and Brown. Yet they were three up and won by four and three.

Beforehand Trevino had rated Calvin Peete and Tom Kite as his best partnership. Both were very straight — much too straight for Langer and Faldo. Out in 33 and two up, they were soon four holes to the good and there was another American point. The third came from Sutton and Craig Stadler, the end here coming swiftly as they took three holes in a row from the thirteenth, only one of them a birdie, to beat Torrance and Clark.

Though they were his own personal selections, Jacklin dropped Faldo and Brown in the afternoon, continued to leave out Rivero and even omitted Lyle, who many thought was better suited to fourball play. But the captain had his reward, for the recovery all stemmed from the top fourball game in which Paul Way and Ian Woosnam beat Green and Fuzzy Zoeller. Way was again the man for the occasion, for it was his drive, two iron and putt for a birdie three at the last which did the trick after they had lost a three-hole lead.

Then came another European point from Ballesteros and Pinero, the former having a run of three consecutive birdies from the fourth and five in all as they beat North and Jacobsen by two and one. Technically this made the two teams level and they stayed there when Langer and Canizares halved their game against Stadler and Sutton. It was probably the right result, because fourteen of the eighteen holes were halved. However, the Americans made sure of an overall lead when Floyd and Wadkins,

having gone two up as early as the fourth, just held on to beat Torrance and Clark, Wadkins' birdie three from 10 yards at the sixteenth being decisive.

For a long time in the fourballs on the Saturday morning there was no shift in the balance of power. Torrance and Clark were mostly in control against Kite and North, particularly after Clark had holed an absolute monster for a birdie at the fifteenth and then chipped in for a three at the sixteenth. Way and Woosnam were four up after only five holes on Green and Zoeller and won comfortably, but equally the United States were having the better of the other two games.

Wadkins and O'Meara, with an outward half of 32, were four up on Ballesteros and Pinero as they went on to record a victory by three and two, and for the most part Stadler and Strange were up on Langer and Lyle, indeed two up with only two to play. It was then that the whole pattern of the Ryder Cup began to change. First Lyle holed a very big putt for an eagle three at the seventeenth, and then at the last there came another even more unexpected and much more crucial twist. Nothing looked more certain than that the hole would be halved in four, but Stadler, left with the sort of tiny putt that in any other circumstances would have been conceded, unaccountably missed and the teams were tied.

At that moment American heads went down as much as European chins went up. By nightfall the pendulum had completely swung. Canizares and Rivero raced away from a seemingly demoralized Kite and Peete in the foursomes to win by seven and five, while Ballesteros and Pinero were six up after eight against Stadler and Sutton and soon home and dry. Certainly there was some American resistance from Strange and Jacobsen, for once they had taken the lead with a birdie at the ninth they quickly opened up a big gap against Way and Woosnam, while for eleven holes Floyd and Wadkins were level with Langer and Brown.

It must be said that Langer and Brown can be two painfully slow players and this almost certainly got on the nerves of Floyd and Wadkins, particularly Wadkins, who wastes no time at all. The six-foot putt he missed for a half in three at the twelfth opened the door, Langer pushed it wider by holing from six yards for a birdie at the fifteenth, and then Brown hit an eight iron stone dead for a three at the sixteenth. Europe had got their third point and were now ahead 9–7.

The atmosphere on the final morning was electric. Players were cheered through avenues of spectators even as they walked to the practice ground, Jacklin never more nervous than when he stood on the first tee seeing them all off. All day he was everywhere, a radio in his hand getting up-to-date information as every putt fell, eyes glued to scoreboards, head turning as roar after roar came up from various parts of the course. By comparison Trevino was more conspicuous by his absence, a point that Jacobsen, for one, was not slow to make.

Unlike the previous Ryder Cup match, Jacklin this time packed his strength not at the top but in the middle. Even so, no one was keener to get into battle than little Pinero, who had jumped up in delight the previous evening when he learned he was to play Wadkins in the leading single. 'That's the man I want,' he said, and he did not fail. Though twice down early on amid some fairly scrappy golf, Pinero was back to all square by the eighth. And then he struck with successive birdies at the tenth and eleventh, made another at the long fifteenth and that left Wadkins too much to do.

This American reverse was promptly cancelled by Stadler, who caught Woosnam on one of his less impressive days, but the normally dependable Floyd lurched from one disaster to another, taking 41 to the turn and standing four down to Way. However, the inward half was a different story and slowly the holes came back until the American was only one down and two to

play. They halved the seventeenth, but at the last Floyd drove into the bunker on the far side of the fairway. It was an all-or-nothing shot from there and, gambling with wood, Floyd topped into the lake. Europe had advanced another step closer to their cherished goal.

But they were not there yet, for Ballesteros had a much rougher time against Kite than most expected, two down at the turn, three down and five to play. In most mortals such a cause would be hopeless, but not for this Spaniard. He sank a colossal putt for a two at the fourteenth and another, a third of the distance but still from 15 feet, at the fifteenth for another birdie. Now the adrenalin was running.

Cutting loose from the seventeenth tee Ballesteros was 60 yards past Kite, who could not get up in two. Ballesteros could, and he was too big. It was the sort of chip he normally lays dead. This time he left it 12 feet short but he holed the putt to draw level, and though Kite had rather the better of the eighteenth, certainly after the drives, they halved.

This was an important moment, for Lyle was up and so was Langer; Torrance was coming back against North, Clark just had his nose in front of O'Meara, Faldo was down to Green, Rivero narrowly ahead of Peete, Canizares deadlocked with Zoeller, but Brown well down to Strange. Europe therefore needed three more points and the first of them came from Lyle, who found his form in the nick of time. Never down against Jacobsen, he was nevertheless only one up with five to play, but Jacobsen three-putted the fifteenth and then, to a great shout, Lyle holed from the back edge of the sixteenth green and there was another win.

Then came Langer as he slowly distanced himself from Sutton, the curious aspect of this game being that only one of their fourteen holes was halved. The American was not at peace with either himself or anyone else, and the end came when Langer, no better than level par, almost sank his tee

Tony Jacklin, resplendent again in collar and tie, shows off the Ryder Cup to admiring spectators at the Belfry

shot to the fourteenth. It was only his second birdie, but he still won by five and four.

And so it was that Torrance, three down after ten holes to North, took the final limelight. 'I told myself just to keep concentrating, keep trying and hopefully my luck would change,' he recalls saying to himself. It did. A par had been good enough to win back the eleventh, but there were still two key strokes. At the fifteenth North, still two up, missed a short putt for the half. At the seventeenth Torrance was deep in the rough with his second shot, but he played a great recovery, sank the putt and had drawn level. Poor North. He may never forget that drive at the last, though it probably did not matter so far as the match result was concerned.

Clark was still there to record a win, and so was Canizares. Faldo admittedly lost to Green, Rivero to Peete and Brown to Strange. But by then the champagne corks were popping, eyes had dried and and hands were being shaken again and again. It had been a long wait; but an even richer moment was still to come.

EUROPE		UNITED STATES
Foursomes (a.m.)		
S. Ballesteros & M. Pinero 2 & 1	beat	C. Strange & M. O'Meara
B. Langer & N. Faldo	lost to	C. Peete & T. Kite 3 & 2
A.W.B. Lyle & K. Brown	lost to	L. Wadkins & R. Floyd 4 & 3
H. Clark & S. Torrance	lost to	C. Stadler & H. Sutton 3 & 2
Fourballs (p.m.)		
P. Way & I. Woosnam 1 hole	beat	F. Zoeller & H. Green
Ballesteros & Pinero 2 & 1	beat	A. North & P. Jacobsen
Langer & J.−M. Canizares	halved with	Stadler & Sutton
Torrance & Clark	lost to	Floyd & Wadkins 1 hole
Fourballs (a.m.)		
Torrance & Clark 2 & 1	beat	Kite & North
Way & Woosnam 4 & 3	beat	Green & Zoeller
Ballesteros & Pinero	lost to	O'Meara & Wadkins 3 & 2
Langer & Lyle	halved with	Stadler & Strange
Foursomes (p.m.)		
Canizares & J. Rivero 7 & 5	beat	Kite & Peete
Ballesteros & Pinero 5 & 4	beat	Stadler & Sutton
Way & Woosnam	lost to	Strange & Jacobsen 4 & 2
Langer & Brown 3 & 2	beat	Floyd & Wadkins

EUROPE		UNITED STATES
Singles		
Pinero 3 & 1	beat	Wadkins
Woosnam	lost to	Stadler 2 & 1
Way 2 holes	beat	Floyd
Ballesteros	halved with	Kite
Lyle 3 & 2	beat	Jacobsen
Langer 5 & 4	beat	Sutton
Torrance 1 hole	beat	North
Clark 1 hole	beat	O'Meara
Faldo	lost to	Green 3 & 1
Rivero	lost to	Peete 1 hole
Canizares 2 holes	beat	Zoeller
Brown	lost to	Strange 4 & 2

Europe 16½ — United States 11½

United States 13 — Europe 15

Played at Muirfield Village, Columbus, Ohio, 25, 26, 27 September 1987

As the teams filed away after the colourful flag-raising ceremony on the eve of Europe's defence of the Ryder Cup at Muirfield Village, Tony Jacklin, the captain, drew Ken Schofield, executive director of the PGA European Tour, to one side and invited him for a drink in the team's headquarters, a sprawling luxury bungalow half hidden by trees and shrubs to the side of the eighteenth fairway. The invitation also included the Tour's chief tournament administrators, Tony Gray, George O'Grady and John Paramor.

If the 'Gang of Four', as they might be termed, expected a pleasant, quiet interlude, they were in for a rude awakening. For two hours they were the victims of some very plain talking as, one after the other, the players laid into them over what they maintained were the unsatisfactory conditions on the European circuit. Anything and everything was seized upon, from the poor practice facilities, substandard practice balls, weak courses, inconsistent greens, uneven fairways and the wrong sand in bunkers to the unsympathetic scheduling of tournaments from one geographical area to another.

Schofield recalls it as being one of the

Ian Woosnam, arm aloft, leads the singing after Europe's victory at Muirfield Village in 1987. Nick Faldo grasps the champagne and Sam Torrance keeps an eye on it just in case there is none left

most intimidating experiences he has had, and he was only thankful that he was not alone. O'Grady recalls Gray and Paramor getting quite upset about it all. For his part, however, O'Grady took a more philosophical stance, seeing it as conceivably all a put-up job by Jacklin to take the players' minds off the golf and its tactics so that they were able, he says, 'to forget the Ryder Cup and come out refreshed the following morning'. In hindsight, Schofield now believes he was probably right. 'I remember thinking,' he says, 'that if the players were in that sort of mood, God help the Americans!'

Three days later I can recall standing at much the same time of day in the press room in the bowels of Muirfield Village's administrative offices and hearing the faint sound of singing through the heavy, almost sound-proofed doors. On investigation there was revealed the most extraordinary sight there has ever been at a golf event as hundreds of European supporters, some carrying flags and others in caps and scarves, swayed together in the big open-air bar singing: 'Eee aye addio, We've won the Cup.' Some were standing on tables, others on chairs, and into their midst came in random sequence their heroes as they in turn led the next chorus, shirts tossed to the crowd, champagne everywhere. If golf had had its moments of patriotic fervour, notably at The Belfry two years earlier, this was something entirely new to the Americans and they could only stand and stare. Perhaps it was only then that many of them realized how much the Ryder Cup meant to those on the other side of the Atlantic. Never before, in all those years going back to the very beginning in 1927, had America been beaten on their own soil. But now they had, 15–13, and it was not something those privileged to have been present were going to let pass without appropriate celebration.

And yet it might never have happened had not Jacklin more than a year earlier dug his toes in. Europe's victory in 1985 had sparked a new American interest in the

Ryder Cup. ABC Television were committed to cover the match live for the first time and at the 1987 Memorial tournament, also at Muirfield Village, a proposition was put to Colin Snape, still executive director of the PGA, to extend the format to four days with an extra series of singles, it making, the Americans argued, a more viable commercial proposition.

Snape then flew to Spain with the new plan and put it to Jacklin, who rejected it. This was nevertheless not the end of the matter and at the Open championship at Turnberry, in July 1986, the proposition was formally tabled again by the American PGA. Jack Nicklaus, appointed American captain because Muirfield Village was 'his course', was present and so was Jacklin, who quite bluntly said that if there was any change in the format he would resign the captaincy. Nicklaus did not want that. 'Let's leave it,' he said; and left it was.

There was one other political skirmish that could have been damaging. This year Johnnie Walker, another branch of Guinness – DCL – had taken over sponsorship from Bell's and shortly before the European team flew by Concorde to the States the PGA was advised that players like Nick Faldo, Sandy Lyle, Bernhard Langer and Ian Woosnam, who were all managed by Mark McCormack's International Management Group, could be in breach of contract if they appeared in clothing provided by the rival manufacturers who had won the Ryder Cup contracts with the PGA. A compromise was reached whereby the said players did in fact wear the official kit but only on condition that the offending logos were blacked out. It was a further example of how some players had become mere pawns within a much bigger game, though it should be pointed out that there were no such difficulties with the Americans.

Behind the euphoria of this first European victory in the States, not enough credit is given to the stern resistance of the US team when their cause was seemingly hopeless.

Ian Woosnam (left) and Nick Faldo were two key figures in Europe's first victory on American soil

From the moment when Europe made a clean sweep of the fourballs on the first day to open up a lead of 6−2, they seemed in total control. With only the singles to come they were 10½−5½ ahead and therefore needed only another four points out of the remaining twelve. Yet where they were going to come from was for a long time a matter of some doubt, and that the Americans closed to within a single point of a tied match reflected still the strongest of hearts. They certainly did not go down without a fight.

And what a showpiece of an arena Muirfield Village made: not a blade of grass out of place, glorious weather and the first all-ticket crowd there had been at a Ryder Cup match with a limit of 25,000 on each of the three days. Some 3000 spectators were reported to be Europeans, and for an uncomfortable hour and a half or so on that opening morning they must have wondered why they had ever bothered; America were quickly up in every foursome. Curtis Strange and Tom Kite won three of the first five holes against Sam Torrance and Howard Clark; Dan Pohl and Hal Sutton were one up after four against Langer and Ken Brown; Larry Mize and Lanny Wadkins three up after three against Faldo and Woosnam; and Payne Stewart and Larry Nelson two up after five against Severiano Ballesteros and Jose-Maria Olazabal, his young fellow countryman.

Nor did the picture significantly change as the four games went through the turn; only

Nelson and Stewart were overhauled and now one down to the two Spaniards. The first of these two foursomes went to its predictable conclusion, but it was the recovery of Faldo and Woosnam from four down that put a whole new complexion on things. Woosnam was largely responsible and it all began with his three iron to five feet at the tenth. Errors from the tee cost the Americans both the twelfth and fourteenth and when Woosnam flew a one iron 250 yards to the shelf of a green at the par five fifteenth, they were level. Woosnam also sank a most missable putt at the seventeenth for the lead, and it was he again who played a glorious bunker shot at the last, so close that Faldo was not asked to putt. Even so, Wadkins did have a putt for a birdie; it caught the rim and spun so far away that Mize missed the next.

Olazabal's form in practice had worried Jacklin and it was only on Ballesteros's insistence that the young Spaniard remained as his partner. Now the senior man had to justify his demand, and justify it he did with some wonderful shot-making to cover his companion's mistakes. There was a three iron picked off the top of the sand, a shot of 190 yards, to save the tenth and they were still one up coming to the eighteenth. Here Olazabal once again drove into a bunker, but again Ballesteros picked a long iron clean and though it left Olazabal a long, wickedly curling putt, he judged it about as well as any man could have done, Ballesteros holing out as safely as he had done all morning. Yet it had been typical of him that as they climbed the slope to the eighteenth green, it was Olazabal's hand he hoisted high above their heads, as if to say that it had been this young man who had done it all.

No one could possibly have foreseen the avalanche that was to follow in the afternoon fourballs. Europe won them all, and not one of them even went as far as the eighteenth. Indeed, the only game that was in any danger was that in which Langer and Lyle found themselves, having earlier been two up, now two down to Calcavecchia and Andy Bean with only five to play. But a birdie at the fourteenth by Lyle gave them new hope and he also saved the sixteenth when it looked for all the world as if they were about to go two down again. Astonishingly neither American could make pars at either the seventeenth or eighteenth, but the Europeans did to be handed a most unlikely victory.

Gordon Brand Junior and Jose Rivero had won the top game comfortably against Simpson and Ben Crenshaw, but it was not until the eleventh hole that Woosnam and Faldo got their noses in front of Sutton and Pohl. There was quite a bit of luck about it, too. Woosnam's second shot to the par five eleventh was flying well wide but it caught a tree, rebounded on to the green and then he added insult to injury by holing the putt for an eagle. Then Faldo promptly sank a putt for a two at the twelfth and the breakthrough had been made. So here was a third point, and a fourth soon followed, for Ballesteros and Olazabal were up from the first hole against Strange and Kite and were never caught. It was a measure of the European performance that of the 68 holes played in the afternoon, America won only 10.

Such was the enthusiasm of the European followers that at that night's press conference Nicklaus said that he felt at times the Americans were playing in Britain. His appeal for greater support rebounded on him. Overnight a flood of small Stars and Stripes flags appeared and they were handed out to spectators as they arrived the following morning. Avenues of flag-wavers then formed between the practice green and the first tee and as the Americans walked through they were accompanied by chants of 'USA! USA! USA!' This was not at all what Nicklaus had had in mind, it rather lowering the golfing tone, and it did not happen again.

If the United States were bent on quick revenge, they did not get it. Though Kite and Strange set a good example in the top

All smiles as Europe retain the Ryder Cup in 1987. Left to right: (back row) Severiano Ballesteros, Gordon Brand junior, Sandy Lyle, Tony Jacklin, Nick Faldo, Sam Torrance, Eamonn Darcy; (front row) Jose Rivero, Jose-Maria Olazabal, Ken Brown, Ian Woosnam, Bernhard Langer, Howard Clark

foursome, quickly recovering from the loss of the first hole and subsequently drawing well clear of Brand and Rivero, Europe increased their lead by another point to 8½−3½. Faldo, unhappy with his game, had been on the point of asking to stand down, but even so he and Woosnam almost beat Sutton and Mize, ahead most of the way due as much as anything to Sutton's inability to hole some crucial putts. However, the Europeans did make a mess of the eighteenth, taking four to reach the green

and therefore ending up all square.

However, Lyle and Langer, all square after ten holes against Wadkins and Nelson, made the breakthrough when at the eleventh Lyle hit a stupendous two iron so close to the hole that the eagle three was conceded. This proved to be the breakthrough, for they quickly became three up and won on the seventeenth green. Another point also looked safe from Ballesteros and Olazabal, though this time it was the younger man who was the steadying influence, particularly on the greens. They were three up after twelve holes against Crenshaw and Stewart, only to make an awful meal of it before they got home on the last green with, of all things, a bogey five. Ballesteros could hardly believe it when his second shot found a bunker behind the green, and was confounded again when his attempted lag after an excellent explosion from Olazabal dribbled six feet beyond the hole. Fortunately for him, Olazabal sank the putt — which he had to do since by then Crenshaw had made up for a duffed pitch into another bunker by sinking his putt for a five as well.

It was in the afternoon fourballs that the fur really flew. 'I never thought that I would live to see the day when I would see golf played like this,' said a drained Jacklin afterwards, and Nicklaus agreed with every word. This time the four games were shared 2−2 for a continuing European lead, now of 10½−5½, though to achieve it they were cumulatively for the 65 holes 29 under par against the Americans' 22.

It was Woosnam (two) and Faldo (three) who set it all off, with five birdies at each of the first five holes to go five up on Kite and Strange. They were out in 29 and ten under par for the fourteen holes it took them to win. But 29 out was also matched by Bean and Stewart, who were eight under par for the first ten holes against Brand and Eamonn Darcy. The Americans were then six up and clearly out of reach. There was, too, another American point from Sutton and Mize, seven under par between them as they inflicted on Ballesteros and Olazabal their one defeat together.

Curiously there were no such fireworks from Lyle and Langer who, though out in 36, were still one up on Wadkins and Nelson, and they moved almost sedately to three up and three to play. It was then that Wadkins, always a tough match player, produced birdies at both the sixteenth and seventeenth and then raised the American roof with a glorious long pitch to the last for yet another certain three. The evening light

was then fading fast but Langer, a seemingly frail and almost lonely figure down there on the fairway, not only matched him but beat him. His eight iron pitched and stopped inches from the hole and all the Americans could do was offer their hands.

Though all Europe needed on that final, pulsating day was four points, Jacklin had a suspicion that they would take some getting. He spent some time discussing the order of play with his team and in the end it was Ballesteros who said, 'Look, Tony, you go into the next room and do it by yourself. We'll play wherever you say.' Suspecting that Nicklaus would lead with strength in the hope that he would recoup whatever he could, Jacklin held back his three aces, Langer, Lyle and Ballesteros, in case of crisis. And crisis there was. Woosnam was unseated by the three twos Bean threw at him, and though Clark and Torrance both won the last hole, the former to beat Pohl and the latter to halve with Mize, the scoreboard at that point told an uncomfortable story. In the remaining nine matches America were up in six, all square in two and down in two. With all games by then through the turn, there was still very little margin for error.

Most disturbing of all was that two of Jacklin's 'bankers', Langer and Lyle, were apparently taking a hammering, the West German at one point three down to Nelson, and Lyle at another four down to Calcavecchia. Only Ballesteros seemed secure, while the less expected bonus of a win from Darcy, three up at the turn against Crenshaw, rapidly disappeared since he was now all square and indeed about to go behind.

Darcy's match was an extraordinary one, for as they left the sixth green, where the Irishman had just gone two up, Crenshaw beat his putter into the ground in annoyance and snapped the shaft. Yet, even though now forced to putt with either his one iron or the leading edge of his sand wedge, the American climbed back and with a three at the short sixteenth took the lead. This, as it

Spaniards in silhouette. Jose-Maria Olazabal (left) and Severiano Ballesteros peer into the setting sun at Muirfield Village

happened, was Europe's darkest moment, for at the next Darcy played a wonderful six iron to the green, sank the putt for a winning birdie and presently became the toast of Europe. Crenshaw had to take a penalty drop after driving into water at the last, but though he was bunkered in three, he still made a five and Darcy therefore needed a four to beat him. Also bunkered, he played a good recovery but his ball came to rest some four or five feet above the hole and that was an awfully treacherous and difficult putt. To his everlasting credit, he got it in.

This was the point Europe needed, for though Faldo against Calcavecchia, Olazabal against Stewart, and Rivero against Simpson all lost, Langer had won three holes in a row from the twelfth against Nelson to draw level, and he stayed there. Curiously, with both players a couple of feet

from the hole in three at the last, Nelson then conceded a halved game which, given the still teetering state of the match, almost exceeded the bounds of generosity.

However, Nelson probably sensed that it hardly mattered, for Ballesteros was now two up and two to play on Strange and with a typically dependable four at the seventeenth, the world's most gifted golfer had the privilege of sinking the putt that won the Ryder Cup. Perhaps there was not quite the theatre about it that there had been when Torrance had sunk the all-important putt at The Belfry two years earlier, but it meant just as much and there was no better man for the honour than Ballesteros who, in his captain's opinion, becomes an entirely different man in the Ryder Cup, the inspiration of the whole side.

UNITED STATES		EUROPE
Foursomes (a.m.)		
C. Strange & T. Kite	beat	S. Torrance & H. Clark
4 & 2		
H. Sutton & D. Pohl	beat	K. Brown & B. Langer
2 & 1		
L. Wadkins & L. Mize	lost to	N. Faldo & I. Woosnam
		2 holes
L. Nelson & P. Stewart	lost to	S. Ballesteros &
		J.−M. Olazabal
		1 hole
Fourballs (p.m.)		
B. Crenshaw &	lost to	G. Brand Jnr & J. Rivero
S. Simpson		3 & 2
A. Bean &	lost to	Langer & A.W.B. Lyle
M. Calcavecchia		1 hole
Sutton & Pohl	lost to	Woosnam & Faldo
		2 & 1
Strange & Kite	lost to	Ballesteros & Olazabal
		2 & 1
Foursomes (a.m.)		
Strange & Kite	beat	Rivero & Brand
3 & 1		
Sutton & Mize	halved with	Faldo & Woosnam
Wadkins & Nelson	lost to	Lyle & Langer
		2 & 1
Crenshaw & Stewart	lost to	Ballesteros & Olazabal
		1 hole

UNITED STATES		EUROPE
Fourballs (p.m.)		
Kite & Strange	lost to	Woosnam & Faldo
		5 & 4
Stewart & Bean	beat	Brand & E. Darcy
3 & 2		
Sutton & Mize	beat	Ballesteros & Olazabal
2 & 1		
Wadkins & Nelson	lost to	Lyle & Langer
		1 hole
Singles		
Bean	beat	Woosnam
1 hole		
Pohl	lost to	Clark
		1 hole
Mize	halved with	Torrance
Calcavecchia	beat	Faldo
1 hole		
Stewart	beat	Olazabal
2 holes		
Crenshaw	lost to	Darcy
		1 hole
Simpson	beat	Rivero
2 & 1		
Nelson	halved with	Langer
Kite	beat	Lyle
3 & 2		
Strange	lost to	Ballesteros
		2 & 1
Sutton	halved with	Brand
Wadkins	beat	Brown
3 & 2		

United States 13 — Europe 15

Europe 14 — United States 14

Played at The Belfry, Sutton Coldfield, 22, 23, 24 September 1989

Such was the injection Europe had given by their victories in 1985 and 1987 that when the Ryder Cup returned to The Belfry in 1989 it was being widely billed as the Match of the Century. If this seemed to be asking a lot, it proved be far from an exaggerated claim, the two sides being of such equal strength that, for the second time in twenty years, they finished deadlocked in a tie at 14—14.

Minds were immediately cast back to that other memorable day at Royal Birkdale in 1969 when Tony Jacklin and Jack Nicklaus, with both teams still level, came out all square in the last single. Now, in somewhat different circumstances, it happened again, the United States clawing their way back from the brink of defeat by winning each of the last four singles, three of them on the eighteenth green.

Yet, if the ultimate relief lay in the American camp, there was a fair share of it too among the Europeans. They too had earlier stared defeat in the face, since at their lowest ebb on this tumultuous warm and sunny final afternoon, they had lost one match, were down in seven more and ahead in only one. Curiously it was not the first time that summer that such agonies had been suffered for at Peachtree, a charming Atlanta club founded by Bobby Jones, Britain had wobbled to their first Walker Cup victory in America, securing the one and half points they needed from eight singles from three players who were all down coming into the last two holes.

Nevertheless the Americans had stopped their Ryder Cup rot and restored, if not all, at least some of their self respect. 'It was an afternoon of a lot of peaks and a lot of valleys,' said Raymond Floyd, their captain, afterwards. 'I doubt that anyone is very happy that we have not won but I sure

Tony Jacklin cuddles the Ryder Cup. 'It ain't going nowhere,' he had said before the match, and he was right

would have hated to lose. The one winner was the game of golf, as I always hoped it would be. The way the players on both sides conducted themselves and the behaviour of the crowds, which worried us when we arrived, could not have been better. They were beautiful.'

Once Concorde had made its now traditional fly-past before the prize giving, indeed before the match was over though at a time when Europe could no longer be beaten, Jacklin made his predictable announcement that he was standing down as captain after being in charge for the last four matches. 'You have got to know when it is time to quit,' he said, 'and this is that moment. It's been an honour and a privilege but the players now need someone who is closer to their own age.'

No one could possibly have served Europe better and if finally he met his equal in Floyd, who had been appointed by the American PGA in the hope that he would be tough and uncompromising, Jacklin knew too that he had forced the American hand. For the first time they gave the captain two hand-picks of his own. It could have been only one but Payne Stewart, who had already qualified on points, also won the PGA championship, that particular event carrying with it a ticket into the Ryder Cup team. Floyd therefore chose Tom Watson and Lanny Wadkins, the former predictably so and the latter less so.

Watson had already had high finishes in both the Open championship at Royal Troon, where he was fourth, and then at the PGA. Wadkins, on the other hand, had missed six cuts in his previous eight tournaments, including the PGA after which the team had to be decided. However it was experience Floyd was counting on for the five newcomers to his team — Paul Azinger, Chip Beck, Fred Couples, Ken Green and Mark McCumber — were, he felt, quite enough.

Eighteen months before the match Jacklin suffered the most grievous of blows when his wife, Vivien, died when she collapsed at the wheel of her car when driving near to their home in Spain. There was speculation that he might give up the captaincy, especially when the more scurrilous of the British tabloid newspapers made revelations that he had become involved with a girl young enough to be his own daughter. Within a matter of months however Jacklin re-married, to a Norwegian divorcee, Astrid Kendall. From a Ryder Cup point of view, she had a difficult role to fill for Vivien had been very much the captain of the 'wives team' and contented spouses mean contented players.

Once again Jacklin was given three selections of his own, but what threw his calculations into disarray was the totally unpredictable run of bad form that overtook Sandy Lyle, who in 1988 had become the first British golfer to win the Masters. After beginning the season very well in America with two seconds and a third, Lyle went into such a slide that in eleven consecutive tournaments either side of the Atlantic, he missed the cut nine times.

By the time of the German Open, the last Ryder Cup points-counting tournament, it was no longer possible, even if he had won the event, for Lyle to qualify for the team automatically. He was as far back as 111th in the money list. Instead Lyle went to the World Series in Akron. But he did not perform well, and on the eve of the team being announced sent a message to Frankfurt asking Jacklin to telephone him.

It was almost midnight European time when Jacklin rang, Lyle coming straight to the point and saying that he did not want to be considered for the team. It was difficult enough, he said, to play for himself when his confidence was so low, let alone for others. He believed the team had to come first. For someone who in 1985 had won the Open championship and in 1988 had followed it with the Masters as well as for much of that season leading the American money list, it was the bravest but also one of the saddest decisions ever to have been made by a sportsman, let alone a golfer.

Consequently Jacklin nominated Bernhard Langer, who had largely conquered the twitch for the second time in his career and very nearly made the team on merit, the experienced Howard Clark and Christy O'Connor junior, who had been bitterly disappointed when he was overlooked for the 1985 team. The only newcomer to Ryder Cup golf therefore was Ronan Rafferty, the leader of the money list and the most automatic of all the automatics.

The planning of the Ryder Cup, still under the very professional sponsorship of

Johnnie Walker, began months beforehand and as early as February Jacklin had his first meeting with the clothing manufacturers over colour schemes. He is a man for the pastel shades.

Austin Reed provided one grey suit, a green blazer, six dress shirts, a pair of natural coloured trousers, seven pairs of socks, two belts, two Ryder Cup ties, two neutral ties and two pairs of cufflinks. Oscar Jacobson provided two pairs each of navy and white gaberdine trousers, one each of grey, beige and black and three more pairs, in case of cold, in cord of grey, beige and black, with one sports belt. Glenmuir provided six white, two navy and two peach coloured shirts; five cashmere sweaters in pale blue, red, pink, white and primrose; three sleeveless pullovers in pink, white and primrose and, for the wives, three matching shirts and three matching sweaters.

Pro Quip provided one teal coloured rain suit (another for wives) and a leisure jacket in the same colour. Titleist/Footjoy provided two pairs of white golf shoes, two pairs of street shoes in black and burgundy, and twelve pairs of socks.

In addition to all this there was a Lark suitcase and a leather Ryder golf bag and hood, head-covers, holdall and ball bag. The total value of all this to each player was in excess of £5000. Two years earlier there had been a dispute over the logos on clothing since many players were contracted to other manufacturers. Consequently the companies who had successfully negotiated the contracts agreed to remove their logos, leaving only the Ryder Cup emblem.

The tented village, with 226 structures covering 350,000 square feet, was the biggest there has ever been at a sporting event in Britain. Including catering and hotel staff, contractors, stewards, exhibitors and tournament staff the working personnel approached 5000.

Media coverage was more intense than it had ever been. There were 380 writers, including more than 50 from America, 170 photographers, 100 broadcasters and more than 500 accreditations for BBC television and the American United Network which was beaming the match live to the United States. The world-wide television audience on the final afternoon was estimated at 200 million, stretching as far as Japan and South Africa.

There was consequently a great deal of hype leading into the match, further fuelled when at the Gala Ball at the Metropole Hotel outside Birmingham, Raymond Floyd introduced his team as 'the twelve greatest players in the world'. If this was meant as a psychological piece of propaganda, there was promptly a stinging, if unpremeditated, response when, at the conclusion of the cabaret, the Band of the Irish Guards gave a rousing rendering of 'Land of Hope and Glory', which had half the assembled company on their feet and the Americans hurrying for the door even as the last strains were floating across the dance floor.

With rain clouds filling the sky it was so gloomy the following morning when, at eight o'clock, the first foursome went off, that had it been a cricket match there would unquestionably have been an immediate appeal for bad light and it would equally unquestionably have been upheld by the umpires. Nor was that the only bizarre note. Amid what seemed to be some general confusion, Ian Woosnam drove off first, Tom Kite having to step back when about to tee up. There had been some speculation the previous evening that because Europe were the holders, they had the honour. In fact this has traditionally been given to the visiting team – both in America and Britain – and the mistake was hastily rectified by the time Payne Stewart led off in the second match.

It proved to be a much better first session for the Americans than it did for the Europeans for they led 3−1 just as they had four years ago on the same course. Indeed the solitary point by the home side came from two halved games, Faldo and

Woosnam against Kite and Strange, and in the third game Ballesteros and Olazabal against Watson and Beck. It was the latter who let the better opportunity slip for they were two up at the turn and three up when Olazabal hit a magnificent three wood to 12 feet at the 275-yard tenth.

The hole draws spectators like a magnet for though it is a short par four of normally 301 yards it is reduced for the Ryder Cup to tempt the players to go for the kidney-shaped green cut slightly to the right and beyond a menacing pond. In the first two days only two players laid up, which seemed to indicate that it was less of a gamble than it should have been.

From three up the Spaniards were nevertheless hauled back to all square within the next four holes, Watson twice obliging with birdie putts and Ballesteros being responsible for the loss of the thirteenth when he drove into a bunker. A rather headstrong putt by Beck lost the Americans the fifteenth but they were handed back the sixteenth in

Nick Faldo holes from a bunker at the seventh in the second series of fourballs. He and Ian Woosnam nevertheless lost to Paul Azinger and Chip Beck

similar vein and there it stayed.

Faldo and Woosnam were two up early on against Kite and Strange but they got into a frightful muddle around the turn and never more so than at the tenth where Faldo missed the green high on the bank to the right of the green. Woosnam's pitch ran through into the water and when Faldo dropped clear under penalty, so he pitched back in again. Now two down, they made birdies at the fourteenth and fifteenth to square, the game coming to a worthy climax at the eighteenth. With the wind against, it was an extremely difficult hole, Kite's second with wood barely making the carry across the lake. However Strange played a fine pitch for a four matched only by an exquisite 25-yard bunker shot from Faldo close enough for Woosnam to hole the putt.

Wadkins and Stewart played the best golf of the morning, round in 68, but even so beating Clark and James only by a single hole. The 25-yard chip Wadkins holed at the seventeenth was the 'killer'. Calcavecchia and Green were nothing like as pressed in beating Langer and Rafferty by two and one for the two Europeans were sadly out of sorts, out in 41 and three down. When they did have a chance to get back to one down at the fifteenth they followed the Americans into the ditch with their second shots and the hole was halved in seven.

By contrast the afternoon belonged totally to Europe as they made a clean sweep of the fourballs, as indeed they had done on the first afternoon at Muirfield Village. The highlight of it was the golf of Ballesteros for after he and Olazabal had won the first five holes against Watson and O'Meara, the elder Spaniard stopped the hint of a slide by making an eagle two at the tenth and then birdies at each of the next three holes to win the match. If he had not played too well in the morning, he certainly did in the afternoon.

There was no better reflection on a thoroughly wretched afternoon for the Americans than the fact that they never once took the lead in any match. Two none-theless came to the last hole, but Brand picked a wonderful bunker shot clean to beat Strange and Azinger while a tight game for Faldo and Woosnam became easier when both Calcavecchia and McCumber failed to clear the water with their seconds.

There was a much greater resolve about the Americans on the second day for both Beck and Azinger, against Brand and Torrance, and Calcavecchia and Green, against O'Connor and Rafferty won their foursomes with comfort. Faldo and Woosnam nevertheless remained unbeaten by defeating Wadkins and Stewart and the key game was therefore between the two Spaniards, Ballesteros and Olazabal, against Kite and Strange.

Three up to the Europeans after eleven holes looked highly promising but they made errors at both the twelfth and thirteenth. The last five holes were consequently balanced on a knife edge, particularly so at the seventeenth and eighteenth where Olazabal twice had to play greenside bunker shots, Ballesteros making no mistake with putts that were eminently missable. It was all riveting stuff and the Americans pressed even harder in the afternoon fourballs.

Here Beck and Azinger played some stupendous golf with a better ball of 30 to the turn and yet still only one up on Faldo and Woosnam. Indeed one or other side made birdies at each of the first eleven holes and eighteen between them when the Americans won on the seventeenth green. Of the eighteen birdies Azinger had seven. Kite and McCumber were seven under par in beating Langer and Canizares by the same margin and so too were Ballesteros and Olazabal as they took good care of Calcavecchia and Green. At 2−1 to the Americans, all depended therefore on Strange and Stewart for the point that would square the whole match at 8−8. Furthermore they were one up with four to play against Clark and James.

Paul Azinger plays out of a bunker at the eighteenth. He then holed the putt to beat Seve Ballesteros and America drew first blood in the singles

However, Clark made a birdie at the sixteenth and the par five seventeenth turned into a nightmare hole for the Americans. With Stewart away in the trees with his second shot, James put the pressure on with a three wood second to the edge of the green. Strange, closest of all to the green, then hit a five wood way out to the right as well and though he still scrambled a five via a bunker, it could not match James's chip and putt birdie four. It was a crucial moment and when James hit a fabulous three iron from the edge of the fairway bunker for a four at the last, he had ensured a European lead of 9–7 with only the singles to come.

Though the first game did not go off until 11.30 the crowds were thick around the course hours earlier, lapping up the atmosphere, and soon the cheers were ring-ing out as Ballesteros against Azinger, Olazabal against Stewart, and Rafferty against Calcavecchia, all quickly went two up in the first four games. But then the Americans began to get the holes back,

Azinger square by the sixth, Stewart by the fifth and Calcavecchia by the sixth.

On top of that Kite played marvellous golf against Clark, out in 31 to be six up, his ultimate victory by eight and seven setting a record. Suddenly nothing was going right for the Europeans, at their lowest point only James being ahead against O'Meara. So much seemed to depend on Ballesteros but Azinger was wonderfully resolute in defending a one-hole lead and never more so than at the eighteenth when, having driven into the water, he played a staggering third shot into a greenside bunker and then got up and down for a five which Ballesteros, who had hit his second into the water, could not beat.

Behind him Beck played beautifully to beat Langer and when the first European points arrived, they did so in unlikely manner. Olazabal had a great tussle with Stewart. He squared for the second time at the seventeenth, where he had a birdie, and then won the match at the last as the American followed Azinger by driving into the water, rolling up his waterproof trousers so that he was ankle deep but taking three to get out.

Unbelievably almost, Calcavecchia did the same against Rafferty, compounding the error by then hitting his third into the water as well. It was nonetheless a fine performance by the young Irishman and a great feather in his cap to beat the reigning Open champion. Soon more cheers greeted James's defeat of O'Meara on the sixteenth green and the tide seemed now to be slowly submerging the Americans.

O'Connor was the next European hero, hanging on to Couples as bravely as any man has ever done and at the last, when all square, hitting the two iron of his life to within four feet of the flag. It so unnerved his opponent that Couples, needing only a nine iron, promptly missed the green, took five and conceded the match to O'Connor, who promptly broke down in understandable tears.

Everything seemed to be happening at the eighteenth and now it was Canizares, the old man of the team, who struck the blows that retained the Cup. Again it was the American nerve which faltered for after Canizares had laid a beautifully judged long putt from the back of the green close to the hole, Green three-putted from the front and lost one down. Green had started for home with five consecutive threes but the Spaniard refused to be daunted and both were round in 68.

A television interviewer was swiftly corrected when he mentioned a European

An impromptu rhumba by Jose-Maria Olazabal and (in the white shirt) Jose-Maria Canizares, whose defeat of Ken Green ensured that the Ryder Cup was retained

victory. 'Not yet,' pointed out Tom Kite tersely, and he was right even though there were still four games out on the course. Watson always had the upper hand on Torrance, McCumber just edged out Brand at the eighteenth and all therefore hinged on the last two singles.

Faldo, down most of the way, finally caught Wadkins at the seventeenth but, when he needed just one more good drive, so he too drove into the water at the eighteenth and the dream of a third victory began to fade. For behind him Strange had pitched beautifully for a four at the seventeenth, his third birdie in a row, for the lead against Woosnam. When the American then cracked a glorious two iron second shot to eight feet at the last, Woosnam needed a birdie to square. Even though hitting six clubs less, an eight iron, he could not get it and there was no point in asking Strange even to putt.

Two hands stretched out, not only across an eighteenth green in the middle of England but also across an ocean that bonds as well as separates Europe from the United States.

EUROPE		UNITED STATES
Foursomes (a.m.)		
N. Faldo & I. Woosnam	halved with	T. Kite & C. Strange
H. Clark & M. James	lost to	L. Wadkins & P. Stewart 1 hole
S. Ballesteros & J–M. Olazabal	halved with	T. Watson & C. Beck
B. Langer & R. Rafferty	lost to	M. Calcavecchia & K. Green 2 & 1
Fourballs (p.m.)		
S. Torrance & G. Brand jnr 1 hole	beat	Strange & P. Azinger
Clark & James 3 & 2	beat	F. Couples & Wadkins
Faldo & Woosnam 1 hole	beat	Calcavecchia & M. McCumber
Ballesteros & Olazabal 6 & 5	beat	Watson & M. O'Meara
Foursomes (a.m.)		
Faldo & Woosnam 3 & 2	beat	Wadkins & Stewart
Brand & Torrance	lost to	Azinger & Beck 4 & 3
C. O'Connor jnr & Rafferty	lost to	Calcavecchia & Green 3 & 2
Ballesteros & Olazabal 1 hole	beat	Kite & Strange
Fourballs (p.m.)		
Faldo & Woosnam	lost to	Azinger & Beck 2 & 1
J. M. Canizares & Langer	lost to	Kite & McCumber 2 & 1
Clark & James 1 hole	beat	Stewart & Strange
Ballesteros & Olazabal 4 & 2	beat	Calcavecchia & Green

EUROPE		UNITED STATES
Singles		
Ballesteros	lost to	Azinger 1 hole
Langer	lost to	Beck 3 & 1
Olazabal 1 hole	beat	Stewart
Rafferty 1 hole	beat	Calcavecchia
Clark	lost to	Kite 8 & 7
James 3 & 2	beat	O'Meara
O'Connor 1 hole	beat	Couples
Canizares 1 hole	beat	Green
Brand	lost to	McCumber 1 hole
Torrance	lost to	Watson 3 & 1
Faldo	lost to	Wadkins 1 hole
Woosnam	lost to	Strange 1 hole

Europe 14 — United States 14

How the British/European team has been chosen

1927 Selection committee comprising Harry Vardon, James Braid and J.H. Taylor.

1929 Five-man selection committee.

1931 Three trial matches at Royal Lytham, Frilford Heath and Fulwell. Team then chosen by committee drawn from PGA regions.

1933 Selection committee.

1935 Selection committee.

1937 Selection committee.

1939 Selection committee; match not played because of outbreak of World War II.

1947 Selection committee who drew up short list of fourteen players. Match-play champion to gain place automatically.

1949 Selection committee who agreed to use 'List of Merit' in compiling shortlist of sixteen.

1951 Selection committee who picked eight players; newly constituted order of merit to act as a guide. Final two places delayed until after Match-play championship.

1953 Selection committee drawn from PGA regions replaced by tournament committee; short list of seventeen who played a sequence of trial matches at Wentworth.

1955 Following meeting with tournament players, decided that the first seven places would be filled from the order of merit following the Open championship. Remaining three places to be decided by PGA tournament sub-committee in consultation with players already chosen.

1957 Team to be chosen from points system. Points awarded to top twenty in all stroke-play events, including the Open. Further points to top ten in Dunlop Masters and last sixteen in Match-play championship.

1959 Leading seven players in order of merit automatic. Remaining places filled by Match-play champion and Dunlop Masters champion or, if already qualified, by ballot among team members and PGA sub-committee.

1961 Open champion and Match-play champion to be added to eight selected from order of merit. Stipulation that players must compete in seven of the nine British tournaments to be eligible.

1963 Points system re-introduced. Points awarded to top forty. Open and Match-play champion to gain places automatically. No points for limited-field events such as Dunlop Masters.

1965 Points system to run over two seasons, beginning with: 1964 Open championship through to Esso tournament of 1965. Open champions automatic, remaining places from points system.

1967–69 Same.

1971 Teams increased to twelve-a-side, six to be automatic from order of merit and remaining six chosen by selection committee.

1973 Points system through August 1972 to August 1973. 30 points for all winners of major PGA tournaments, then 24 points, 23, 22 down to one for twenty-fifth place. Eight players to gain selection automatically, four by invitation.

1975 Leading eight players from order of merit (technically the money list); remaining four by invitation from selection committee of three chaired by the captain.

1977 Same.

1979 Leading ten from money list; two by invitation. Team to include players from Continent of Europe.

1981 Same.

1983 Whole team decided on money list.

1985 Leading nine from money list; three at sole discretion of the captain.

1987 Same.

1989 Same.

How the American team has been chosen

1927 All 'homebreds'. Eight players chosen based 'entirely on performance during last three years'. Information compiled by Melvin Taylor of the USGA Executive Committee.

1929 No records found.

1931 Five selected at 1930 annual meeting. Three others chosen from fourteen players invited to compete in 72-hole competition at Scioto week before Ryder Cup.

1933 Team selected by vote of PGA executive committee and section presidents.

1935 Selection based on playing records of previous two years. Automatic qualifiers: Walter Hagen, team captain; Paul Runyan, 1934 PGA champion; Olin Dutra, 1934 US Open champion; Sam Parks, 1935 US Open champion; and six players based on scoring average.

1937 Six chosen; four more added after performance in US Open.

1939 Team announced in May but match cancelled because of World War II.

1941 US Ryder Cup team chosen and played match 23, 24 August at Detroit CC against a team of other prominent professionals under Ryder Cup rules. Challenge team led by Bobby Jones. Jones team, scoring 8½−6½, 'upset'; Jones beat Henry Picard 2 and 1.

1947 Points system used for first time, devised by George Schneiter, chairman of PGA Tournament Committee. Current US Open and PGA champions automatic. Balance of team selected by PGA Executive Committee largely based on points list. Points awarded to top ten in all events, except PGA Championship, where only last eight earned points. Points accrued from 1 January 1946 through 1 September 1947. Winners of PGA Championship and US Open receive 100 points, winner of Masters 95, winner of Western Open 80, winners of all other PGA co-sponsored events 70.

1949 Same.

1951 Same.

1953 PGA Executive committee adds off-year PGA champion Jim Turnesa, 1952, to automatic list, along with 1953 PGA champion, Walter Burkemo. Others from points list.

1955 Same.

1957 Team members must have played in both 1956 and 1957 PGA championships; 1957 PGA champion automatic.

1959 Points standings from 1 August 1957 through 7 September 1959.

1961 Same.

1963 Selection based on two-year points standings through 1963 PGA championship.

1965 Same.

1967 Same.

1969 Teams chosen on points through 1968−69 PGA championship.

1971 Same.

1973 Same.

1975 Same.

1977 Points earned from July 1976 through July 1977. Bonus points for 1976 PGA championship and World Series of Golf. Winners of 1977 PGA championship and World Series automatic.

1979 Top twelve from points list.

1981 Top twelve from points list, plus 1981 PGA champion.

1983 Same.

1985 Based on points from 1 January 1985 through 1985 PGA championship. Bonus points for PGA championship, US Open and Tournament Players championship. Current US Open and PGA champions automatic.

1987 Based on points from 1 January 1986 through 1987 PGA championship. Bonus points awarded for 1986 and 1987 PGA championship. Current US Open and PGA champions automatic.

1989 Bonus points awarded for PGA championship, US Open, British Open and Masters. 1989 PGA champion automatic. US captain given two nominations of his own provided PGA champion already qualified: otherwise one choice.

Sidelights

Most Times on Ryder Cup Teams

GB & I	10 Christy O'Conner	1955 to 1973	Consecutive matches
	10 Dai Rees	1937 to 1961	Played in 9 matches. Selected 1939 – match not played.
USA	9 Sam Snead	1937 to 1959	Played in 7 matches. Selected 1939 and 1941 – matches not played.
	8 Billy Casper	1961 to 1975	Consecutive matches

Most Matches Played

GB & I	40 Neil Coles
USA	37 Billy Casper

Most Matches Won

GB & I/	16 Nick Faldo
EUROPE	14 Peter Oosterhuis
USA	22 Arnold Palmer
	20 Billy Casper

Most Matches Lost

GB & I	21 Neil Coles
	21 Christy O'Connor
USA	13 Ray Floyd
	10 Billy Casper

Most Matches Halved

GB & I/	8 Tony Jacklin
EUROPE	7 Neil Coles
USA	8 Gene Littler
	7 Billy Casper

Largest Winning Margin by Team

USA	1947 11−1	at Portland, Oregon	36-hole matches
	1967 23½−8½	at Houston, Texas	18-hole matches
GB & I	1957 7½−4½	at Lindrick, England	36-hole matches
EUROPE	1985 16½−11½	at The Belfry, England	18-hole matches

Largest Margin of Victory in Individual Matches

Over 36 holes (1927−1959)

Foursomes	1931 10 and 9	Walter Hagen and Densmore Shute (USA) over George Duncan and Arthur Havers (GB & I)
	1947 10 and 9	Lew Worsham and Ed Oliver (USA) over Henry Cotton and Arthur Lees (GB & I)
Singles	1929 10 and 8	George Duncan (GB & I) over Walter Hagen (USA)
	1929 9 and 8	Leo Diegel (USA) over Abe Mitchell (GB & I)
	1933 9 and 8	Abe Mitchell (GB & I) over Olin Dutra (USA)

Over 18 holes (1961 to date)

Foursomes	1979 7 and 6	Hale Irwin and Tom Kite (USA) over Ken Brown and Des Smyth (Europe)
	1983 7 and 5	Lanny Wadkins and Gil Morgan (USA) over Sam Torrance and Jose-Maria Canizares (Europe)
	1985 7 and 5	Jose-Maria Canizares and Jose Rivero (Europe) over Tom Kite and Calvin Peete (USA)
Fourballs	1981 7 and 5	Lee Trevino and Jerry Pate (USA) over Nick Faldo and Sam Torrance (Europe)
	1989 8 and 7	Tom Kite (USA) over Howard Clark (Europe)
Singles	1969 7 and 6	Miller Barber (USA) over Maurice Bembridge (GB & I)
	1971 7 and 6	Lee Trevino (USA) over Brian Huggett (GB & I)

Most Consecutive Team Victories

7 BY THE UNITED STATES 1935−55
7 BY THE UNITED STATES 1971−83

Teams Winning all the Foursomes or Fourballs Form of the Matches

1947 USA won the Foursomes 4−0
1963 USA won the second series of Foursomes 4−0
1975 USA won the first series of Foursomes 4−0
1981 USA won the second series of Foursomes 4−0
1967 USA won the first series of Fourballs 4−0
1971 USA won the first series of Fourballs 4−0
1987 EUROPE won the first series of Fourballs 4−0
1989 EUROPE won the first series of Fourballs 4−0

Oldest Competitors

GB & I	Ted Ray 1927	50 years 2 months 5 days	
	Christy O'Connor 1973	48 years 8 months 30 days	
USA	Don January 1977	47 years 9 months 26 days	
	Julius Boros 1967	47 years 7 months 17 days	

Youngest Competitors

GB & I	Nick Faldo 1977	20 years 1 month 28 days
Europe	Paul Way 1983	20 years 7 months 2 days
GB & I	Bernard Gallacher 1969	20 years 7 months 9 days
USA	Horton Smith 1929	21 years 0 months 4 days

Years	Format
1927−1959	Two days, 36-hole matches, four foursomes and eight singles. 12 points available
1961	Two days, matches reduced to 18 holes, two series of four foursomes day one, two series of eight singles day two. 24 points available
1963−71	Three days, addition of two series of four fourball matches: Day one−two series of four foursomes. Day two−two series of four fourballs. Day Three−two series of eight singles. 32 points available
1973−75	One series of four foursomes and one of four fourballs on each of the first two days. Day three−two series of eight singles. 32 points available
1977	Day one−five foursomes. Day two−five fourballs. Day three−ten singles. 20 points available
1979	(European team with inclusion of continentals) Days one and two−four foursomes and four fourball matches each day. Day three−two series of six singles. 28 points available
1981−	Days one and two as for 1979 match. Day three−twelve singles. 28 points available

Ryder Cup Captains

Year	Great Britain & Ireland/Europe	United States of America		Year	Great Britain & Ireland/Europe	United States of America
1927	Ted Ray	Walter Hagen		1961	Dai Rees	Jerry Barber
1929	George Duncan	Walter Hagen				[3]Ed Oliver
1931	Charles Whitcombe	Walter Hagen		1963	[1]John Fallon	Arnold Palmer
1933	[1]J.H. Taylor	Walter Hagen		1965	[1]Harry Weetman	[1]Byron Nelson
1935	Charles Whitcombe	Walter Hagen		1967	[1]Dai Rees	[1]Ben Hogan
1937	Charles Whitcombe	[1]Walter Hagen		1969	[1]Eric Brown	[1]Sam Snead
[2]1939		Walter Hagen		1971	[1]Eric Brown	[1]Jay Hebert
		[3]Vic Ghezzi		1973	[1]Bernard Hunt	[1]Jack Burke Jnr
[2]1941		Walter Hagen		1975	[1]Bernard Hunt	[1]Arnold Palmer
1947	Henry Cotton	Ben Hogan		1977	[1]Brian Huggett	[1]Dow Finsterwald
		[3]Walter Hagen		1979	[1]John Jacobs	[1]Billy Casper
		[3]Craig Wood		1981	[1]John Jacobs	[1]Dave Marr
1949	[1]Charles Whitcombe	[1]Ben Hogan		1983	[1]Tony Jacklin	[1]Jack Nicklaus
		[3]Ed Dudley		1985	[1]Tony Jacklin	[1]Lee Trevino
1951	[1]Arthur Lacey	Sam Snead		1987	[1]Tony Jacklin	[1]Jack Nicklaus
1953	[1]Henry Cotton	Lloyd Mangrum		1989	[1]Tony Jacklin	[1]Raymond Floyd
1955	Dai Rees	Chick Harbert				
		[3]Lloyd Mangrum				
1957	Dai Rees	Jack Burke Jnr				
1959	Dai Rees	Sam Snead				

Notes

[1] Non-playing captain. [2] USA teams selected but no matches played. GB & I named eight players only for the proposed 1939 match. [3] Honorary captain

Match Results

Dates played	Venues	Winners	Winners' score	Losers' score
3, 4 June 1927	Worcester Country Club, Worcester, Massachusetts	USA	9½	2½
26, 27 May 1929	Moortown Golf Club, Leeds, England	GB & I	7	5
26, 27 June 1931	Scioto Country Club, Columbus, Ohio	USA	9	3
26, 27 June 1933	Southport and Ainsdale Golf Club, Southport, England	GB & I	6½	5½
28, 29 Sept 1935	Ridgewood Country Club, Ridgewood, New Jersey	USA	9	3
29, 30 June 1937	Southport and Ainsdale Golf Club, Southport, England	USA	8	4

(Ryder Cup not contested in 1939, 1941, 1943 and 1945 as a result of World War II)

Dates played	Venues	Winners	Winners' score	Losers' score
1, 2 Nov. 1947	Portland Golf Club, Portland, Oregon	USA	11	1
16, 17 Sept. 1949	Ganton Golf Club, Scarborough, England	USA	7	5
2, 4 Nov. 1951	Pinehurst Country Club, Pinehurst, North Carolina	USA	9½	2½
2, 3 Oct. 1953	Wentworth Golf Club, Virginia Water, England	USA	6½	5½
5, 6 Nov. 1955	Thunderbird Ranch and Country Club, Palm Springs, California	USA	8	4
4, 5 Oct. 1957	Lindrick Golf Club, Sheffield, England	GB & I	7½	4½
6, 7 Nov. 1959	Eldorado Country Club, Palm Desert, California	USA	8½	3½
13, 14 Oct. 1961	Royal Lytham and St Anne's Golf Club, St Anne's, England	USA	14½	9½
11, 12, 13 Oct. 1963	East Lake Country Club, Atlanta, Georgia	USA	23	9
7, 8, 9 Oct. 1965	Royal Birkdale Golf Club, Southport, England	USA	19½	12½
20, 21, 22 Oct. 1967	Champions Golf Club, Houston, Texas	USA	23½	8½
18, 19, 20 Sept. 1969	Royal Birkdale Golf Club, Southport, England	(Tie)	16	16
16, 17, 18 Sept. 1971	Old Warson Country Club, St Louis, Missouri	USA	18½	13½
20, 21, 22 Sept. 1973	The Honourable Company of Edinburgh Golfers, Muirfield, Scotland	USA	19	13
19, 20, 21 Sept. 1975	Laurel Valley Golf Club, Ligonier, Pennsylvania	USA	21	11
15, 16, 17 Sept. 1977	Royal Lytham and St Anne's Golf Club, St Anne's, England	USA	12½	7½
14, 15, 16 Sept. 1979	The Greenbrier, White Sulphur Springs, West Virginia	USA	17	11
18, 19, 20 Sept. 1981	Walton Health Golf Club, Tadworth, England	USA	18½	9½
14, 15, 16 Oct. 1983	PGA National Golf Club, Palm Beach Gardens, Florida	USA	14½	13½
13, 14, 15 Sept. 1985	The Belfry, Sutton Coldfield, England	EUROPE	16½	11½
25, 26, 27 Sept. 1987	Muirfield Village Golf Club, Dublin, Ohio	EUROPE	15	13
22, 23, 24 Sept. 1989	The Belfry, Sutton Coldfield, England	EUROPE	14	14

United States 21 wins, Great Britain & Ireland/Europe 5 wins, two tied matches

Ryder Cup Appearance Analysis
Great Britain & Ireland/Europe

Name	Years	No.	matches played				Singles				Foursomes				Fourballs			
			P	W	L	H	P	W	L	H	P	W	L	H	P	W	L	H
Jimmy Adams	39 47 49 51 53	5	7	2	5	0	3	1	2	0	4	1	3	0	0	0	0	0
Percy Alliss	29* 33 35 37	4	6	3	2	1	3	2	1	0	3	1	1	1	0	0	0	0
Peter Alliss	53 57 59 61 63 65 67 69	8	30	10	15	5	12	5	4	3	11	4	6	1	7	1	5	1
Laurie Ayton	49*	1	0	0	0	0	0	0	0	0	0	0	0	0	0	0	0	0
Severiano Ballesteros	79 83 85 87 89	5	25	13	8	4	5	1	2	2	10	7	2	1	10	5	4	1
Harry Bannerman	71	1	5	2	2	1	2	1	0	1	1	1	0	0	2	0	2	0
Brian Barnes	69 71 73 75 77 79	6	25	10	14	1	10	5	5	0	6	2	4	0	9	3	5	1
Maurice Bembridge	69 71 73 75	4	16	5	8	3	5	1	3	1	8	3	5	0	3	1	0	2
Aubrey Boomer	27 29	2	4	2	2	0	2	1	1	0	2	1	1	0	0	0	0	0
Ken Bousfield	49 51 55* 57 59 61	6	10	5	5	0	4	2	2	0	6	3	3	0	0	0	0	0
Hugh Boyle	67	1	3	0	3	0	1	0	1	0	1	0	1	0	1	0	1	0
Harry Bradshaw	53 55 57	3	5	2	2	1	3	1	1	1	2	1	1	0	0	0	0	0
Gordon Brand Jnr	87 89	2	7	2	4	1	2	0	1	1	2	0	2	0	3	2	1	0
Gordon J Brand	83	1	1	0	1	0	1	0	1	0	0	0	0	0	0	0	0	0
Eric Brown	53 55 57 59	4	8	4	4	0	4	4	0	0	4	0	4	0	0	0	0	0
Ken Brown	77 79 83 85 87	5	13	4	9	0	4	2	2	0	5	1	4	0	4	1	3	0
Stewart Burns	29*	1	0	0	0	0	0	0	0	0	0	0	0	0	0	0	0	0
Richard Burton	35 37 39 49	4	5	2	3	0	3	0	3	0	2	2	0	0	0	0	0	0
Jack Busson	35	1	2	0	2	0	1	0	1	0	1	0	1	0	0	0	0	0
Peter Butler	65 69 71 73	4	14	3	9	2	5	2	3	0	5	1	4	0	4	0	2	2
Jose-Maria Canizares	81 83 85 89	4	11	5	4	2	4	2	1	1	3	2	1	0	4	1	2	1
Alex Caygill	69	1	1	0	0	1	0	0	0	0	0	0	0	0	1	0	0	1
Clive Clark	73	1	1	0	1	0	0	0	0	0	0	0	0	0	1	0	1	0
Howard Clark	77 81 85 87 89	5	13	6	6	1	5	3	2	0	3	0	3	0	5	3	1	1
Neil Coles	61 63 65 67 69 71 73 77	8	40	12	21	7	15	5	6	4	13	4	8	1	12	3	7	2
Archie Compston	27 29 31	3	6	1	4	1	3	1	2	0	3	0	2	1	0	0	0	0
Henry Cotton	29 37 39 47	4	6	2	4	0	3	2	1	0	3	0	3	0	0	0	0	0
Bill Cox	35 37	2	3	0	2	1	1	0	0	1	2	0	2	0	0	0	0	0
Allan Dailey	33*	1	0	0	0	0	0	0	0	0	0	0	0	0	0	0	0	0
Fred Daly	47 49 51 53	4	8	3	4	1	4	1	2	1	4	2	2	0	0	0	0	0
Eamonn Darcy	75 77 81 87	4	11	1	8	2	4	1	3	0	2	0	1	1	5	0	4	1
William Davies	31 33	2	4	2	2	0	2	1	1	0	2	1	1	0	0	0	0	0
Peter Dawson	77	1	3	1	2	0	1	1	0	0	1	0	1	0	1	0	1	0
Norman Drew	59	1	1	0	0	1	1	0	0	1	0	0	0	0	0	0	0	0
George Duncan	27 29 31	3	5	2	3	0	2	2	0	0	3	0	3	0	0	0	0	0
Syd Easterbrook	31 33	2	3	2	1	0	1	1	0	0	2	1	1	0	0	0	0	0
Nick Faldo	77 79 81 83 85 87 89	7	27	16	9	2	7	4	3	0	10	6	2	2	10	6	4	0
John Fallon	55	1	1	1	0	0	0	0	0	0	1	1	0	0	0	0	0	0
Max Faulkner	47 49 51 53 57	5	8	1	7	0	4	0	4	0	4	1	3	0	0	0	0	0
George Gadd	27*	1	0	0	0	0	0	0	0	0	0	0	0	0	0	0	0	0
Bernard Gallacher	69 71 73 75 77 79 81 83	8	31	13	13	5	11	4	3	4	11	5	6	0	9	4	4	1
John Garner	71 73*	2	1	0	1	0	0	0	0	0	0	0	0	0	1	0	1	0
Antonio Garrido	79	1	5	1	4	0	1	0	1	0	2	1	1	0	2	0	2	0
Eric Green	47*	1	0	0	0	0	0	0	0	0	0	0	0	0	0	0	0	0
Malcolm Gregson	67	1	4	0	4	0	2	0	2	0	1	0	1	0	1	0	1	0
Tom Haliburton	61 63	2	6	0	6	0	2	0	2	0	3	0	3	0	1	0	1	0
Jack Hargreaves	51*	1	0	0	0	0	0	0	0	0	0	0	0	0	0	0	0	0

Name	Selections Years	No.	matches played				Singles				Foursomes				Fourballs			
			P	W	L	H	P	W	L	H	P	W	L	H	P	W	L	H
Arthur Havers	27 31 33	3	6	3	3	0	3	2	1	0	3	1	2	0	0	0	0	0
Jimmy Hitchcock	65	1	3	0	3	0	2	0	2	0	1	0	1	0	0	0	0	0
Bert Hodson	31	1	1	0	1	0	1	0	1	0	0	0	0	0	0	0	0	0
Reg Horne	47*	1	0	0	0	0	0	0	0	0	0	0	0	0	0	0	0	0
Tommy Horton	75 77	2	8	1	6	1	3	1	1	1	2	0	2	0	3	0	3	0
Brian Huggett	63 67 69 71 73 75	6	25	9	10	6	7	3	3	1	10	5	3	2	8	1	4	3
Bernard Hunt	53 57 59 61 63 65 67 69	8	28	6	16	6	10	4	3	3	11	1	9	1	7	1	4	2
Geoffrey Hunt	63	1	3	0	3	0	1	0	1	0	1	0	1	0	1	0	1	0
Guy Hunt	75	1	3	0	2	1	1	0	1	0	1	0	1	0	1	0	0	1
Tony Jacklin	67 69 71 73 75 77 79	7	35	13	14	8	11	2	8	1	13	8	1	4	11	3	5	3
John Jacobs	55	1	2	2	0	0	1	1	0	0	1	1	0	0	0	0	0	0
Mark James	77 79 81 89	4	14	5	8	1	4	1	2	1	4	1	3	0	6	3	3	0
Edward Jarman	35	1	1	0	1	0	0	0	0	0	1	0	1	0	0	0	0	0
Herbert Jolly	27	1	2	0	2	0	1	0	1	0	1	0	1	0	0	0	0	0
Michael King	79	1	1	0	1	0	1	0	1	0	0	0	0	0	0	0	0	0
Sam King	37 39 47 49	4	5	1	3	1	3	1	1	1	2	0	2	0	0	0	0	0
Arthur Lacey	33 37	2	3	0	3	0	2	0	2	0	1	0	1	0	0	0	0	0
Bernhard Langer	81 83 85 87 89	5	22	10	8	4	5	2	1	2	9	4	5	0	8	4	2	2
Arthur Lees	47 49 51 55	4	8	4	4	0	4	2	2	0	4	2	2	0	0	0	0	0
Sandy Lyle	79 81 83 85 87	5	18	7	9	2	5	1	4	0	7	3	3	1	6	3	2	1
Jimmy Martin	65	1	1	0	1	0	0	0	0	0	1	0	1	0	0	0	0	0
Peter Mills	57 59*	2	1	1	0	0	1	1	0	0	0	0	0	0	0	0	0	0
Abe Mitchell	27** 29 31 33	4	6	4	2	0	3	1	2	0	3	3	0	0	0	0	0	0
Ralph Moffitt	61	1	1	0	1	0	1	0	1	0	0	0	0	0	0	0	0	0
Christy O' Connor Jnr	75 89	2	4	1	3	0	1	1	0	0	2	0	2	0	1	0	1	0
Christy O'Connor	55 57 59 61 63 65 67 69 71 73	10	36	11	21	4	14	2	10	2	13	6	6	1	9	3	5	1
Jose-Maria Olazabal	87 89	2	10	7	2	1	2	1	1	0	4	3	0	1	4	3	1	0
John O'Leary	75	1	4	0	4	0	1	0	1	0	2	0	2	0	1	0	1	0
Peter Oosterhuis	71 73 75 77 79 81	6	28	14	11	3	9	6	2	1	10	3	6	1	9	5	3	1
Alf Padgham	33 35 37 39	4	6	0	6	0	3	0	3	0	3	0	3	0	0	0	0	0
John Panton	51 53 61	3	5	0	5	0	1	0	1	0	4	0	4	0	0	0	0	0
Alf Perry	33 35 37	3	4	0	3	1	2	0	1	1	2	0	2	0	0	0	0	0
Manuel Pinero	81 85	2	9	6	3	0	2	2	0	0	4	2	2	0	3	2	1	0
Lionel Platts	65	1	5	1	2	2	2	1	1	0	1	0	1	0	2	0	0	2
Eddie Pollard	73	1	2	0	2	0	0	0	0	0	1	0	1	0	1	0	1	0
Ted Ray	27	1	2	0	2	0	1	0	1	0	1	0	1	0	0	0	0	0
Ronan Rafferty	89	1	3	1	2	0	1	1	0	0	2	0	2	0	0	0	0	0
Dai Rees	37 39 47 49 51 53 55 57 59 61	10	18	7	10	1	10	5	5	0	8	2	5	1	0	0	0	0
Jose Rivero	85 87	2	5	2	3	0	2	0	2	0	2	1	1	0	1	1	0	0
Fred Robson	27 29 31	3	6	2	4	0	3	0	3	0	3	2	1	0	0	0	0	0
Syd Scott	55	1	2	0	2	0	1	0	1	0	1	0	1	0	0	0	0	0
Des Smyth	79 81	2	7	2	5	0	2	0	2	0	3	1	2	0	2	1	1	0
Dave Thomas	59 63 65 67	4	18	3	10	5	5	0	4	1	7	3	2	2	6	0	4	2
Sam Torrance	81 83 85 87 89	5	18	4	10	4	5	1	2	2	6	1	5	0	7	2	3	2
Peter Townsend	69 71	2	11	3	8	0	3	0	3	0	4	2	2	0	4	1	3	0
Brian Waites	83	1	4	1	3	0	1	0	1	0	1	0	1	0	2	1	1	0
Charles Ward	47 49 51	3	6	1	5	0	3	0	3	0	3	1	2	0	0	0	0	0
Paul Way	83 85	2	9	6	2	1	2	2	0	0	3	1	2	0	4	3	0	1
Harry Weetman	51 53 55 57 59 61 63	7	15	2	11	2	8	2	6	0	6	0	4	2	1	0	1	0
Charles Whitcombe	27 29 31 33 35 37 39	7	9	3	2	4	4	1	2	1	5	2	0	3	0	0	0	0
Ernest Whitcombe	29 31 35	3	6	1	4	1	3	0	2	1	3	1	2	0	0	0	0	0

Name	Selections Years	No.	matches played P W L H	Singles P W L H	Foursomes P W L H	Fourballs P W L H
Reg Whitcombe	35 39	2	1 0 1 0	1 0 1 0	0 0 0 0	0 0 0 0
George Will	63 65 67	3	15 2 11 2	4 0 3 1	6 2 3 1	5 0 5 0
Norman Wood	75	1	3 1 2 0	1 1 0 0	1 0 1 0	1 0 1 0
Ian Woosnam	83 85 87 89	4	17 7 7 3	4 0 4 0	5 2 1 2	8 5 2 1
Totals		310	870 292 471 107	314 104 169 41	338 116 192 30	218 72 110 36

Notes:
* Denotes selected and present but did not participate in the matches
** In 1927 Abe Mitchell was selected but was ill and did not travel to the USA

Ryder Cup Appearance Analysis United States of America

Name	Selections Years	No.	matches played P W L H	Singles P W L H	Foursomes P W L H	Fourballs P W L H
Tommy Aaron	69 73	2	6 1 4 1	2 0 2 0	2 1 1 0	2 0 1 1
Skip Alexander	49 51	2	2 1 1 0	1 1 0 0	1 0 1 0	0 0 0 0
Paul Azinger	89	1	4 3 1 0	1 1 0 0	2 1 0 1	1 1 0 0
Jerry Barber	55 61	2	5 1 4 0	3 0 3 0	2 1 1 0	0 0 0 0
Miller Barber	69 71	2	7 1 4 2	2 1 1 0	3 0 3 0	2 0 0 2
Herman Barron	47	1	1 1 0 0	0 0 0 0	1 1 0 0	0 0 0 0
Andy Bean	79 87	2	6 4 2 0	2 2 0 0	1 0 1 0	3 2 1 0
Frank Beard	69 71	2	8 2 3 3	2 0 1 1	3 0 2 1	3 2 0 1
Chip Beck	89	1	4 3 1 0	1 1 0 0	2 1 0 1	1 1 0 0
Homero Blancas	73	1	4 2 1 1	2 1 1 0	0 0 0 0	2 1 0 1
Tommy Bolt	55 57	2	4 3 1 0	2 1 1 0	2 2 0 0	0 0 0 0
Julius Boros	59 63 65 67	4	16 9 3 4	6 3 2 1	7 5 0 2	3 1 1 1
Gay Brewer	67 73	2	9 5 3 1	4 2 1 1	1 0 1 0	4 3 1 0
Billy Burke	31 33	2	3 3 0 0	1 1 0 0	2 2 0 0	0 0 0 0
Jack Burke Jnr	51 53 55 57 59*	5	8 7 1 0	4 3 1 0	4 4 0 0	0 0 0 0
Walter Burkemo	53	1	1 0 1 0	0 0 0 0	1 0 1 0	0 0 0 0
Mark Calcavecchia	87 89	2	7 3 4 0	2 1 1 0	2 2 0 0	3 0 3 0
Billy Casper	61 63 65 67 69 71 73 75	8	37 20 10 7	10 6 2 2	15 8 5 2	12 6 3 3
Bill Collins	61	1	3 1 2 0	1 0 1 0	2 1 1 0	0 0 0 0
Charles Coody	71	1	3 0 2 1	1 0 1 0	1 0 1 0	1 0 0 1
Fred Couples	89	1	2 0 2 0	1 0 1 0	0 0 0 0	1 0 1 0
Wilfred Cox	31	1	2 2 0 0	1 1 0 0	1 1 0 0	0 0 0 0
Ben Crenshaw	81 83 87	3	9 3 5 1	3 2 1 0	2 1 1 0	4 0 3 1
Jimmy Demaret	41 47 49 51	4	6 6 0 0	3 3 0 0	3 3 0 0	0 0 0 0
Gardner Dickinson	67 71	2	10 9 1 0	3 2 1 0	4 4 0 0	3 3 0 0
Leo Diegel	27 29 31 33	4	6 3 3 0	3 2 1 0	3 1 2 0	0 0 0 0
Dave Douglas	53	1	2 1 0 1	1 0 0 1	1 1 0 0	0 0 0 0

Name	Selections Years	No.	matches played				Singles				Foursomes				Fourballs			
			P	W	L	H	P	W	L	H	P	W	L	H	P	W	L	H
Dale Douglass	69	1	2	0	2	0	1	0	1	0	0	0	0	0	1	0	1	0
Ed Dudley	29 33 37	3	4	3	1	0	1	1	0	0	3	2	1	0	0	0	0	0
Olin Dutra	33 35	2	4	1	3	0	2	1	1	0	2	0	2	0	0	0	0	0
Lee Elder	79	1	4	1	3	0	1	0	1	0	1	0	1	0	2	1	1	0
Al Espinosa	27* 29 31	3	4	2	1	1	2	1	0	1	2	1	1	0	0	0	0	0
Johnny Farrell	27 29 31	3	6	3	2	1	3	1	2	0	3	2	0	1	0	0	0	0
Dow Finsterwald	57 59 61 63	4	13	9	3	1	6	3	3	0	5	4	0	1	2	2	0	0
Ray Floyd	69 75 77 81 83 85	6	23	7	13	3	6	3	3	0	8	2	6	0	9	2	4	3
Doug Ford	55 57 59 61	4	9	4	4	1	5	2	2	1	4	2	2	0	0	0	0	0
Ed Furgol	57	1	1	0	1	0	1	0	1	0	0	0	0	0	0	0	0	0
Marty Furgol	55	1	1	0	1	0	1	0	1	0	0	0	0	0	0	0	0	0
Al Geiberger	67 75	2	9	5	1	3	3	2	0	1	3	2	1	0	3	1	0	2
Vic Ghezzi	39 41	2	0	0	0	0	0	0	0	0	0	0	0	0	0	0	0	0
Bob Gilder	83	1	4	2	2	0	1	1	0	0	2	0	2	0	1	1	0	0
Bob Goalby	63	1	5	3	1	1	2	2	0	0	1	1	0	0	2	0	1	1
Johnny Golden	27 29	2	3	3	0	0	1	1	0	0	2	2	0	0	0	0	0	0
Lou Graham	73 75 77	3	9	5	3	1	2	1	1	0	4	1	2	1	3	3	0	0
Hubert Green	77 79 85	3	7	4	3	0	3	3	0	0	1	0	1	0	3	1	2	0
Ken Green	89	1	4	2	2	0	1	0	1	0	2	2	0	0	1	0	1	0
Ralph Guldahl	37 39	2	2	2	0	0	1	1	0	0	1	1	0	0	0	0	0	0
Fred Haas Jnr	53	1	1	0	1	0	1	0	1	0	0	0	0	0	0	0	0	0
Jay Haas	83	1	4	2	1	1	1	0	1	0	1	1	0	0	2	1	0	1
Walter Hagen	27 29 31 33 35	5	9	7	1	1	4	3	1	0	5	4	0	1	0	0	0	0
Bob Hamilton	49	1	2	0	2	0	1	0	1	0	1	0	1	0	0	0	0	0
Chick Harbert	49 55	2	2	2	0	0	2	2	0	0	0	0	0	0	0	0	0	0
Chandler Harper	55	1	1	0	1	0	0	0	0	0	1	0	1	0	0	0	0	0
E.J. 'Dutch' Harrison	47 49 51*	3	3	2	1	0	2	2	0	0	1	0	1	0	0	0	0	0
Fred Hawkins	57	1	2	1	1	0	1	1	0	0	1	0	1	0	0	0	0	0
Mark Hayes	79**	1	3	1	2	0	1	1	0	0	1	0	1	0	1	0	1	0
Clayton Heafner	49 51	2	4	3	0	1	2	1	0	1	2	2	0	0	0	0	0	0
Jay Hebert	59 61	2	4	2	1	1	2	0	1	1	2	2	0	0	0	0	0	0
Lionel Hebert	57	1	1	0	1	0	1	0	1	0	0	0	0	0	0	0	0	0
Dave Hill	69 73 77	3	9	6	3	0	3	3	0	0	3	1	2	0	3	2	1	0
Jimmy Hines	39	1	0	0	0	0	0	0	0	0	0	0	0	0	0	0	0	0
Ben Hogan	41 47 51	3	3	3	0	0	1	1	0	0	2	2	0	0	0	0	0	0
Hale Irwin	75 77 79 81	4	16	11	4	1	5	3	1	1	5	4	1	0	6	4	2	0
Tommy Jacobs	65	1	4	3	1	0	2	1	1	0	0	0	0	0	2	2	0	0
Peter Jacobsen	85	1	3	1	2	0	1	0	1	0	1	1	0	0	1	0	1	0
Don January	65 77	2	7	2	3	2	2	0	1	1	3	0	2	1	2	2	0	0
Herman Keiser	47	1	1	0	1	0	1	0	1	0	0	0	0	0	0	0	0	0
Tom Kite	79 81 83 85 87 89	6	24	13	7	4	6	4	0	2	11	6	4	1	7	3	3	1
Ted Kroll	53 55 57	3	4	3	1	0	1	0	1	0	3	3	0	0	0	0	0	0
Ky Laffoon	35	1	1	0	1	0	1	0	1	0	0	0	0	0	0	0	0	0
Tony Lema	63 65	2	11	8	1	2	4	3	0	1	4	3	0	1	3	2	1	0
Bruce Lietzke	81	1	3	0	2	1	1	0	0	1	1	0	1	0	1	0	1	0
Gene Littler	61 63 65 67 69 71 75	7	27	14	5	8	10	5	2	3	8	4	3	1	9	5	0	4
Mark McCumber	89	1	3	2	1	0	1	1	0	0	0	0	0	0	2	1	1	0
Jerry McGee	77	1	2	1	1	0	1	0	1	0	1	1	0	0	0	0	0	0
Harold McSpaden	39 41	2	0	0	0	0	0	0	0	0	0	0	0	0	0	0	0	0
John Mahaffey	79	1	3	1	2	0	1	1	0	0	1	0	1	0	1	0	1	0
Tony Manero	37	1	2	1	1	0	1	0	1	0	1	1	0	0	0	0	0	0
Lloyd Mangrum	41 47 49 51 53	5	8	6	2	0	4	3	1	0	4	3	1	0	0	0	0	0
Dave Marr	65	1	6	4	2	0	2	2	0	0	2	1	1	0	2	1	1	0

Name	Selections Years	No.	matches played				Singles				Foursomes				Fourballs			
			P	W	L	H	P	W	L	H	P	W	L	H	P	W	L	H
Billy Maxwell	63	1	4	4	0	0	1	1	0	0	1	1	0	0	2	2	0	0
Dick Mayer	57	1	2	1	0	1	1	0	0	1	1	1	0	0	0	0	0	0
Bill Mehlhorn	27	1	2	1	1	0	1	1	0	0	1	0	1	0	0	0	0	0
Dick Metz	39	1	0	0	0	0	0	0	0	0	0	0	0	0	0	0	0	0
Cary Middlecoff	53 55 59	3	6	2	3	1	3	1	2	0	3	1	1	1	0	0	0	0
Johnny Miller	75 81	2	6	2	2	2	2	0	2	0	2	2	0	0	2	0	0	2
Larry Mize	87	1	4	1	1	2	1	0	0	1	2	0	1	1	1	1	0	0
Gil Morgan	79 83	2	6	1	2	3	2	0	1	1	2	1	0	1	2	0	1	1
Bob Murphy	75	1	4	2	1	1	2	2	0	0	1	0	1	0	1	0	0	1
Byron Nelson	37 39 41 47	4	4	3	1	0	2	1	1	0	2	2	0	0	0	0	0	0
Larry Nelson	79 81 87	3	13	9	3	1	3	2	0	1	6	4	2	0	4	3	1	0
Bobby Nichols	67	1	5	4	0	1	2	1	0	1	2	2	0	0	1	1	0	0
Jack Nicklaus	69 71 73 75 77 81	6	28	17	8	3	10	4	4	2	9	8	1	0	9	5	3	1
Andy North	85	1	3	0	3	0	1	0	1	0	0	0	0	0	2	0	2	0
Ed Oliver	47 51 53	3	5	3	2	0	2	1	1	0	3	2	1	0	0	0	0	0
Mark O'Meara	85 89	2	5	1	4	0	2	0	2	0	1	0	1	0	2	1	1	0
Arnold Palmer	61 63 65 67 71 73	6	32	22	8	2	11	6	3	2	12	9	3	0	9	7	2	0
Johnny Palmer	49	1	2	0	2	0	1	0	1	0	1	0	1	0	0	0	0	0
Sam Parks Jnr	35	1	1	0	0	1	1	0	0	1	0	0	0	0	0	0	0	0
Jerry Pate	81	1	4	2	2	0	1	0	1	0	1	1	0	0	2	1	1	0
Calvin Peete	83 85	2	7	4	2	1	2	2	0	0	3	2	1	0	2	0	1	1
Henry Picard	35 37 39	3	4	3	1	0	2	2	0	0	2	1	1	0	0	0	0	0
Dan Pohl	87	1	3	1	2	0	1	0	1	0	1	1	0	0	1	0	1	0
Johnny Pott	63 65* 67	3	7	5	2	0	2	1	1	0	3	2	1	0	2	2	0	0
Dave Ragan	63	1	4	2	1	1	1	1	0	0	1	1	0	0	2	0	1	1
Henry Ransom	51	1	1	0	1	0	0	0	0	0	1	0	1	0	0	0	0	0
Johnny Revolta	35 37	2	3	2	1	0	1	1	0	0	2	1	1	0	0	0	0	0
Juan Rodriguez	73	1	2	0	1	1	0	0	0	0	2	0	1	1	0	0	0	0
Bill Rogers	81	1	4	1	2	1	1	0	0	1	2	1	1	0	1	0	1	0
Bob Rosburg	59	1	2	2	0	0	1	1	0	0	1	1	0	0	0	0	0	0
Mason Rudolph	71	1	3	1	1	1	1	0	1	0	1	0	0	1	1	1	0	0
Paul Runyan	33 35 39	3	4	2	2	0	2	1	1	0	2	1	1	0	0	0	0	0
Doug Sanders	67	1	5	2	3	0	2	0	2	0	1	0	1	0	2	2	0	0
Gene Sarazen	27 29 31 33 35 37 41	7	12	7	2	3	6	4	1	1	6	3	1	2	0	0	0	0
Densmore Shute	31 33 37	3	6	2	2	2	3	1	1	1	3	1	1	1	0	0	0	0
Dan Sikes	69	1	3	2	1	0	1	1	0	0	1	1	0	0	1	0	1	0
Scott Simpson	87	1	2	1	1	0	1	1	0	0	0	0	0	0	1	0	1	0
Horton Smith	29 31* 33 35 37* 39 41	7	4	3	0	1	3	2	0	1	1	1	0	0	0	0	0	0
Jesse 'J.C.' Snead	71 73 75	3	11	9	2	0	4	3	1	0	3	2	1	0	4	4	0	0
Sam Snead	37 39 41 47 49 51 53 55 59	9	13	10	2	1	7	6	1	0	6	4	1	1	0	0	0	0
Ed Sneed	77	1	2	1	0	1	0	0	0	0	1	0	0	1	1	1	0	0
Mike Souchak	59 61	2	6	5	1	0	3	3	0	0	3	2	1	0	0	0	0	0
Craig Stadler	83 85	2	8	4	2	2	2	2	0	0	3	1	2	0	3	1	0	2
Payne Stewart	87 89	2	8	3	5	0	2	1	1	0	4	1	3	0	2	1	1	0
Ken Still	69	1	3	1	2	0	1	0	1	0	1	0	1	0	1	1	0	0
Dave Stockton	71 77	2	5	3	1	1	2	1	0	1	2	1	1	0	1	1	0	0
Curtis Strange	83 85 87 89	4	17	6	9	2	4	2	2	0	7	4	2	1	6	0	5	1
Hal Sutton	85 87	2	9	3	3	3	2	0	1	1	4	2	1	1	3	1	1	1
Lee Trevino	69 71 73 75 79 81	6	30	17	7	6	10	6	2	2	10	5	3	2	10	6	2	2
Jim Turnesa	53	1	1	1	0	0	1	1	0	0	0	0	0	0	0	0	0	0
Joe Turnesa	27 29	2	4	1	2	1	2	0	2	0	2	1	0	1	0	0	0	0
Ken Venturi	65	1	4	1	3	0	1	0	1	0	2	0	2	0	1	1	0	0

RYDER CUP APPEARANCE ANALYSIS

Name	Selections Years	No.	matches played				Singles				Foursomes				Fourballs			
			P	W	L	H	P	W	L	H	P	W	L	H	P	W	L	H
Lanny Wadkins	77 79 83 85 87 89	6	25	15	9	1	6	3	2	1	11	6	5	0	8	6	2	0
Art Wall Jnr	57 59 61	3	6	4	2	0	2	2	0	0	4	2	2	0	0	0	0	0
Al Watrous	27 29	2	3	2	1	0	2	1	1	0	1	1	0	0	0	0	0	0
Tom Watson	77 79** 81 83 89	5	15	10	4	1	4	2	2	0	6	4	1	1	5	4	1	0
Tom Weiskopf	73 75	2	10	7	2	1	3	2	0	1	4	3	1	0	3	2	1	0
Craig Wood	31 33 35 41	4	4	1	3	0	2	1	1	0	2	0	2	0	0	0	0	0
Lew Worsham	47	1	2	2	0	0	1	1	0	0	1	1	0	0	0	0	0	0
Fuzzy Zoeller	79 83 85	3	10	1	8	1	3	0	2	1	2	0	2	0	5	1	4	0
Totals		321	870	471	292	107	314	169	104	41	338	192	116	30	218	110	72	36

Notes:

* Denotes selected and present but did not participate in the matches

** Tom Watson was selected for the 1979 matches but withdrew because of the impending birth of his wife Linda's first baby. Mark Hayes substituted.

Index